Machine Learning for Physicists

A hands-on approach

Online at: https://doi.org/10.1088/978-0-7503-4957-4

Machine Learning for Physicists

A hands-on approach

Sadegh Raeisi

Department of Physics, Sharif University of Technology, Azadi Avenue, Tehran, Iran

Sedighe Raeisi

MCI R&D Center, No 3, Dabir St, Yazdanpanah St, Nelson Mandela Blvd, Tehran, Iran

IOP Publishing, Bristol, UK

ISBN   978-0-7503-4957-4 (ebook)
ISBN   978-0-7503-4955-0 (print)
ISBN   978-0-7503-4958-1 (myPrint)
ISBN   978-0-7503-4956-7 (mobi)

DOI   10.1088/978-0-7503-4957-4

Version: 20231101

IOP ebooks

British Library Cataloguing-in-Publication Data: A catalogue record for this book is available from the British Library.

Published by IOP Publishing, wholly owned by The Institute of Physics, London

IOP Publishing, No.2 The Distillery, Glassfields, Avon Street, Bristol, BS2 0GR, UK

US Office: IOP Publishing, Inc., 190 North Independence Mall West, Suite 601, Philadelphia, PA 19106, USA

To Mom and Dad, Farah and Hadi

For having our backs every step of the way and for being there for us all these years.

Contents

Preface

This book is based on a course that I have been teaching at the Sharif University of Technology [1]. The book is mainly inspired by the needs of my students and my colleagues for using these concepts for their research.

The machine learning concepts are not difficult and are usually fairly accessible for someone with a background in physics or mathematics. However, there is an initial barrier that many find it difficult to break through.

Many of the books and resources for machine learning are not helpful for speeding up the learning curve. They are usually too technical and put too much emphasis on the theoretical foundations of machine learning. While these foundations are interesting and necessary for research in machine learning, they are not as critical for a physics student who wants to use these ideas in their research, at least not initially. In this book, we try to take a slightly modified approach to machine learning and try to ease the learning curve and entry into this field. Also, we try to put more emphasis on the practical aspects of machine learning. The goal is for the reader to be able to use these concepts in their everyday tasks.

The experience of teaching this as a course has provided me with excellent feedback and has helped me to iterate and fine-tune different parts of this book over the course of the past five years. A relatively large portion of the students on this course have managed to use machine learning to conduct novel research as a part of their course projects and in many cases this has led to scientific publications. In fact, I believe the best approach to teaching this book is to apply it to a specific research project. In my course, students have a course project with four milestones. The first milestone is focused on the problem definition and collection of the required data. The second milestone focuses on the application of traditional machine learning techniques to their problem. For their third milestone, they move forward to apply deep learning techniques, and finally for their last milestone, they write a manuscript that summarizes their work and results. In many cases, they ended up publishing their final manuscript after some revisions and improvements.

Based on the description above, you can see that this book is tuned toward physics or similar students who are interested in utilizing machine learning for their research. The goal here is to provide a relatively optimized path towards the point that people with a physics or similar background can start using machine learning for their everyday tasks. This involves the ability to quickly identify the right machine learning tool for the problem that they are working on and then implement it. The former may seem obvious, but I have seen many papers where neural networks are used for simple problems that are better suited to traditional techniques.

Another objective is to improve the ability to map a physics problem or parts of it to a machine learning problem. Based on my experience, this is the biggest skill that students struggle with when they are first exposed to machine learning.

Once the physics problem is translated into a machine learning problem or expressed in the machine learning language and once the right machine learning techniques for the problem are identified, it is time to implement it. Fortunately, the machine learning community has been actively developing open-source tools for machine learning techniques and, in most cases, one does not need to implement machine learning techniques and can use the existing libraries. For instance, if a specific problem requires a convolutional neural network, there are libraries such as Keras or PyTorch that allow you to implement your desired architecture in a few lines of code. These libraries are extremely optimized and maintained by a large community of machine learning practitioners. This means that for the implementation of most machine learning techniques, you only need to be familiar with the right tools, i.e. the libraries that have been developed for that task.

However, the reader should use this book as the starting point. This book does not provide an in-depth review of all the different techniques that have been developed in machine learning. For instance, when we review supervised techniques, there are many techniques that will not be covered here. This is partly because it is not possible to fit all the details of all of these techniques in one book. There are books dedicated to many of the subjects in this book. For instance, you can find books on the different generative techniques.

It also helps the learning process to go and research these techniques on your own. Machine learning is an active field of research. Many of the key developments of this field have been happening in recent years. For instance, the generative adversarial network (GAN) was only introduced in 2014 [2]. Most likely, from the day you started reading this book to the time you finish it, there will be some new advances and techniques. It is not possible to include a the entirety of dynamic field such as this in a single book. More importantly, this is part of what the reader needs to learn, i.e. that to keep up with the field, they need to do their own research.

We also do not go into great depth on the theoretical aspects of machine learning and the details behind the techniques that we introduce. For instance, there are a variety of mathematical theorems related to neural networks or the K-means algorithm that are not covered here. This is not to say that they are not interesting or important. They are just not within the subject of this book. For the practical and hands-on experience that we are aiming for, the theoretical foundations of machine learning are not as important. We still try to provide a high-level understanding and present the intuition behind the techniques and ideas that we review.

Once again, this book is meant to be a starting point and help the reader climb their learning curve and help pave their way utilizing machine learning for research in physics and projects, and we hope that this will make some contribution towards the progress of physics in this new era.

References

[1] Raeisi S 2022 Machinelearning_physics *GitHub* https://github.com/sraeisi/MachineLearning_ Physics
[2] Goodfellow I J, Pouget-Abadie J, Mirza M, Xu B, Warde-Farley D, Ozair S, Courville A and Bengio Y 2014 Generative adversarial nets *Proc. 27th Int. Conf. on Neural Information Processing Systems (NIPS'14) vol 2* (Cambridge, MA: MIT Press)

Acknowledgements

This book started as courses that we thought for a few years and if it was not for the curious and smart questions of our students, it would have not matured to this book. So we would like to express our deepest appreciation to our brilliant students who have taken our courses and provided us with valuable feedback that helped improve this book.

We are also grateful to our colleagues who have provided us with their insights and expertise, especially Dr Shant Baghram, Dr Fakhteh GhanbarNejad and Dr Saman Moghimi for investing so much of their time helping with our machine-learning-related student projects.

Finally, we would like to thank our friends and family for their unwavering support and encouragement throughout this journey. In particular, we would like to thank our mom and dad, Farah and Hadi, our uncle, Hassan Akbari and our cousins, Taha and Tania Akbari who have been extremely supportive and inspiring to us through this journey.

Author biographies

Sadegh Raeisi

 **Sadegh Raeisi** has a PhD in Physics and quantum computing from the institute for Quantum Computing at the University of Waterloo. He is an assistant professor at Sharif University of Technology. He is also a co-founder and the CEO at Foqus Technologies Inc where they leverage proprietary Quantum technologies and Machine Learning algorithms to enhance Medical Imaging with MRI.

Sadegh is known for his pioneering works in Quantum Thermodynamics and specifically on algorithmic cooling, including finding the cooling limit of Heat-bath Algorithmic Cooling (HBAC) techniques which was an open problem for a decade, and for inventing the Blind HBAC technique, which is the only optimal and practical HBAC technique. He is also recognized for his pioneering work on the foundations of quantum mechanics, macroscopic quantumness and in particular, discovering the first technique for verifying macroscopic quantum entanglement.

Sedighe Raeisi

 **Sedighe Raeisi** has a PhD in elementary particle physics from Ferdowsi University of Mashhad.
She has been a lecturer at Ferdowsi University of Mashhad and is currently working as an artificial intelligence scientist at MCI R&D center, which is the largest telecommunication operator company in Iran.

She has expertise and extensive experience in graph neural networks, machine vision, natural language processing, time series forecasting, non-linear dynamics, and chaotic physics.

IOP Publishing

Machine Learning for Physicists
A hands-on approach
Sadegh Raeisi and Sedighe Raeisi

Chapter 1

Preliminaries

In this chapter, we review some of the prerequisites that will help optimize the learning process for this book.

The main target audience of this book is university students in physics or similar disciplines. This means that we are assuming that the audience has some basic understanding of undergraduate physics, statistics, and mathematics. Students with a strong statistics background will find many of the concepts in this book familiar. Many machine learning techniques have their roots in statistics. We will point out some of these concepts as we encounter them.

In addition, the audience needs some basic understanding of linear algebra. This is needed in particular for understanding the mechanics of neural networks (NNs), and it has applications in other techniques such as principal component analysis (PCA) as well.

1.1 Python

Another critical requirement of this book is proficiency in a programming language and, ideally, in Python. Different programming languages and tools such as R, MATLAB, Mathematica, and Java are used for machine learning. However, Python is arguably the most commonly used language for machine learning applications. This means that there is a large community of Python programmers who can help you find the answers to your questions. Also, many of the machine learning and deep learning tools are built for Python. Please note that this does not mean that Python is better than other programming languages, only that, from a practical view, it is more convenient.

For this book, basic familiarity with programming and basic Python syntaxes are essential. Additionally, there are libraries such as NumPy, pandas, and Matplotlib that are extremely helpful for handling and visualization of the data and are used

Table 1.1. Cheat sheets for some of the most common tools that we will be using in this book.

Library/tool	Description	Link to cheat sheet
Python	The programming language that will be used for this course.	Python
NumPy	A Python library that provides strong and efficient tools for the manipulation of high-dimensional arrays.	NumPy
SciPy	A Python library, built on NumPy, for mathematical and scientific computing.	SciPy
pandas	A Python library, built on NumPy, that provides efficient tools for the handling and analysis of data.	Pandas-1 Pandas-2
Visualization (Matplotlib, Seaborn)	Some of the most common Python libraries for data visualization.	MatplotlibSeaborn
scikit-learn	A Python library that provides a nice and fairly efficient implementation of most machine learning techniques and ideas.	scikit-learn
Neural networks (Keras, PyTorch)	These are some of the most common Python libraries that provide a high-level and easy-to-use interface for deep learning.	PyTorchKeras
Project Jupyter	An interactive environment for programming.	Project Jupyter
Git	A strong infrastructure for version control. GitHub is web-based hosting service for version control and it also provides services for collaboration.	Git

frequently in this context. The reader is thus encouraged to become familiar with them.

In table 1.1 we have collected a list of tools that are helpful for machine learning applications. Also, for each tool, a link to a cheat sheet is provided. This list includes some libraries that are used for machine learning applications. We will provide a brief introduction to these libraries when we reach their corresponding sections.

1.2 GitHub library

In each section, the code snippet for the implementation of the related technique is provided.

An extended version of these codes can be found on the course GitHub page at the MachineLearning_Physics page.

1.3 Datasets

Throughout this book, we will be using some datasets for examples and questions. These are summarized in table 1.2.

Table 1.2. A list of some of the datasets that we use for practice in this book. To use the datasets, you can use the code snippet here.

Dataset ID	Title	Description
DTS-BBR	Black body radiation	The data for energy density at different frequencies for the black body radiation. These data are collected from [1].
DTS-SF	Spring force	The data for the force exerted by a spring. These data are collected from the laboratory reports of students in Phys Lab III.
DTS-SC	Superconductivity critical temperature	This dataset contains information of different superconductors and the task is to predict the critical temperature of superconductors [2, 3].
DTS-NASA	Star type classification	The data contain different star samples, such as red dwarf, brown dwarf, white dwarf, main sequence, super giants, hyper giants. The task is to classify them [4].
DTS-ED	Entanglement detection	The dataset contains random quantum states of two quantum spins and the task is to identify if they are entangled [5, 6].
DTS-PI	Particle identification from detector responses	The dataset is for the classification of particles and contains four types of particles: positron, pion, kaon, and proton [7].
DTS-GSE	Ground state energies of molecules	The dataset contains different samples with their ground state energies and their different chemical bonds [8, 9].
DTS-SS	Sunspots	These data contain the mean value of the number of sunspots for each month from 1749 [10].
DTS-GT	Average temperature of earth surface	These data contain the average temperature of the surface of Earth since 1850 [11, 12].
DTS-GZ2	Galaxy Zoo II	The dataset is taken from the Galaxy Zoo II survey [13].

References

[1] Fowler M Black body radiation *University of Virginia* http://galileo.phys.virginia.edu/classes/252/black_body_radiation.html (Accessed 2023)

[2] Hamidieh K Superconductivity data *UCI Machine Learning Repository* https://archive.ics.uci.edu/ml/datasets/superconductivty+data (Accessed 2023)

[3] Hamidieh K 2018 A data-driven statistical model for predicting the critical temperature of a superconductor *Comput. Mater. Sci.* **154** 346–54

[4] Dincer B Star type classification/NASA *kaggle* https://www.kaggle.com/datasets/brsdincer/star-type-classification (Accessed 2023)

[5] Yosefpor M Autoencoder entanglement detection optimizer/Quantum machine learning *GitLab* https://gitlab.com/quantum-machine-learning/autoencoder-entanglement-detection-optimizer/-/tree/master/Data (Accessed 2023)

[6] Yosefpor M, Mostaan M R and Raeisi S 2020 Finding semi-optimal measurements for entanglement detection using autoencoder neural networks *Quantum Sci. Technol.* **5** 045006

[7] Harrison N Particle identification from detector responses *kaggle* https://www.kaggle.com/datasets/naharrison/particle-identification-from-detector-responses (Accessed 2023)

[8] Burakh Ground state energies of 16242 molecules *kaggle* https://www.kaggle.com/datasets/burakhmmtgl/energy-molecule (Accessed 2023)

[9] Himmetoglu B 2016 Tree based machine learning framework for predicting ground state energies of molecules *J. Chem. Phys.* **145** 134101

[10] Royal Obervatory of Belgium Sunspot number graphics *Solar Influences Data Analysis Center* https://www.sidc.be/silso/ssngraphics (Accessed 2023)

[11] National Centers for Environmental Information 2023 Global time series *Climate at a Glance* https://www.ncei.noaa.gov/access/monitoring/climate-at-a-glance/global/time-series (Accessed 19 April 2023)

[12] Rhode R 2021 Global temperature report for 2020 *Berkeley Earth* https://berkeleyearth.org/global-temperature-report-for-2020/ (Accessed 2023)

[13] Willett K W *et al* 2013 Galaxy Zoo 2: detailed morphological classifications for 304 122 galaxies from the Sloan Digital Sky Survey *Mon. Not. R. Astron. Soc.* **435** 2835–60

IOP Publishing

Machine Learning for Physicists
A hands-on approach
Sadegh Raeisi and Sedighe Raeisi

Chapter 2

Introduction

Over the past decade, there has been a surge in papers and research projects empowered by machine learning (ML) [1–20]. In this chapter, we will provide a basic introduction to machine learning and its applications, especially in physics.

2.1 What is machine learning?

Let us start with what machine learning (ML) is. It is not easy to define exactly what qualifies as ML. It is a diverse field and there are many different approaches. It is also a moving target in the sense that there are new techniques and applications every day and the definition is being expanded.

We can probably define it by what it is not. The traditional approach to computer programming has been based on algorithmic programming. For instance, to classify apples and oranges, one would need to specify a set of if/else conditions and find an algorithmic way to identify apples and oranges.

With ML, there is no programming of an algorithm for the classification of apples and oranges. You start with a generic classification algorithm and present it with a dataset containing samples of apples and oranges. This leads to a model that 'learns' to classify apples and oranges.

What is nice about this approach is that if you change the problem to the classification of dogs and cats, you do not need to change the algorithm, you just need to retrain the model with the cat and dog dataset. In contrast, with the traditional approach, you would need to find new if/else conditions that would work for dogs and cats.

It also has the added benefit that sometimes we may not even know what the conditional clauses for classification should be. For the ML approach, we do not need a deep understanding of processes or samples.

doi:10.1088/978-0-7503-4957-4ch2

However, we do need to have the right data for most ML techniques—and this is not always easy. For classification tasks we need data with labels that indicate the classes of the samples. As we will see, the data are the key ingredient of ML and, almost always, the quality of our ML model is tied to the quality of the data we have.

2.2 Applications of machine learning

Machine learning has revolutionized our lives over the past few years. From self-driving cars [21, 22] to natural language processing [23–25], from financial fraud detection [26] to navigation using Google Maps [27], we are surrounded by different technologies that would have been impossible without ML. Machine learning is being used in healthcare for drug discovery [28] and understanding the structure of proteins [29]. It is even being used to speed up and enhance MRI [30, 31]. In natural language processing, we have language models [24] that can aggregate all the knowledge on the Internet and every book and answer our questions in a way that is almost indistinguishable from human interaction [32].

What is more fascinating is that most of these advances happened over a relatively short period of time. Although ML has been around for a few decades [33], most of this ML-powered progress occurred over the past decade.

In this book, we are primarily interested in the applications of ML in physics and science. Machine learning has enabled physicists and scientists, in general, to explore the vast amount of data that different labs, telescopes, and observatories are collecting. For instance, CERN data centers store more than 30 petabytes of data [34]. Similarly, observatories and laboratories all around the world collect unprecedented amounts of data. Processing these data with classical techniques, which usually involve a graduate student reviewing them, is impossible. In fact, this is one of the main areas of application of ML in physics [35].

These applications are not limited only to processing large amounts of data. Physicists have been using ideas from ML in novel ways, from mapping the phase spaces of many body systems using the inability of ML models [36, 37] to learn patterns, to finding the measurements that are the most informative for entanglement detection [38]. For one of these interesting applications, an ML agent was trained using a technique called reinforcement learning and learned, or 'discovered', modern experimental quantum optics techniques [39].

In some ways, the new wave of research that uses ML may remind us of when computer simulations started to be used in physics [40]. The applications of computer simulations over the past few decades have significantly sped up scientific research and have even changed our scientific methods. Today, numerical simulations are a well-accepted scientific method next to experimentation. A similar pattern seems to be emerging for the applications of ML in scientific research. If this is anything like the wave of progress that we experienced with numerical simulation, we are in for an interesting ride and what we have seen so far seems to be only the tip of the iceberg.

However, this has not been a one-way street, in the sense that physics and physicists have also been contributing to the progress in ML. A lot of ML techniques are based on or inspired by ideas from physics [41]. Some of these ideas, such as physics-informed ML, help to improve the performance or the training speed of established machine learning techniques [42]. There are even new ML techniques and approaches invented based on ideas from physics [43], such as restricted Boltzmann machine (RBM) models. There is also a lot of research on building new ML techniques using quantum algorithms that could be faster than their classical analogs [44–47].

2.3 Different types of machine learning

There are different categorizations of ML techniques.
The main categories are:

- Supervised.
- Unsupervised.
- Reinforcement learning.

Each of these categories can be broken down into subcategories. For example, supervised techniques are usually sub-categorized into classification and regression techniques.

Similarly, there are different types of unsupervised techniques. Some of these include:

- Clustering.
- Dimensionality reduction.
- Feature engineering.
- Anomaly detection.

There are also generative models that are sometimes categorized under unsupervised techniques.

Similarly, there are different types of reinforcement learning algorithms [48].

2.4 Structure of the book

This book is divided into two parts—supervised and the unsupervised techniques. Each part is divided into several chapters. The general trend is that we start with the introduction of the classical and traditional techniques and then introduce the more modern, often neural network (NN)-based, techniques.

For the supervised techniques, the first chapter covers the basics of a supervised ML model. This includes the problem statement as well as the general approach to solving the problem.

In the following chapter, we review NNs and their applications for supervised ML problems. We then introduce some of the more specific supervised tasks and the NN architectures that are designed for these tasks.

Then we move on to the second part of the book which is focused on unsupervised techniques. There are more variations for unsupervised tasks. We will review some of the more important ones, such as clustering. We also cover the generative models under unsupervised techniques. Not everyone agrees with this categorization. Some categorize generative models under supervised techniques or as a separate category. It will become clear that based on the definition that we work with, generative models fall more naturally under unsupervised techniques.

Throughout this book we try to engage the reader with exercises and questions. The difference between the exercises and questions is that the answer for the exercises is usually provided immediately after them. The reader is encouraged to figure out the answer on their own and check their answers against the ones provided. These exercises are designed to facilitate the learning process and the book will be more effective if the reader spends some time solving them on their own. However, if you cannot do this, the solution—which is usually an important part of the subject—is provided.

Questions, on the other hand, are problems that are designed to strengthen the readers' skills or knowledge of the related topic. The answers to the questions are not provided, although hints or references may be provided to guide the reader to find the answer.

Finally, for each technique, we usually start with an intuitive problem statement and then introduce the technique. We usually give some intuition as to why the technique works or is suitable for the related problem. Then we may review some examples. Finally, we try to provide the code snippet for the implementation of the technique. These codes will help the reader obtain some hands-on experience on the topic.

References

[1] Wang Z, Gehring C, Kohli P and Jegelka S 2018 Batched large-scale Bayesian optimization in high-dimensional spaces *Proc. Machine Learning Res.* **84** 745–54 https://proceedings.mlr.press/v84/wang18c.html

[2] Alvarez-Melis D, Jaakkola T and Jegelka S 2018 Structured optimal transport *Proc. Machine Learning Res.* **84** 1771–80 https://proceedings.mlr.press/v84/alvarez-melis18a.html

[3] Louizos C, Shalit U, Mooij J M, Sontag D, Zemel R and Welling M 2017 Causal effect inference with deep latent-variable models *Advances in Neural Information Processing Systems* ed Guyon I, Von Luxburg U, Bengio S, Wallach H, Fergus R, Vishwanathan S and Garnett R (Red Hook, NY: Curran) vol 30 https://proceedings.neurips.cc/paper_files/paper/2017/file/94b5bde6de888ddf9cde6748ad2523d1-Paper.pdf

[4] Shalit U, Johansson F D and Sontag D 2017 Estimating individual treatment effect: generalization bounds and algorithms *Proc. Machine Learning Res.* **70** 3076–85 https://proceedings.mlr.press/v70/shalit17a.html

[5] Jernite Y, Choromanska A and Sontag D 2017 Simultaneous learning of trees and representations for extreme classification and density *Proc. Machine Learning Res.* **70** 1665–74 https://proceedings.mlr.press/v70/jernite17a.html

[6] Krishnan R G, Shalit U and Sontag D 2017 Structured inference networks for nonlinear state space models *Proc. 31st AAAI Conf. on Artificial Intelligence* vol 31 pp 2101–9

[7] Zhang Y, Barzilay R and Jaakkola T 2017 Aspect-augmented adversarial networks for domain adaptation *Trans. Assoc. Comput. Linguist.* **5** 515–28

[8] Alvarez Melis D and Jaakkola T 2017 A causal framework for explaining the predictions of black-box sequence-to-sequence models *Proc. 2017 Conf. Empirical Methods in Natural Language Processing* (Copenhagen: Association for Computational Linguistics) pp 412–21

[9] Lei T, Jin W, Barzilay R and Jaakkola T 2017 Deriving neural architectures from sequence and graph kernels *Proc. Machine Learning Res.* **70** 2024–33 https://proceedings.mlr.press/v70/lei17a.html

[10] Mueller J, Reshef D, Du G and Jaakkola T 2017 Learning optimal interventions *Proc. Machine Learning Res.* **54** 1039–47 https://proceedings.mlr.press/v54/mueller17a.html

[11] Zhao M, Yue S, Katabi D, Jaakkola T and Bianchi M 2017 Learning sleep stages from radio signals: a conditional adversarial architecture *Proc. Machine Learning Res.* **70** 4100–9 https://proceedings.mlr.press/v70/zhao17d.html

[12] Mueller J, Jaakkola T and Gifford D 2018 Modeling persistent trends in distributions *J. Am. Stat. Assoc.* **113** 1296–310

[13] Coley C W, Barzilay R, Jaakkola T, Green W H and Jensen K F 2017 Prediction of organic reaction outcomes using machine learning *ACS Cent. Sci.* **3** 434–43

[14] Alvarez-Melis D and Jaakkola T 2017 Tree structured decoding with doubly recurrent neural networks *Int. Conf. on Learning Representations* (Appleton, WI: ICLR)

[15] Wang Z, Jegelka S, Kaelbling L P and Lozano-Perez T 2017 Focused model-learning and planning for non-Gaussian continuous state-action systems *IEEE Int. Conf. on Robotics and Automation (ICRA)* https://doi.org/10.1109/ICRA.2017.7989433

[16] Shulkind G, Jegelka S and Wornell G W 2017 Multiple wavelength sensing array design *2017 IEEE Int. Conf. on Acoustics, Speech and Signal Processing (ICASSP)* pp 3424–8

[17] Song H O, Jegelka S, Rathod V and Murphy K 2017 Deep metric learning via facility location *Int. Conf. on Computer Vision and Pattern Recognition (CVPR)* pp 2206–14

[18] Staib M and Jegelka S 2017 Robust budget allocation via continuous submodular functions *Int. Conf. on Machine Learning (ICML)* 1049–79

[19] Wang Z and Jegelka S 2017 Max-value entropy search for efficient Bayesian optimization *Int. Conf. on Machine Learning (ICML)*

[20] Wang Z, Li C, Jegelka S and Kohli P 2017 Batched high-dimensional Bayesian optimization via structural kernel learning *Int. Conf. on Machine Learning (ICML)* https://doi.org/10.48550/arXiv.1703.01973

[21] Daily M, Medasani S, Behringer R and Trivedi M 2017 Self-driving cars *Computer* **50** 18–23

[22] Spoehel E and Banik S 2020 Self-driving cars: all you need to know *2020 Int. Conf. on Computational Science and Computational Intelligence (CSCI)* pp 655–8

[23] Melis G, Dyer C and Blunsom P 2017 On the state of the art of evaluation in neural language models arXiv preprint arXiv:1707.05589

[24] Kasneci E *et al* 2023 ChatGPT for good? On opportunities and challenges of large language models for education *Learn. Individ. Differ.* **103** 102274

[25] Singh S P, Kumar A, Darbari H, Singh L, Rastogi A and Jain S 2017 Machine translation using deep learning *2017 Int. Conf. on Computer, Communications and Electronics (Comptelix)* (Piscataway, NJ: IEEE) pp 162–7

[26] Bao Y, Hilary G and Ke B 2022 Artificial intelligence and fraud detection *Innovative Technology at the Interface of Finance and Operations* (Berlin: Springer) pp 223–47

[27] Derrow-Pinion A *et al* 2021 Eta prediction with graph neural networks in google maps *Proc. 30th ACM Int. Conf. on Information & Knowledge Management* pp 3767–76 https://arxiv.org/abs/2108.11482

[28] Vamathevan J, Clark D, Czodrowski P, Dunham I, Ferran E, Lee G, Li B, Madabhushi A, Shah P and Spitzer M *et al* 2019 Applications of machine learning in drug discovery and development *Nat. Rev. Drug Discov.* **18** 463–77

[29] Jumper J *et al* 2021 Highly accurate protein structure prediction with AlphaFold *Nature* **596** 583–9

[30] Foqus Technologies Inc 2023 https://foqus.ca/.

[31] Wang S and Summers R M 2012 Machine learning and radiology *Med. Image Anal.* **16** 933–51

[32] Petroni F, Rocktäschel T, Lewis P, Bakhtin A, Wu Y, Miller A H and Riedel S 2019 Language models as knowledge bases? arXiv preprint (arXiv:1909.01066)

[33] Haenlein M and Kaplan A 2019 A brief history of artificial intelligence: on the past, present, and future of artificial intelligence *Calif. Manage. Rev.* **61** 5–14

[34] Gaillard M July 2017 accessed in 2023 CERN data centre passes the 200-petabyte milestone *CERN* https://home.cern/news/news/computing/cern-data-centre-passes-200-petabyte-milestone

[35] Van Der Veken F *et al* 2020 SISSA: machine learning in accelerator physics: applications at the CERN Large Hadron Collider *Proc. Sci.* **372** 044

[36] Gökmen D E, Biswas S, Huber S D, Ringel Z, Flicker F and Koch-Janusz M 2023 Machine learning assisted discovery of exotic criticality in a planar quasicrystal arXiv preprint (arXiv:2301.11934)

[37] Carrasquilla J and Melko R G 2017 Machine learning phases of matter *Nat. Phys.* **13** 431–4

[38] Yosefpor M, Mostaan M R and Raeisi S 2020 Finding semi-optimal measurements for entanglement detection using autoencoder neural networks 2020 *Quantum Sci. Technol.* **5** 045006

[39] Melnikov A A, Poulsen Nautrup H, Krenn M, Dunjko V, Tiersch M, Zeilinger A and Briegel H J 2018 Active learning machine learns to create new quantum experiments *Proc. Natl Acad. Sci.* **115** 1221–6

[40] Heermann D W 1986 *Computer Simulation Methods in Theoretical Physics* (Berlin: Springer) https://doi.org/10.1007/978-3-642-75448-7

[41] Carleo G, Cirac I, Cranmer K, Daudet L, Schuld M, Tishby N, Vogt-Maranto L and Zdeborová L 2019 Machine learning and the physical sciences *Rev. Mod. Phys.* **91** 045002

[42] Karniadakis G E, Kevrekidis I G, Lu L, Perdikaris P, Wang S and Yang L 2021 Physics-informed machine learning *Nat. Rev. Phys.* **3** 422–40

[43] Zhang N, Ding S, Zhang J and Xue Y 2018 An overview on restricted Boltzmann machines *Neurocomputing* **275** 1186–99

[44] Lloyd S, Mohseni M and Rebentrost P 2013 Quantum algorithms for supervised and unsupervised machine learning (arXiv preprint arXiv:1307.0411)

[45] Biamonte J, Wittek P, Pancotti N, Rebentrost P, Wiebe N and Lloyd S 2017 Quantum machine learning *Nature* **549** 195–202

[46] Dunjko V and Wittek P 2020 A non-review of quantum machine learning: trends and explorations *Quantum Views* **4** 32

[47] García D P, Cruz-Benito J and García-Peñalvo F J 2022 Systematic literature review: quantum machine learning and its applications arXiv preprint (arXiv:2201.04093)

[48] Li Y 2017 Deep reinforcement learning: an overview arXiv preprint (arXiv:1701.07274)

Part I

Supervised learning

Chapter 3

Supervised learning

In this chapter, we will introduce supervised learning. This is one of the most widely used types of machine learning. We start with problem definitions and terminologies. We break the supervised learning task into its key ingredients and study them one by one. We will later extend this modular approach to understand neural networks.

The first type of ML that we study is called 'supervised learning'. This is one of the most widely used types of ML. Supervised learning is usually used for parameter estimation or prediction.

Imagine that we are interested in a target quantity which we refer to as the 'label', and we are given a set of instances or samples. For each instance, we know the value of the target quantity as well as the circumstances of the specific instance. For example, in figure 3.1 you can see the first five rows of a dataset of stars. This dataset contains seven columns: the temperature in kelvins, relative luminosity, relative radius, absolute magnitude, visible color, spectral class, and type of each star. Here,

Features						Label
Temperature in Kelvin	Relative Luminosity	Relative Radius	Absolute Magnitude	Visible Color	Spectral Class	Star Type
2700	0.00018	0.13	16.05	Red	M	0
3600	0.0029	0.51	10.69	Red	M	1
25000	0.056	0.0084	10.58	Blue White	B	2
39000	204000	10.6	-4.7	Blue	O	3
33750	220000	26	-6.1	Blue	B	4
3490	270000	1520	-9.4	Red	M	5

Figure 3.1. NASA star type classification dataset [1].

the first six columns are features of the model and the last column, the type of star, is the target. These data are taken from [1].

The goal is to build a model that can estimate or predict the value of the target quantity.

Supervised learning can be divided into two classes: classification problems and regression problems. For classification problems the target quantity is a categorical quantity. An example of a classification problem is identifying if an object in the sky is a planet or a star. For regression the target is a numerical quantity. Often this is a continuous value. For instance, we may want to use astronomical data to estimate or predict the mass of a star or planet.

We can turn a classification problem into a regression one. For instance, we can assign a probability to a sample belonging to different classes and use a regression model to estimate the probability. For the classification task, we can use the class with the highest probability. This is called logistic regression and sometimes is regarded as its own category of supervised learning problems.

3.1 Definitions, notations, and problem statement

We start with the notation and the problem specification. Then we use these to describe the elements of a supervised learning model and investigate the details of each element.

The following covers some of the major terminology that will be used frequently in this book.

Sample: Also known as a data sample or data instance. This refers to the samples in our dataset. For example, in figure 3.1 each row of the table corresponds to a sample in the dataset.

Features: Features are the attributes that describe each sample. These features are given to the model to be used for the prediction of the target values or labels. In figure 3.1 the features for each sample are the different columns indicated in blue. For instance, each star is described by its temperature, relative luminosity, relative radius, absolute magnitude, visible color, and a spectral class.

Label: The label is the target property of a sample. In supervised learning tasks, we are building models to estimate or predict the labels. A trained model uses features of a sample to predict the label. In the example of figure 3.1 the labels are {0, 1, 2, 3, 4, 5}, which refer to the type of star and correspond to red dwarf, brown dwarf, white dwarf, main sequence, supergiants, and hypergiants, respectively. We will see examples of regression where the labels are real-valued numbers.

Figure 3.2 shows a schematic sample. We used the first column to indicate the sample. This often is a sample ID. The second part refers to the features and is

Sample 1	Features of Sample 1	Label of Sample 1
$\vec{X}^1$	$X_1^1, X_2^1, X_3^1, \cdots, X_{nf}^1$	Y^1

Figure 3.2. Sample 1.

sometimes called the feature vector. The last part is the label. The label may also be multi-valued, in which case it can be represented by a vector.

It is common to use X to refer to the features of the samples and Y or y to refer to the labels.

Data: A collection of samples, each of which has some features and one or more labels.

Figure 3.3 shows the same data as the table in figure 3.1. However, the samples, features, and labels are indicated.

The dataset for a supervised learning task is usually specified with two matrices, the feature matrix, X, and the label vector/matrix, Y. In the left panel of figure 3.4, these are indicated in blue and yellow. Also, we sometimes refer to the features of a sample X as the feature vector and show it by $\vec{X}$. Each element of the vector points to the corresponding feature of the sample X.

Also, we use n_s to refer to the number of samples in the data. Similarly, we use n_f to refer to the number of features. This means that the feature matrix has n_s rows and n_f columns.

Question: How many rows does Y have?

It is also common to use the superscript to refer to the sample index and use the subscript to refer to the feature index. For example, X_2^7 refers to the second feature of the seventh sample. The right panel of figure 3.4 shows this schematically.

	Feature 1	Feature 2	Feature 3	Feature 4	Feature 5	Feature 6	Label
	Temperature in Kelvin	Relative Luminosity	Relative Radius	Absolute Magnitude	Visible Color	Spectral Class	Star Type
Sample 1	2700	0.00018	0.13	16.05	Red	M	0
Sample 2	3600	0.0029	0.51	10.69	Red	M	1
Sample 3	25000	0.056	0.0084	10.58	Blue White	B	2

Figure 3.3. Data, a collection of samples.

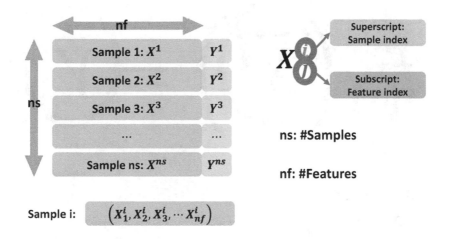

Figure 3.4. Notation used for the data.

Training data are a subset of the data that are used for training the model. We use $(X_{\text{training}}, Y_{\text{training}})$ for the training data.

Test data are a subset of the data that are used for testing the performance of a trained model. We use $(X_{\text{test}}, Y_{\text{test}})$ for the test data.

The purpose of using two separate sets for testing and training comes from statistics. This is to make sure that the model cannot cheat and memorize the labels. This is especially important for characterizing how well the models generalize beyond the data on which they are trained. We will discuss this subject extensively later.

Model/hypothesis: The model or hypothesis is the central piece of any supervised learning task. You may be familiar with hypotheses from statistics. This is an educated guess for how the labels depend on the features of each sample. For instance, for a spring, you may guess that the force has a linear dependence on the displacement of the spring. This is a linear hypothesis or model.

Often, we work with hypotheses that have some free parameters and tune those parameters to match our data. In the case of the spring, these are the two constants of the linear functions, the slope and the intercept.

We use f_w to denote a hypothesis with free parameters w. Figure 3.5 shows schematically how a model is used to map a sample with feature vector $\vec{X}^i$ to its corresponding label.

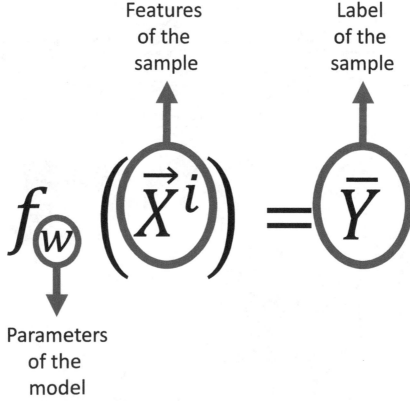

Figure 3.5. Schematic image of how a model/hypothesis is used to map a sample with feature vector $\vec{X}^i$ to its corresponding label.

Free parameters, w: Also known as the trainable parameters or the weights. These are the free parameters of the hypothesis. For a supervised problem, the training involves finding the set of free parameters that give the correspondence between the features and labels of the samples in the dataset.

Classification: This is the type of supervised learning problem where the labels are classes, often identified by a set of integers, e.g. $\{0, 1,...\}$.

Regression: This is the type of supervised learning problem where the labels are numerical values, often real. Note that the labels for a regression problem may also be integers. What distinguishes this from classification is that for classification the relation between the numbers does not mean anything. For example, in the star type dataset in figure 3.1, the different classes are identified by integers, however, as class indicators, class 0 and class 2 are the same with respect to class 1, and it is not as if class 0 is less or class 2 is more than class 1.

Feature space: This is the space formed by the different features of the samples. For instance, in the example of the spring, there was only one feature, displacement. So the corresponding feature space is a 1D space. Figure 3.6 shows a schematic feature space expanded by features X_1 and X_2. For low-dimensional data, the feature space can be a powerful tool for developing an intuition into the structure of the data, in particular for classification tasks.

Decision boundary: This is used for classification tasks. The decision boundary is a hyper-plane in the feature space that separates samples from different classes. Figure 3.6 shows one such decision boundary.

Finding the decision boundary is equivalent to finding the classification model.

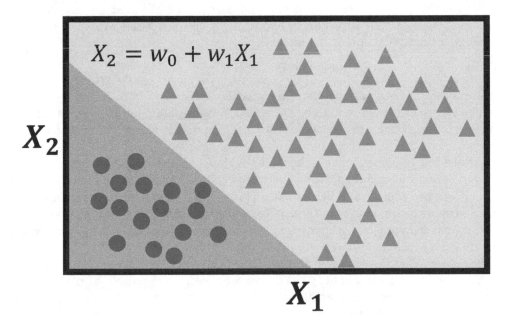

Figure 3.6. A sample decision boundary for a binary classification problem.

Predictions: These are estimations or predictions for the labels provided by a model. When we train a model, it uses feature vectors to predict the labels. We sometimes use $\tilde{Y}$ to distinguish them from the actual values of the labels.

Ground truth: These are the actual values of the labels. We use labels and ground truth interchangeably.

We start with a loose definition of supervised learning.

Supervised learning: Given X and Y, find a model f, such that $f(X)$ closely approximates the labels, Y.

It seems simple enough. The goal is to find a model that, given the features of a sample, can predict or estimate the labels.

There are three main types of supervised learning techniques which are determined by the types of labels that we want to predict. These categories are:

- *Classification*: The label is a category, for instance, types of variable stars [2, 3] or entangled or separable states [4, 5].
- *Regression*: The label is a numerical value, for instance, the mass of a particle or the force of a spring.
- *Logistic regression*: The label is a probability, i.e. a value between 0 and 1. Logistic regression can be seen as a regression problem. At the same time, it can also be used for classification, where the probability of a sample belonging to each category is estimated.

In some categorizations, the logistic regression is not included as a separate category and is described as a special case of the other categories.

The process of building a supervised learning model starts with a model/hypothesis with some free parameters and then fitting the free parameters. For example, one may start with a linear hypothesis. This means that we expect the label (s) to be a linear function of the features, i.e.

$$f(X) = w_0 + w_1 X_1 + w_2 X_2 + \cdots + w_{n_f} X_{n_f}, \tag{3.1}$$

where w_i are the free parameters of the model.

The choice of hypothesis can be motivated by our domain knowledge. In the case of the force of the spring, we know that the force depends linearly on the displacement of the spring. In the absence of domain knowledge, we are often interested in hypotheses that are flexible enough to capture any dependence between the target quantity and the features. In other words, we are interested in models that can universally capture and fit any data. This is one of the main reasons behind the popularity of neural networks (NNs). We will get to this in the next chapter.

For a given hypothesis, a supervised learning task reduces to fit the parameters of the model f_w such at $f_w(X)$ is close to Y.

Exercise: What does it mean for $f_w(X)$ to be close to Y.

For this, we need to quantify the distance between the predictions of the model and the actual values of the target quantity. This is known as the 'loss function'. The training of a supervised learning model translates to optimizing the parameters w such that the distance between Y and $f_w(X)$ is minimized.

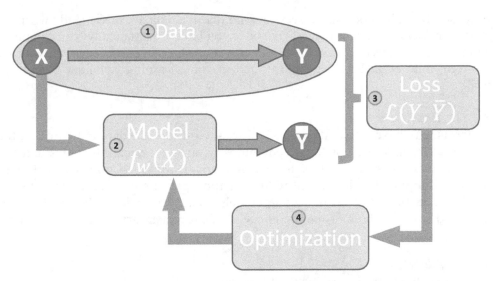

Figure 3.7. A schematic diagram of the pipeline for training a supervised learning model.

Overall, a supervised learning problem has four main ingredients: the data, model or hypothesis, loss function, and optimization method. Figure 3.7 shows the pipeline of training a supervised learning model and how the different elements work with each other. Next, we will go through these four elements and study them in more detail.

3.2 Ingredients of supervised learning

3.2.1 Data

The data are the key ingredient of most ML techniques and one of the most important steps of every ML project is collecting the right data and finding the right representation that can be processed by the machine.

For instance, imagine that you want to build a model that classifies different types of stars [1]. We need a dataset of stars. We need the dataset to include features that are relevant to the star classification task and we need to find a representation for those features that can be processed. Some of the attributes of the star may be irrelevant to its type. This means that we probably would not want to keep them as a feature. Also, some of these features may be categorical. In the example of figure 3.1, the visible color might be an important feature, but we need to find the right representation for this.

In this section, we review different types of data as well as different preprocessing techniques. We will discuss some of the common practices for preparing the data.

In my experience, the data collection and its preprocessing are the most time-consuming aspects of ML. Note that we are not usually provided with a clean dataset. There are some cleaned-up datasets that are often used for educational purposes, but it is important to keep in mind that the data are rarely ready when we start a problem. You will soon see that once you have the data ready, you can make complicated models and train them with only a few lines of code. However, without the right data even the most sophisticated machine learning technique cannot do well.

3.2.1.1 Data types

Datasets may have different types of features. Consider the data in figure 3.1, the 'temperature in kelvin' or 'relative luminosity' are numerical attributes, cut the 'visible class' or 'spectral class' are not numerical. Most ML models work with numerical inputs. It is important to find an appropriate numerical representation of all the features to feed into these models. Here, we review different types of data and some of the most common encodings for them are covered in the next section.

Types of data

There usually are two major types of features.

- *Numerical features* are gathered from quantitative observation or measurements. Therefore, these attributes are given by numerical variables. These can be either continuous, such as temperature, or discrete, such as the number of planets in a solar system.
- *Categorical features* can take values from a discrete, usually limited, and fixed set. These could be qualitative measurements such as color.

Let us see some examples.

In figure 3.8 you can see some of the features of the superconductor dataset (DTS-SC 1.2).

Exercise: In this, dataset, the 'number of elements' is the number of chemical elements in the superconductor material. Is this a numerical or categorical feature?

Although the 'number of elements' is a discrete attribute, it is a numerical one, because the integers do not refer to different categories.

Exercise: How about the 'critical temperature'?

This is a continuous numerical feature.

Often if the features are taken from a qualitative measurement, they are categorical. There are two different types of categorical features, the 'nominal' features, and the 'ordinal' features. The nominal features are the results of observations that are not given with numbers and are expressed with words or

Number of elements	Mean atomic mass	wtd mean atomic mass	Gmean atomic mass	Wtd range atomic_mass	...	Critical Temperature
4	88.94447	57.86269	66.36159	31.79492	...	29
5	92.72921	58.51842	73.13279	36.16194	...	26

Figure 3.8. Superconductor dataset.

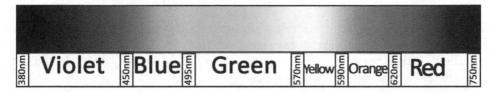

Figure 3.9. Spectrum of light with wavelength, an ordinal categorical attribute.

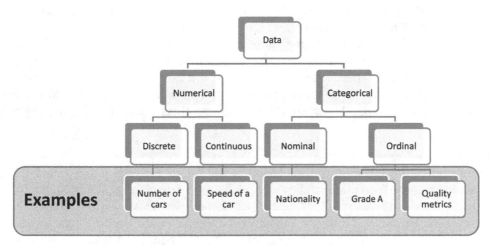

Figure 3.10. Data types. This flowchart illustrates some of the commonly used data types.

characters. There is also no ordinal relation between different categories. In figure 3.1 the 'star type' is a nominal, categorical feature. As you can see, in general, there is no superiority between categories labeled 1 and 2 (although there is a superiority between some of them in evolution and aging, it is not common between all categories and it does not matter for this representation).

In contrast, we have ordinal categorical features. These are features extracted from qualitative observations. For example, in figure 3.1 the 'visible color' is an ordinal categorical attribute. In this case, these categories, i.e. colors, refer to different ranges of wavelength in visible light, see figure 3.9. The red color has a higher wavelength with respect to the blue color. So there is a natural order between these categories.

Another example is a qualitative feature referring to speed, which could be slow or fast. This is an ordinal categorical feature.

Figure 3.10 summarizes different types of features and gives some examples.

Question: Try to find more examples for each data type.

Question: Imagine that your data are the text from a book. What type of data are those?

3.2.1.2 Encodings

Most machine learning models work with numerical features. Therefore, we should transform the categorical attributes into numerical values. This process is called 'encoding'. This is the first type of preprocessing that we usually apply to the data.

Exercise: How would you encode a categorical feature?

There are different types of encodings. Here, we review some of the more common ones.

Label encoding

Label encoding is the most simple encoding. In this encoding, we replace each category with an integer. This could start from 0 and go up.

The main issue with this encoding is that we induce some order between different categories. This is because, for the machine, the value 1 is less than 2 and greater than 0. So if there is an order between the categories, we should carefully specify it, and if there is no order between different categories, we should use this encoding with caution. There are other encodings that are better at handling this issue.

Ordinal encoding

Ordinal encoding is similar to label encoding but is only used when the attributes are ordinal categorical. In this encoding we usually replace each category with an integer between zero and the index of categories minus one. However, we assign these integers as the order of numeric encodes corresponds to the order of categories.

Consider a color feature in the example above. There is an order according to their wavelength between these categories, so we assign the integer labels of the categories based on their orders. We consider zero for the blue, which has the lowest wavelength. Then, we assign one for the orange which has a wavelength greater than the blue and less than red. Finally, we encode red into two:

$$\lambda_{\text{Blue}} < \lambda_{\text{Orange}} < \lambda_{\text{Red}} \Rightarrow \begin{cases} \text{Blue} \to 0 \\ \text{Orange} \to 1. \\ \text{Red} \to 2 \end{cases} \qquad (3.2)$$

In Python, we can use the sklearn library to implement this encoding. Listing 3.1 shows how to do this.

One-hot encoding

As explained, a categorical attribute should transform into a numerical value. If we have a nominal categorical attribute, we cannot use an ordinal encoding. Since there is no order between different categories, we cannot just replace each category with a different numerical value. The one-hot encoding provides a smart alternative to label encoding that resolves this issue. In this encoding, we replace each category with a 'one-hot' vector. This is a binary vector. Its length is the same as the number of categories. All the elements of the vector are zero (off) except for the one at the index that corresponds to the category.

```
1 from sklearn.preprocessing import OrdinalEncoder
2 encoder=OrdinalEncoder(categories=
3                        [['Blue',
4                         'Orange',
5                         'Red']])      ## Construct an object of
6                                       ## the type Ordinal Encoder
7                                       ## with a given order
8                                       ## of categories.
9 encoder.fit(X)                        ## Trains/Set the parameters
10                                      ## of the object.
11 X_encoded=encoder.transform(X)       ## Use the encoder object to
12                                      ## encode the X.
```

Listing 3.1. Ordinal encoding.

Original Data	Ordinal Encoded	One-Hot Encoded		
Feature	Feature	Category_1	Category_2	Category_3
Category_1	0	1	0	0
Category_2	1	0	1	0
Category_3	2	0	0	1

Figure 3.11. Encodings.

```
1 from sklearn.preprocessing import OneHotEncoder
2 encoder=OneHotEncoder()              ## Construct an object of
3                                      ## the type OneHotEncoder
4 encoder.fit(X)                       ## Trains/Set the parameters
5                                      ## of the object.
6 X_encoded=encoder.transform(X)       ## Use the encoder object to
7                                      ## encode the X.
```

Listing 3.2. One-hot encoding.

Let us look at an example. Assume that in figure 3.3, the feature, 'spectral class' has three different categories: 'M', 'B', and 'O'. Then the one-hot vector would be

$$M \rightarrow (1 \quad 0 \quad 0)$$
$$B \rightarrow (0 \quad 1 \quad 0) \tag{3.3}$$
$$O \rightarrow (0 \quad 0 \quad 1).$$

Figure 3.11 gives a comparison between ordinal and one-hot encodings for a three-category case.

We can use the Sklearn library to implement the one-hot encoding, as shown in listing 3.2.

3.2.1.3 Data transformation

After finding the right representation for the input features, we often need to do some more preprocessing on the data before we start building our model. These preprocessing operations could serve a wide range of purposes. One of the typical issues with data is that different features are on different scales. For instance, one feature may change between 0 and 1 while another feature may vary between 1 and 1000. As we will see later, this could complicate the training of the model and slow the process.

Another type of preprocessing is data reduction or dimensionality reduction. Imagine that your data has too many features for each sample. These could include features that are not necessarily relevant to the problem. For instance, for the star classification problem, the name of the star is unlikely to be relevant to its type (category). So we may remove the ID or the name of the star. Reducing the unnecessary features could help with the reducing computation resources required for training the model. But it has a more significant impact. Often the required number of data samples required for a successful training increases with the features. So the more features we have, the more samples we need to train a good model.

In this section, we will review some of the more common preprocessing methods that are applied to the data.

3.2.1.4 Standardization and scaling

From a physical point of view, all the features should be specified on their appropriate scales. Typically, this is given by a physical scale relevant to that quantity. For instance, imagine that as a feature, we want to specify the displacements of a spring. Clearly, kilometer is not a good scale to specify the displacement. Similarly, nanometers would not be an appropriate scale either.

Figure 3.12 shows some sample data for the force of a spring and its displacement. You can visually see that if the data are not displayed on the right scale, it would be hard to make sense of it.

It is thus important to represent the data on the right scale. This could significantly affect the performance of the training. To this end, one of the key and common preprocessing steps is to rescale the data.

Exercise: How would you find the right scale for some given numerical feature?

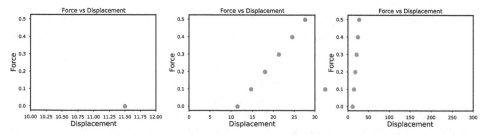

Figure 3.12. Data scale. The three plots show the force of spring versus its displacement. All the plots show the same data but on different scales. This illustrates why it is important to use the right scale for the data. If the scale is too big, all the values are practically identical, if the scale is too small, the range gets too big and it becomes challenging to capture the whole range.

```
1  from sklearn.preprocessing import StandardScaler
2
3  scaler = StandardScaler()          ## Construct an object of
4                                     ## the type StandardScaler
5
6  scaler.fit(X)                      ## Trains/Set the parameters of
7                                     ## the object, i.e. mean and variance.
8
9  X_scaled = scaler.transform(X)     ## Use the scaler object to transform
10                                    ## and standardize the feature Matrix
       X.
```

Listing 3.3. Standardization.

There are different ways to scale the features in the data. For a feature with normal distribution, it is common to rescale the variance to one and bring the mean to zero. This is called 'standardization'. Mathematically, it is

$$\bar{x} = \frac{x - \mu}{\sigma}, \tag{3.4}$$

where μ is the average of x and σ is the standard deviation. Note that x can be any of the features and the average and the standard deviations are calculated over the different samples.

This can be done easily in Python, as shown in listing 3.3.

Another method of data scaling is called min–max scaling. In this method we transform the feature to the range of zero and one. In other words, first the feature is shifted such that the minimum is moved to zero. Then all the features are scaled such that the maximum goes to one. This way, we are rescaling the feature from its range to [0, 1].

Mathematically, the min–max scaling is given by

$$\bar{x} = \frac{x - x_{\min}}{x_{\max} - x_{\min}}, \tag{3.5}$$

where $x_{\max}$ and $x_{\min}$ are the maximum and minimum values of variable x.

The code snippet in listing 3.4 shows how this can be implemented in Python.

3.2.1.5 Data reduction

Imagine that we are trying to estimate the force of a spring on a mass. We may use the mass as one of the features. However, as we know from the physics of the spring, the mass does not play any role and we can get rid of it. Similarly, when we are solving a problem, we need to identify features that are not relevant to the problem and remove them.

Data reduction helps in two major ways. First, it reduces the computational resources required for training a model. This may include the memory or number of processing units. It may also affect the time required to train a model. Second, data reduction can help improve the quality of the models that we train. This is because, with more features, we need more data samples to train a model. To obtain a better sense of this, consider this example. Assume that we are building a linear model. As discussed in equation (3.1), the number of free parameters is $n_f + 1$. This means that the more features we have, the more parameters we need to fit to build our model. However, to find more parameters,

```
1  from sklearn.preprocessing import MinMaxScaler
2
3  scaler = MinMaxScaler()        ## Construct an object of
4                                 ## the type MinMaxScaler
5  scaler.fit(X)                  ## Trains/Set the parameters of
6                                 ## the object, i.e. mean and variance.
7
8  X_scaled = scaler.transform(X) ## Use the scaler object to transform
9                                 ## and standardize the feature Matrix
      X.
```

Listing 3.4. Min–max scaling.

we need more data. If we have a limited number of samples, having too many features that provide little information about the label could affect the performance of the model. Data reduction can help us use our data more efficiently.

Exercise: Imagine that you are given a dataset with some features and a label. How would you reduce the data?

There are two major ways to reduce the data, feature selection and feature transformation. We will now discuss them in more detail.

Feature selection
The first approach is to reduce the features by selecting a subset of the features. There are different circumstances in which we can do this. For instance, if a feature is constant or is almost constant, we are not learning anything from it. Similarly, if a feature is not relevant to the label, it can be removed.

Question: How can you check if a feature is not related to the labels?

One can use the correlation between the labels and a given feature. If the correlation is small, you may be tempted to remove the feature. But you need to be careful. Sometimes, a single feature may seem uncorrelated with the labels, but combined with a different feature, it may provide a lot of information.

There are different techniques to do so.

The first one is removing features that have small variances, i.e. are almost constant. These features are not going to be helpful for predicting the label. In this technique, we need to specify a threshold for the variance. Let us call it ϵ. This feature selection technique would remove the feature if its variance is smaller than the threshold, ϵ. Note that this technique only uses the feature itself and does not rely on the label for feature selection and, in some sense, is an unsupervised data reduction technique. Listing 3.5 shows how to implement this in python using the scikit-learn library.

Question: Write a Python function that takes a dataset (X, Y) and a threshold ϵ and implements the feature selection as we described it here.

Exercise: If we use a standard scaler on the feature, it would scale the variance to one. How can we decide if the variance of the feature is large enough to keep?

One of the major challenges of feature selection based on variance is that we need to specify the threshold. Fortunately, physical quantities usually have a natural scale. For instance, we are measuring the displacement of a spring with a ruler, the scale is centimeters. If the changes in the displacement are on the orders of a few micrometers (which will not be even visible with the ruler), we take that to be of fixed

```
1 from sklearn.feature_selection import VarianceThreshold
2 VT = VarianceThreshold(threshold=epsilon)     ## Construct an object of
    the VarianceThreshold type
3                                                ## Need to provide the
    threshold for variance, i.e. the epsilon
4
5 var_thrshld_X = VT.fit_transform(X)            ## Use the object to apply
    the feature selection to the feature matrix.
```

Listing 3.5. Feature selection based on variance.

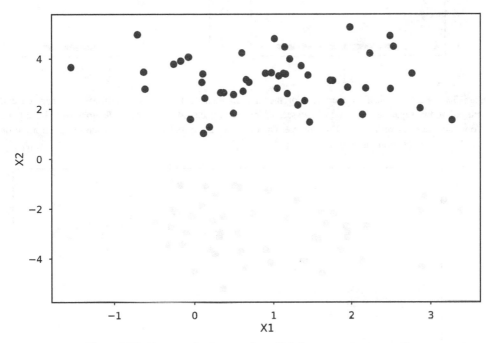

Figure 3.13. Feature selection exercise: which feature can be removed?

length. The physical scale of the problem can be used to set the threshold for this technique which means that we need to rely on our domain knowledge.

Another approach is to check how much a feature could contribute to predicting the label. There are different ways to use labels to reduce the data. To obtain a better sense of the problem, let us first do an exercise.

Exercise: Look at the data shown in figure 3.13. Propose a way to use the labels to decide which features can be removed.

It might be helpful if we separate the features and look at the dependence of the labels on each feature. Figure 3.14 shows how the label depends on the two features.

From figure 3.14 you can probably guess that correlation might be a good starting point. It also works for regression. This approach favors features that have strong correlations with the labels and removes the ones that have small correlations.

However, you need to be careful because, in some situations, a feature may not have a strong correlation on its own with the labels, but when combined with

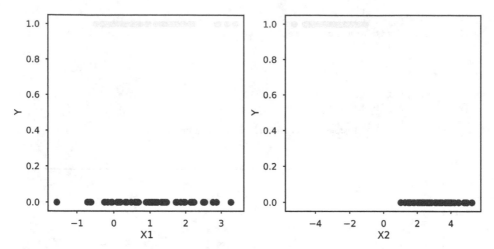

Figure 3.14. Feature selection exercise. For the data in figure 3.13, the two features are separated and displayed on two separate plots. As you can see, $X2$ is enough to classify the samples. Samples with $X2 < 0$ are yellow and the ones with $X2 > 0$ are purple. On the other hand, X1 does not provide much information towards the classification on its own.

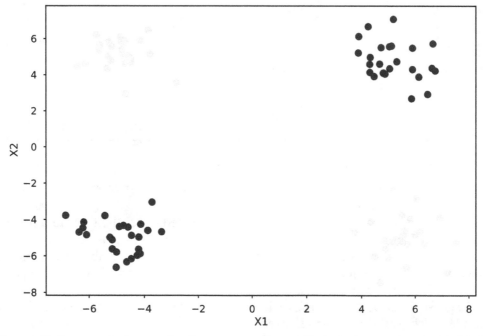

Figure 3.15. Feature selection exercise. In contrast to figure 3.13, both features are essential for the classification.

another feature, it would be relevant, even critical for predicting the labels. Figure 3.15 shows one such example.

Another approach is to use information gain. You can learn more about information gain in [6, 7]. The intuition is that we have some uncertainty about each sample belonging to a class, and each feature provides some information about the label. For instance, imagine that initially, without knowing the features of a given sample, the odds of the two classes are the same, i.e. $P(y = 1) = 0.5$. Knowing the features of the sample would change this probability. One way to characterize the importance of a feature is to calculate how much this probability changes on average when we learn the feature. For an informative feature, this probability would go to 0 or 1, i.e. $P(y = 1|x) = 0$ or 1 where x is the feature of interest. On the other hand, for a non-informative feature, the probability does not change, i.e. $P(y = 1|x) \approx P(y = 1)$.

Probably a better approach is to test if the feature is really helping with the learning task. We can train a model and see how much a specific feature contributes to the process. If a feature is not contributing to the training process and the final performance, we can remove it.

As we will discuss, some of the machine learning models can attribute a notion of importance to the features. For instance, for a linear model, the weights of the model can be used to characterize the significance of the corresponding features, i.e. a successfully trained model would assign greater weights to the more important features and smaller weights to the less important ones.

Exercise: Imagine that you are building a linear model as was described in equation (3.1). After training the model, the fitted parameters are shown in figure 3.16. If you wanted to reduce the data and remove one of the features, which ones would you get rid of and why?.

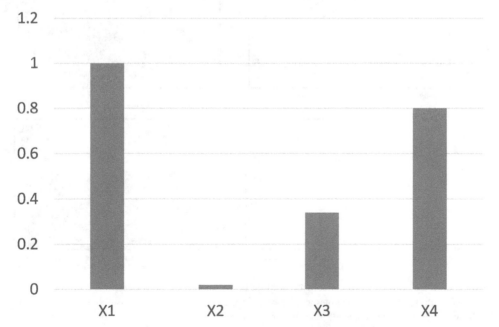

Figure 3.16. Feature importance: this plot shows the importance of four features in the classification of some sample dataset. Which one can be removed?

It is not hard to decide which feature to remove. Many supervised learning models have mechanisms for ranking the value of the different features of their process. We will see some of these when we get to the next section and introduce some of the supervised learning models.

Even if the model does not provide a mechanism for ranking the importance of the features, we can still use the performance of the trained model to characterize the significance of features. More specifically, we can train the model once with and once without a specific feature and see how much the performance changes. If the performance is significantly reduced when we remove the feature, this means that the corresponding feature is important for predicting the label and cannot be removed. However, if the performance stays unchanged, then this indicates that the corresponding features do not have a significant contribution to the prediction of the label, at least not with that specific hypothesis.

This technique requires training a model. When we reach the models for supervised learning, we will provide some examples of this approach.

Feature transformation

Imagine that we have two features that both provide some information about the label, however, they are not independent. For example, see figure 3.17. In the

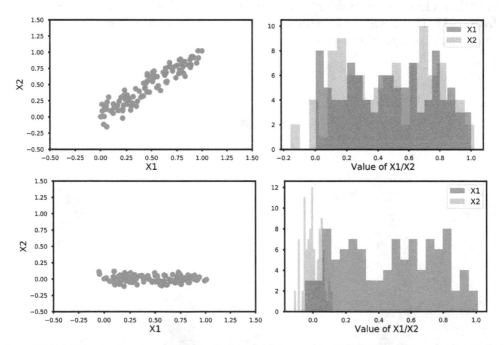

Figure 3.17. Data reduction: these plots show the idea behind one of the techniques for data reduction. In the top panel, both X_1 and X_2 have variations. However, it is clear that these are mostly one-dimensional data. The lower panel shows the same data where the features are rotated. It illustrates that only one of the features (the new X_1) changes, while the other feature (the new X_2) is practically constant. The plots on the right show the histograms of the features. In the top panel, both features are distributed over the whole range. In the bottom panel, the right plot shows that after the rotation, the second feature has a small variance.

top-left panel, you can see that the two features X_1 and X_2 are correlated. In such a circumstance, we may not need both of the features. But how can we reduce the data in this case?

We can use an idea similar to the feature selection based on the threshold in the variance. The issue, however, is that both features have relatively large variances. This can be seen from their histogram on the top right panel of 3.17.

One solution is to transform the feature. In the case of the data in figure 3.17, if we rotate the data, we obtain the data in the bottom left panel. Now you can see that one of the features has low variance and is almost constant. We can use the variance threshold to reduce the data. But for this, we first need to transform the data.

This is the general idea that we will review for the rest of the data reduction section.

In situations such as the one in figure 3.17, we cannot simply remove a specific feature. However, there is still some redundancy in the data that we can and need to remove. The goal here is to find a transformation that takes the features to a new set of features that are easier to reduce. Mathematically, we make a new set of features that depend on the original features, i.e.

$$\bar{X}_j = \mathcal{F}_j(X_1, X_2, \ldots, X_{nf}). \tag{3.6}$$

where $\bar{X}_j$ is the jth features after transformation and $\mathcal{F}_j$ describes how the new feature depends on the original features.

Intuitively, we want the transformation to reduce the correlation or redundancies between the features. In the case of figure 3.17, you can see that the new features are not correlated where the original ones were strongly correlated. You can also see that once this is done, one feature is enough to encompass all the required data.

One of the most famous ways for data reduction using feature transformation is the 'principal component analysis' (PCA).

3.2.1.6 Principal component analysis
PCA is one of the most commonly used data reduction techniques. Here we will review how it works. It is indeed one of the most simple and brilliant techniques in ML.

To better understand PCA, let us follow a schematic example. Imagine that you are given a dataset with n_s samples and n_f features. This means that the feature matrix is $n_s \times n_f$ matrix.

As explained, there could be some correlation between different features (see figure 3.17). For PCA, we try to find the transformation that leads to features with the maximum possible variance. This means that the new features are such that the first one, $\bar{X}_1$, is the linear combination of the original features with the maximum variance. The second one, $\bar{X}_2$, is the linear combination of the original features with the second largest variance, and so on. If we want to reduce m features and reduce the data to $n_f - m$ features, we can remove the last m transformed features.

To do this, we can use the covariance matrix and the Lagrange multiplier approach for the optimization. This leads to finding the eigenvectors of the covariance matrix and ranking them based on their corresponding eigenvalue.

We start with the covariance matrix. Mathematically the covariance is given by

$$\Sigma_{j,k} = \frac{\sum_{i=1}^{n}(X_j^i - \bar{X}_j) \times (X_k^i - \bar{X}_k)}{n}. \tag{3.7}$$

The $\bar{X}_j$ is the average value of the jth feature of the dataset over all samples. Note that subtracting each feature from its average shifts the corresponding feature and sets its average at zero. We refer to the shifted features as the centralized features.

The covariance matrix is an $n_f \times n_f$ matrix that is usually used to study the correlation of different features. This is a symmetric matrix. The off-diagonal elements correspond to the correlation of the features and the diagonal elements of the matrix are the variance of each feature.

The zero off-diagonal elements of this matrix indicate that there is no correlation between the corresponding features.

To reduce the correlation between the transformed features, we want the off-diagonal elements of their covariance matrix to be minimized and ideally to zero. In other words, we are looking for a transformation that gives a diagonal covariance matrix. This means that we are looking for a transformation that diagonalizes the covariance matrix. Thus, next we need to solve the eigenvalue equation, which gives

$$\Sigma \vec{v} = \lambda \vec{v}. \tag{3.8}$$

Solving this equation leads to finding the eigenvalues and eigenvectors and we obtain

$$\bar{\Sigma} = U\Sigma U^{\dagger}, \tag{3.9}$$

where $\bar{\Sigma}$ is the new covariance matrix for the transformed features, U is the unitary transformation that diagonalizes the covariance matrix and $\dagger$ represents the complex conjugate and transposition of the matrix. The matrix U is built by stacking the normalized eigenvectors together. We also assume that the transformation is done such that the eigenvalues on the diagonal of $\bar{\Sigma}$ are sorted decreasingly.

To reduce the data, we want to remove the m features with the smallest eigenvalues and keep the $n_f - m$ features with the largest eigenvalues. This is because these eigenvalues are the variance of the new features and the larger the eigenvalue, the larger the variance.

Exercise: What are the reduced set of features? Note that so far, we have not specified the transformed features.

We can transform the dataset to the new set of coordinates using the diagonalization transformation. We can calculate all the transformed features and then remove the m new features that correspond to the smallest eigenvalues of Σ. However, it is more efficient to do the transformation for only the features that we are keeping. To this end, we use the $n_f - m$ eigenvectors corresponding to the

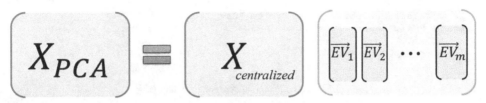

Figure 3.18. In order to find the PCA of the feature matrix, we multiply the centralized dataset with the transformation matrix. Columns of the transformation matrix are eigenvectors of the covariance matrix which are arranged in descending order. If we want to reduce the data and keep only m features, we can keep eigenvectors of the m largest values of λ_i. The new feature matrix would have m non-zero columns.

larger eigenvalues and make a transformation matrix. The eigenvectors are columns of this transformation matrix and are arranged descendingly based on the magnitude of their eigenvalues. Then we multiply the centralized feature matrix, X, by this transformation matrix. Mathematically that is

$$\bar{X}_{\text{PCA}} = X \cdot \left((\vec{v}_1) \ \ (\vec{v}_2) \ \cdots \ (\vec{v}_{n_f - m}) \right) \tag{3.10}$$

You can check that the reduced feature matrix $\bar{X}_{\text{PCA}}$ is $n_s \times (n_f - m)$.

Figure 3.18 shows the transformation schematically.

The combination of primary features that makes the new set of features is called the principal components. Intuitively, these are the components that have zero correlation with each other. If we calculate the covariance matrix for this new dataset, we would have

$$\Sigma_{\text{PCA}} = \begin{pmatrix} \lambda_1 & 0 & 0 & 0 \\ 0 & \lambda_2 & 0 & 0 \\ 0 & 0 & \ddots & 0 \\ 0 & 0 & 0 & \lambda_{n_f - m} \end{pmatrix}. \tag{3.11}$$

Question: Verify equation (3.11).

As we can see the off-diagonal elements vanished. This means there is no correlation between the new set of features, and the principal components. The diagonal elements of the covariance matrix, i.e. the eigenvalues, are the variance of principal components.

This section was meant to give you a basic understanding of PCA and does not cover all the mathematical details of PCA. For more information, you are encouraged to read [8].

The algorithm is summarized in the following pseudo-code.

Algorithm 1: The PCA algorithm.

Data: Feature matrix X

1. Calculate the covariance matrix, Σ;
2. Calculate the eigenvectors and eigenvalues of Σ;
3. Remove the m eigenvectors with the smallest eigenvalues;

```
1 from sklearn.decomposition import PCA
2 pca = PCA(n_components=m)                    ## Cunstruct an object of
3                                              ## PCA
4 X_pca = pca.fit_transform(X)                 ## Implement the PCA   on
5                                              ## dataset.
```

Listing 3.6. Principal component analysis.

4. Form the transformation matrix from the remaining $n_f - m$ eigenvectors;

5. Apply the transformation to the centralized feature matrix.

For more information on PCA, see [8–10].

Question: Implement the PCA algorithm.

Question: How can you check if your implementation is working properly?

Listing 3.6 shows a simple Python code that uses the scikit-learn library and allows you to apply the PCA algorithm.

It helps to do a few examples to get a better sense of how PCA works.

Question: The following matrix shows a feature matrix with three features and four samples. Imagine that we want to keep only two features. Apply PCA and find the transformed features.

$$X = \begin{bmatrix} x_1 & x_2 & x_3 \\ 1 & 1 & 5 \\ 1 & 2 & 4 \\ 1 & 3 & 7 \\ 1 & 4 & 6 \end{bmatrix}. \tag{3.12}$$

Exercise: Apply the PCA algorithm to the ground-state energy dataset, DST-GSE (table 1.2).

  A. Plot the eigenvalues.

  B. Visualize the principal components.

Use the Python code in listing 3.6 to transform the data. Figure 3.19 visualizes the eigenvalues and the principal components.

The left panel shows how rapidly the eigenvalues drop to close to zero. Note that this is on a logarithmic scale.

The right panel illustrates the principal components. The color bar shows the value of the matrix elements. Blue indicates close to zero values, and red and other colors indicate components that contribute to the corresponding principal component.

At this point, you may be wondering what a good choice for m is. If m is too small, we may end up keeping a lot of principal components with small variances. On the other hand, if we make m too big, we may end up losing principal components that are important.

Question: Find a way to choose the parameter m.

In addition to techniques that use linear transformation, we can also use non-linear transformations. Manifold learning techniques are a class of techniques that use non-linear functions to capture the essence of the data with fewer features.

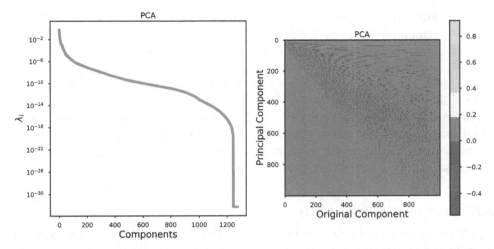

Figure 3.19. PCA for the GSE data. The plot on the left shows the Schmidt values. It is evident that except for a few of them, the rest are extremely small and can be neglected. Note that this is on a logarithmic scale. The plot on the right shows the principal components in terms of the original components.

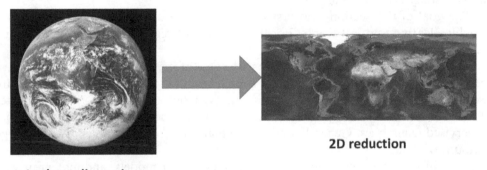

Figure 3.20. Non-linear feature transformation. One example of a non-linear transformation that is commonly used for data reduction is transformations such as mapping the 3D surface of the Earth onto 2D maps. Clearly, they cannot preserve all the information in the original data, but they provide a good representation. For instance, it may seem from this map that Russia is bigger than the whole continent of Africa, but this is not true, it is just due to the non-linear transformation. (Image credit: NASA (left); NASA Goddard Space Flight Center, Image by Reto Stöckli (right).)

To make some analogy, think about all the maps of Earth that you have seen (figure 3.20). We know that the Earth is a three-dimensional object. Maps represent only the surface of the Earth which is two-dimensional. However, with normal coordinates (e.g. Cartesian or polar), every point is specified with three parameters (i.e. features). Maps apply a non-linear transformation on these points and project them into a two-dimensional space.

Question: If you were to make a map of the surface of the Earth, what kind of transformation would you use?

There are a wide range of non-linear techniques used for data reduction. They are known as 'manifold learning'. We do not cover manifold learning techniques here. The reader is encouraged to see [11, 12] for an in-depth introduction to manifold learning techniques.

We will, however, review some unsupervised non-linear techniques for data reduction later in the book.

So far in this chapter, we have reviewed the first ingredient of supervised learning algorithms, namely the data. We studied different types of data as well as different preprocessing techniques. Next, we move on to the model, which may be considered as the heart of any supervised learning task.

3.2.2 Supervised learning models

There are different techniques to build models that will map the input features to the corresponding labels in the data. In this section we will review some of the more well-recognized supervised techniques.

We break these techniques into two groups, traditional supervised learning models and NNs. Here we focus on traditional techniques. In the next chapter, we will study NNs in detail.

The goal of this section is to first give you a sense of how the full pipeline of a machine learning project works. For this, it does not really matter if we are using a linear model or a complex NN.

The second goal is to familiarize you with some of the classic techniques that have been used for years before the hype of deep learning. Some of these techniques are extremely powerful and in some cases can even outperform NNs. We will later discuss when it is appropriate to use NNs and when to resort to traditional supervised techniques. Generally, NNs are great for complex problems with a large amount of data.

We will start with the simplest techniques, i.e. linear models, and make our way toward more complicated traditional models.

For the most part, we will be focusing on classification. However, most of these techniques can be extended to regression as well. In fact, for many of these techniques, the model finds a decision boundary $f_w(X)$. Then the category of a sample is specified by whether it falls above the decision boundary, i.e. $f_w(X) \geqslant 1$, or below it i.e. $f_w(X) \leqslant 1$.

3.2.2.1 Linear models

We introduced a linear model in equation (3.1). For a classification problem, the goal is to find a linear fit to the decision boundary. If different classes can be separated by a linear decision boundary, the data are said to be 'linearly separable'. It is not always possible to separate different classes with a linear decision boundary. See the example in figure 3.21. Panel (A) demonstrates linearly separable data. However, for panel (B) it is evident that it is not possible to find a linear decision boundary.

One can represent a linear model with a vector of the free parameters, i.e.

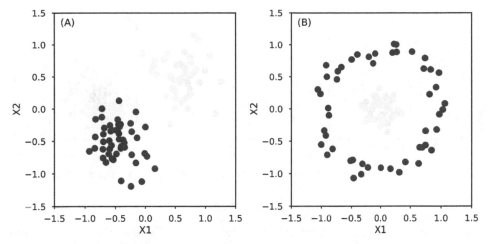

Figure 3.21. Examples of datasets that (A) are and (B) are not linearly separable.

$$\vec{W} = (w_0, w_1, \ldots, w_{n_f}).\qquad(3.13)$$

The linear model can be expressed as

$$f_w(X) = \vec{W} \cdot \vec{X},\qquad(3.14)$$

where · represents the inner product between the two vectors. Also

$$\vec{X} = (1, X_1, X_2, \ldots, X_{n_f}).$$

This provides a compact representation that we will use frequently throughout this book. In the next chapter, we will see that this representation is also computationally more efficient. In other words, it is more efficient to use the vectorized representation and turn the for-loop into matrix multiplication.

The $f_w(X)$ gives a hyper-plane in the n_f dimensional feature space. For the task of supervised learning, the goal is to find a hyper-plane that separates the samples from different classes.

Up to this point, we have not provided any algorithm for finding the free parameters, $\{w_i\}$. At this stage, we are not really concerned with the performance of the linear models. Later, we will explain how we use the loss function and an optimization technique to find the set of parameters that would provide a good fit to the data. But to give you a sense, do the following exercise.

Question: For the data in figure 3.21(A), try different values for the $\vec{W}$ and find the model that gives a good classification.

Question: Is there a unique model that gives the best result? If not, is there any preference between different models that may classify all the samples correctly?

The next algorithm provides a systematic approach to the last question. It tries to find a model that maximizes the margins of the decision boundary from the two classes.

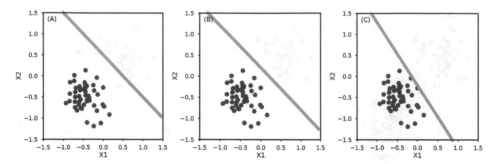

Figure 3.22. Three different classifications. Which one do you think is a better classification?

3.2.2.2 Support vector machines

From the last question, you probably have learned that there could be many models with the same performance, and even a model that classifies all the samples perfectly is not unique. Figure 3.22 shows three such decision boundaries. Which one do you think is a better classification?

You probably chose (B).

Exercise: Why do you feel (B) gives a better classification?

The decision boundary in (B) leaves a relatively large distance from both of the clusters. Intuitively, this minimizes the probability of misclassification.

With the intuition above, we have two expectations from an ideal linear decision boundary:

- To segregate the samples from different classes as much as possible.
- To maximize the distances of samples from the decision boundary.

For the first condition, ideally, we are hoping for perfect classification, however, if the data are not linearly separable, that is not possible.

The second condition is what defines the support vector machines (SVMs) [13]. A linear SVM is a linear model in that the decision boundary is optimized to have the maximum margins from the samples of each class. Maximizing the margins helps with the confidence of the results of the classification. It means that not only does the model provides a good classification for the training data, but it is also more likely to generalize well for new samples.

We give a brief overview of how the training process works for an SVM.

We use the points which are close to the decision boundary. These points are called support vectors. We want to maximize the distance of these points from the decision boundary.

For simplicity, let us focus on the data in the example above where there are only two features. The decision boundary is a line and we need to find the slope and intercept of the line. Figure 3.23(a) shows three options for the decision boundary.

The equation of a line is given by

$$\vec{W} \cdot \vec{X} - b = 0, \tag{3.15}$$

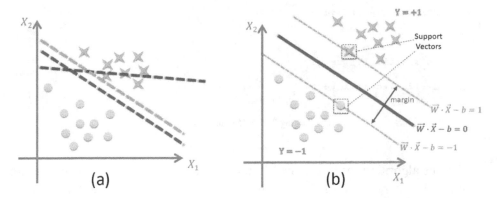

Figure 3.23. (a) The red hyper-plane is a suitable choice with respect to two other hyperplanes. Since it segregates two classes and also has a maximum margin. (b) Different elements of the SVM.

or in the expanded form

$$W_1 X_1 + W_2 X_2 - b = 0. \tag{3.16}$$

Normally, the classification is given by whether a sample falls above or below the decision boundary. The issue is that the points close to the decision boundary are more likely to be misclassified. It is hard to trust a classification that can change by moving the decision boundary slightly.

For the SVM, we want more confidence, so we set a higher bar for the classification condition, i.e.

$$\vec{W} \cdot \vec{X} - b \geqslant 1, \tag{3.17}$$

for the first class and

$$\vec{W} \cdot \vec{X} - b \leqslant -1 \tag{3.18}$$

for the second class. With these two conditions, if a sample is classified to be in the first category, it is not just above the decision boundary, it is also outside the margin of the decision boundary. This provides a classification with a higher level of confidence in the results.

Note that in equation $\vec{W} \cdot \vec{X} - b$ the $\vec{W}$ and b are specified after training and $\vec{X}$ is the coordinate of the point. In the SVM algorithm, the decision boundary should classify the points correctly and has the maximum possible margin.

For the example above, the margins are indicated with the two gray dashed lines in figure 3.23(b). Mathematically, they are

$$\vec{W} \cdot \vec{X} - b = 1 \tag{3.19}$$

$$\vec{W} \cdot \vec{X} - b = -1. \tag{3.20}$$

```
1  from sklearn import svm
2
3  clf = svm.SVC()                 ## Construct an object of
4                                  ## the SVM classifier
5  clf.fit(x_train, y_train)       ## Train the parameters of
6                                  ## the object
7  y_pred=clf.predict(x_test)      ## Use the trained
8                                  ## classifier for predication
```

Listing 3.7. SVM classifier.

Thus this algorithm looks for the $\vec{W}$ and b which both segregate the classes and maximize the margins. With $\vec{W}$ and b we have the decision boundary. For the example above, this is schematically depicted as the red line in figure 3.23.

For more information about the SVMs, see [13].

To implement an SVM model in Python, you can use the scikit-learn library, see listing 3.7. It has most of the models that we cover in this section implemented and you can use them with a few lines of code.

For almost all ML models implemented in the scikit-learn library, the process of training a model is similar to what we did for SVM. That is:

- (1) Create an object of the type of model that you want to build, e.g. SVM.
- (2) All model objects come with a method called 'fit' which takes X and Y and trains the model.
- (3) All model objects come with a method called 'predict' which predicts the labels for a given set of samples.

The predict function can be applied to the samples in the data that are used for training as well as new samples that the model has not seen yet. Also note that for the predict function, the model needs to be trained first. Before training, the model is usually initialized randomly.

Here we focused on applications of SVM for linear models. However, SVMs can be used to build powerful non-linear models as well. This requires using kernels which we will be introducing soon.

Question: We explained how to use SVMs for classification problems. Try to expand this idea for regression. (*Hint*: If you need help, see [14].)

3.2.2.3 *Logistic regression*

Logistic regression refers to a class of supervised learning tasks that assigns probabilities to the samples [15].

For instance, consider a binary classification problem with $\{0, 1\}$ classes. A logistic regression model for this problem returns the probability of the sample being in class 1, i.e. $P(Y = 1)$.

This means that the outputs of the model should be valid probabilities, i.e. positive numbers and less than one. To build a logistic regression model, we use the sigmoid function which is defined as

$$\text{Sigmoid}(z) = \frac{1}{1 + e^{-z}}. \qquad (3.21)$$

The sigmoid function can map the function in equation (3.14) to probabilities between zero and one. Mathematically, the logistic regression model is

$$f_w(X) = \text{Sigmoid}(\vec{W}.\vec{X}). \qquad (3.22)$$

We will discuss the sigmoid function in more detail later.

For a more in-depth introduction to logistic regression models, see [15].

3.2.2.4 Polynomial models

Often, supervised learning problems are not simple enough to be done with linear models and we need to use non-linear models. Figure 3.24 shows a schematic example where there are two classes and they are not linearly separable.

For such examples, we need non-linear models. There is a wide range of non-linear models. We are going to start with one of the simplest ones.

Perhaps the easiest way to extend the linear hypothesis is to use polynomial models. These are models that in addition to the linear terms, allow for the higher-order (non-linear) terms

As an example, consider a quadratic model for a problem with two input features, i.e. $n_f = 2$. The quadratic model is described as

$$f_w(\bar{X}) = w_0 + w_1X_1 + w_2X_2 + w_3X_1^2 + w_4X_2^2 + w_5X_1 \times X_2,$$

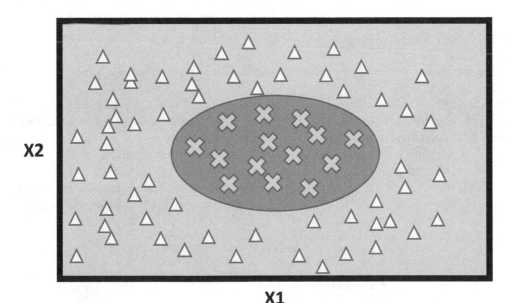

Figure 3.24. Non-linear classification. Often the classes are not linearly separable and we need to resort to non-linear and more complex models.

where the w_i are the free parameters of the model.

One of the key advantages of polynomial models is that the non-linearity can be controlled by the degree of the non-linearity. For instance, if for a specific problem, based on your domain knowledge, you know that the label is a polynomial of degree two of the features, you can make a model that captures exactly that level of complexity. One such example is the entanglement classification problem for two qubits or spins. There is a method based on the negativity of the partial transpose of the density matrix. Since the density matrix is a 4×4 matrix, one can show that this leads to a polynomial of degree 4. This indicates that a polynomial model of $d = 4$ is enough and we do not need to go beyond that.

Exercise: Why do we need to keep the complexity (degree) of the model as low as possible?

Before we answer this question, answer the following question.

Question: For a dataset with n_f feature, how many free parameters do we get with a polynomial model of degree d?

How does the number of free parameters scale?

As you can see, it is computationally expensive to add non-linearity by increasing the degree of the polynomial models. This slows down the training process and also would require more data to fit all the free parameters.

One more drawback is that high-degree polynomial models do not generalize well beyond the training data. We will talk more about this later. Usually, less complex (low-degree) models are more desirable.

One easy way to build polynomial models is to transform the data and add the non-linear terms as new features. This means that instead of processing each sample through the model we transform the features and add new features. For instance, for the example above with two features, for $d = 2$ we obtain

$$\Phi_{d=2}([X_1, X_2]) = [1, X_1, X_2, X_1^2, X_2^2, X_1 X_2]. \tag{3.23}$$

Now instead of building a polynomial model for X, we can build a linear model for $\Phi_d(\bar{X})$.

Question: Verify that for $d = 2$, both approaches give the same results.

This provides an alternative for building polynomial models that in some cases can be more convenient than building the model directly.

You can use scikit-learn to apply this feature transformation to the feature matrix, see listing 3.8.

Note that this is an unsupervised transformation. For such transformations in scikit-learn, you can call 'fit_trasnform' which automatically transforms the data.

```
1 from sklearn.preprocessing import PolynomialFeatures
2 poly = PolynomialFeatures(degree=n)   ## Cunstruct an object of
3                                        ## PolynomialFeatures, with
4                                        ## n degrees.
5 X_poly = poly.fit_transform(X)              ## Use the object to
    make new
6                                        ## set of features.
```

Listing 3.8. Polynomial features.

The challenge with polynomial techniques, as we described it here, is that if there are too many features and we want to build a model with a high degree, the number of parameters scales as n_f^d with d the degree of the polynomial.

Handling the complexity, in particular if we are building the model as described above, could be challenging. In some cases we can avoid this challenge by using kernels. In the next section, we will briefly explain what kernels are and how this idea works.

3.2.2.5 Kernels

For a lot of machine learning techniques, we work with the inner product of the feature vectors and do not necessarily need the feature vectors themselves. For instance, for SVMs there is an equivalent formulation that relies on the calculation of the inner product between feature vectors of every of the two samples [13].

In such cases, one can use the 'kernel trick' [16–18]. To better understand this, let us first use the technique described in the previous section for making non-linear models. For simplicity, the following transformation does not include the linear terms or the intercept:

$$\Phi\left(\begin{bmatrix} X_1 \\ X_2 \end{bmatrix}\right) = \begin{bmatrix} X_1^2 \\ X_2^2 \\ \sqrt{2}\,X_1 X_2 \end{bmatrix}. \tag{3.24}$$

Now imagine that for our algorithm we need the inner product of two feature vectors. That is

$$\left\langle \Phi\left(\begin{bmatrix} X_1 \\ X_2 \end{bmatrix}\right), \Phi\left(\begin{bmatrix} Z_1 \\ Z_2 \end{bmatrix}\right) \right\rangle = \cdots = X_1^2 Z_1^2 + X_2^2 Z_2^2 + 2 X_1 X_2 Z_1 Z_2. \tag{3.25}$$

Question: In the equation above, we skipped the middle calculations. Derive the final result.

Now imagine that we define a kernel as

$$K(\vec{X}, \vec{Z}) = \langle \vec{X}, \vec{Z} \rangle^2. \tag{3.26}$$

Exercise: Apply the kernel above to

$$\vec{X} = \begin{bmatrix} X_1 \\ X_2 \end{bmatrix}, \vec{Z} = \begin{bmatrix} Z_1 \\ Z_2 \end{bmatrix}.$$

You can see that the kernel gives

$$K(\vec{X}, \vec{Z}) = (X_1 Z_1 + X_2 Z_2)^2,$$

which is the same as the result we obtained with feature transformation.

The key point is that we did not need to transform all the samples and using the kernel can avoid the computationally expensive transformation that is needed for building a polynomial model.

Kernels have been studied extensively in mathematics and machine learning [17, 19]. There are kernels for higher-order polynomials or even kernels that keep all orders with decaying weights. The reader is encouraged to see [17, 18] if they are interested to learn more about this topic.

3.2.2.6 K-nearest neighbors (KNN)

Polynomial techniques are not the only non-linear method for supervised learning. Here we will review one of the most intuitive supervised learning techniques.

Exercise: Imagine that you are given the data illustrated in figure 3.25, where there are two classes. Consider the three samples indicated as red circles. The labels of these samples are not known.

- Label the red samples.
- What is your intuition for your choice?
- Which one was harder to classify? Why?

You probably classified sample 1 as a green cross and 2 as a yellow rectangle. But why? Our intuition is that if it is surrounded by samples from a specific class, then it should belong to the same class. For instance, in the case of sample 1, it is surrounded by green samples.

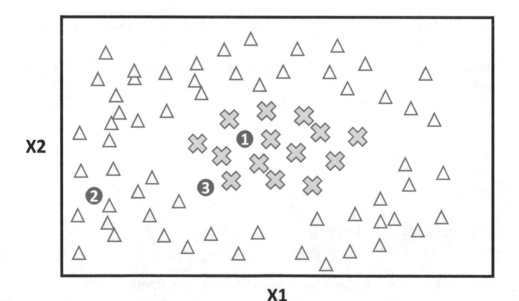

Figure 3.25. Classify the three samples indicated in red.

```
1 from sklearn.neighbors import KNeighborsClassifier
2 clf = KNeighborsClassifier(n_neighbors=k)  ## Cunstruct an object of
3                                            ## KNN, with k neighbors
4
5 clf.fit(x_train,y_train)                   ## Train the parameters of
6                                            ## the object
7 y_pred=clf.predict(x_test)                 ## Use the object to make
8                                            ## predication.
```

Listing 3.9. *K*-nearest neighbor classifier.

Probably the most challenging one is sample 3 as it is between the two classes. You may classify it based on its closest neighbor or the majority of its 3 or 5 closest neighbors.

This approach makes the basis for one of the most natural supervised learning techniques. In this technique, we use samples with similar or close feature vectors to predict the label of a new sample. This technique is known as '*K*-nearest neighbors' (KNN) [20, 21].

Specifically, to predict the label for a given sample, we calculate its distance from every other sample in the dataset. We pick *K*-nearest neighbors of the sample, hence the name. We then use the labels of the k neighbors to predict the label of the new sample. For this, we can take a majority vote between the labels of the neighbors. For instance, if $k = 5$ and 3 of them are from class 0, then we predict the sample to be of class 0. We can also weigh the contribution of the k neighbors based on their distances from the target sample.

Question: What happens if we take $k = 0$?

Question: What happens if we take $k = n_s$?

Question: We usually take k to be an odd number, especially when we use majority voting for predicting the label. Can you explain why?

The scikit-learn library has an implementation of the KNN algorithm, see listing 3.9. The code below shows how to train a KNN model. Like other models, we start with building an object of the KNN class. We then call the 'fit' method to train the object. For the case of KNN, this is really memorizing all the feature vectors. Next, when the 'predict' method is called for a new sample, the model calculates its distance from all the samples in the dataset, finds the k closest ones, and determines the label based on the labels of the neighbors.

Distance metrics

One of the key ingredients of KNN is the measure that is used to define the distance. Note that there is no unique choice for this. The metric used to calculate the distance can affect the predictions significantly.

There are different choices of metric, and here we review some of the more common ones.

Euclidean distance

By far the most popular distance is the Euclidean distance. Mathematically, that is

$$d(X, Z) = \sqrt{\sum_i^{n_f}(X_i - Z_i)^2}, \tag{3.27}$$

where X and Z represent two points in the space. In the case of KNN, these are the feature vectors corresponding to samples.

Minkowski distance

Euclidean distance is a member of a bigger family, the Minkowski distances which are defined as

$$d_p(X, Z) = \left(\sum_{i=1}^{n_f}|X_i - Z_i|^p\right)^{\frac{1}{p}}, \tag{3.28}$$

where p can be any positive integer. For $p = 2$, we obtain the Euclidean distance. $p = 1$ is another popular choice.

Manhattan distance

For $p = 1$ the distance metric is called the Manhattan distance.

$$d(X, Z) = \sum_{i=1}^{n_f}|X_i - Z_i|. \tag{3.29}$$

Chebyshev distance

For $p = \infty$ the distance metric is known as the Chebyshev metric. You can check that mathematically, for $p = \infty$ the Minkowski distance gives

$$d_\infty(X, Z) = \max_i(|X_i - Z_i|). \tag{3.30}$$

This distance put emphasis on the feature that has the largest distinction between the two samples.

Figure 3.26 compares these different distances schematically.

There are other distances that are not based on the Minkowski distance. Here we review some of them.

Exercise (Hamming distance): Imagine that you are given two binary vectors, i.e. vectors with elements $\in \{0, 1\}$. What would you use to characterize the distance between the two vectors?

One of the common choices for this application is the 'Hamming distance'. It counts the number of indices where the two vectors are different.

This is particularly good for categorical features.

Exercise: Find a mathematical expression for the Hamming distance.

We can add the two binary vectors and count the number of non-zero elements. Remember that in the binary representation, $0 + 0 = 1 + 1 = 0$. So we can use

$$d_H(X, Z) = \sum_i(X + Z)_i. \tag{3.31}$$

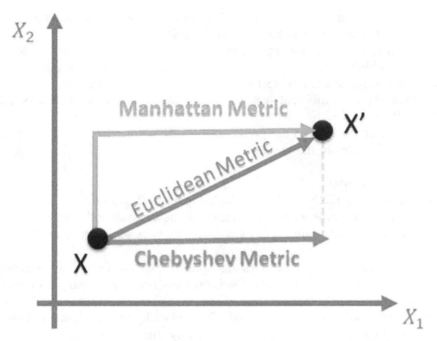

Figure 3.26. Distance of two points, X and X', in different metrics.

Cosine metric: In some situations, we are only interested in the angular distance between two points. This means that we may be not interested in the scale of the vectors. For instance, consider the distance between two vectors $\vec{v}$ and $2 \times \vec{v}$. Each of the distance functions above would indicate some distance between the two vectors. However, if we do not care about the scale of the vectors, they are essentially the same vectors. For such circumstances, the angular distance provides a good alternative. For the example above, the angular distance between the two vectors is zero.

We can use the cosine between the two vectors as a measure of similarity, i.e.

$$\cos \theta = \frac{\langle \vec{X}, \vec{Z} \rangle}{|\vec{X}| \; |\vec{Z}|}, \tag{3.32}$$

where θ is the angle between $\vec{X}$ and $\vec{Z}$. Cosine is not a distance, it is a measure of similarity. For two identical vectors, we obtain $\cos \theta = 1$, and for two vectors perpendicular to each other (i.e. max distance), we obtain $\cos \theta = 0$.

For the distance, we can use the angle itself. Although it is common to use cosine as a measure of similarity.

For more information on distance functions, see [22].

Using these different distance functions and playing with the sale of the different features could give different results for the final classification than you obtain from KNN. For example, it may be that, based on your domain knowledge, one feature plays a more important role in the classification task. For such a case, we can define a distance that puts more emphasis on that specific feature.

KNN can also be used for regression. We leave this as a question to the reader.

Question: Think about how we can use KNN for a regression model.

Before we move to the next technique, let us ask a few questions.

Question: How do different features contribute to the supervised task using a KNN model?

Question: Can we explain the prediction of a KNN model for a specific sample based on the features of the sample?

3.2.2.7 Decision trees

The predictions of a KNN model, despite being natural, are usually hard to explain. It is not easy to find some set of rules that would describe or make sense of the result of a KNN model. Explainability is a key factor that for some applications, becomes important.

Some machine learning techniques are easier to explain. One of these methods is the decision tree technique [23, 24]. Decision trees provide a clear set of rules and conditions to predict the labels.

Let us take a look at an example. The left panel in figure 3.27 shows some samples in the feature space with their labels indicated by their shape and color.

Exercise: Find a set of conditions that would give an accurate classification of the samples in the left panel of figure 3.28.

For such a problem, one can write the flowchart as the one in the right panel of figure 3.27 to classify the samples.

The tree in the right panel of figure 3.27 is called a 'decision tree' [23, 24].

To better understand this concept, let us add a little more complexity to the problem.

Question: Build a decision tree for the samples in figure 3.28. Note that there is a yellow sample in the bottom left quadrant.

As you can see, it is easy to understand and explain a decision tree. The tree provides a set of conditions based on the features of a sample. The sample is

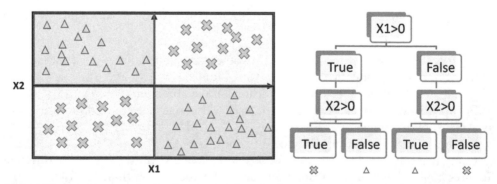

Figure 3.27. A decision tree classification. On the left we are given the feature space of a classification problem. On the right we have the decision tree that can classify the samples from the feature space correctly.

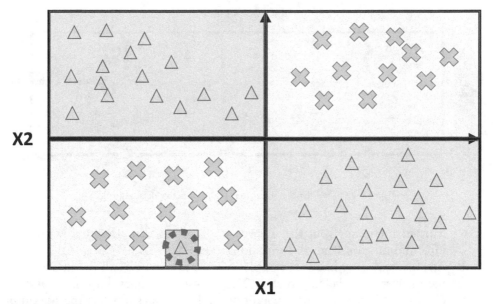

X2

X1

Figure 3.28. The feature space in this plot is similar to the one in figure 3.27. However, there is an additional point that is yellow but based on the classification of the tree in figure 3.27, falls in the green zone. Build a tree that classifies all the samples correctly.

classified based on which conditions are met. It is relatively easy to understand the role and contribution of each feature to the decision-making.

In some ways, decision trees are the closest ML technique to traditional algorithmic techniques. The main difference is that, for decision trees, we learn the conditions from the data.

Exercise: How do we train a decision tree? More specifically, given a set of data samples, how can we automatically choose the 'decision rules'?

One way to do this is to find decision rules that have the highest information gain. We briefly explained what information gain is. In this context, there is some uncertainty regarding the category of each sample. Each decision rule is like asking a question and getting an answer to that question about the data. The information gain describes how much the uncertainty is reduced by knowing the answer to that question.

This, of course, would be more concrete if we used the concept of information and entropy. But let us try to gain some intuition with some examples. Imagine that we have a binary classification problem (i.e. only two classes) and that the dataset is balanced (i.e. the two classes have the same population). Given a new sample, initially, we are as uncertain as we can be, the sample has the same probability for both classes. Now, let us say that we ask a first question that splits the samples into two categories, one for when the answer is yes and one for the answer is no. For the subcategories, we may have the following possibilities.

   A. The subcategories are still balanced, meaning that each subcategory has the same number of samples from each class. This means that we have not

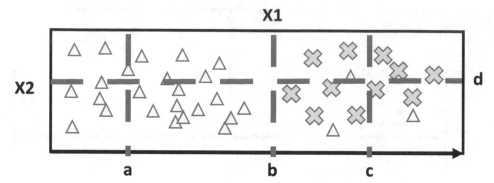

Figure 3.29. Find the condition that makes a better deciding rule.

learned anything from the answer to this question. In other words, the information gain from this question is zero.

B. Each subcategory has only samples from one class, e.g. all the samples with the answer 'yes', belong to class 0, and all the samples with 'no' belong to class two. This is the ideal condition and that question has the maximum information gain.

C. The population of the subcategories changes but not as much as in (B). This is what usually happens. After the question, we gain some partial information but it may not be enough to identify the exact class. In such a situation, we need to ask more questions.

We can use the information gain to train a decision tree. The process involves finding the decision rules that provide the highest information gain. However, as some of you may not be familiar with entropy and information gain, we will introduce an alternative approach. For more details about information theory see [6, 7], and for details of training decision trees based on information gain see [23, 24].

The alternative approach to training a decision tree is to find deciding rules that provide the maximum reduction in variance. Let us see what that means.

Exercise: Consider the example in figure 3.29. Out of the following four conditions, which one do you think is a better deciding rule?

1. $X1 > a$.
2. $X1 > b$.
3. $X1 > c$.
4. $X2 > d$.

Let us start with $X2 > d$. This breaks the set into the upper and lower subset. However, both subsets have relatively the same variance between the two classes as the original box. So this condition is not effective in reducing the variance. Note that you can count the number of samples and evaluate the variance, but here we are more interested in qualitative insight.

Next, there is $X1 > a$. For the left subset, all the samples are yellow (the variance is zero) but the right subset has both yellow and green samples (variance > 0). So the

```
1  from sklearn import tree
2  clf = tree.DecisionTreeClassifier()        ## Cunstruct an object of
3                                              ## DecisionTree.
4  clf = clf.fit(x_train, y_train)            ## Train the parameters of
5                                              ## the object
6  y_pred=clf.predict(x_test)                 ## Use the object to make
7                                              ## predication.
8  tree.plot_tree(clf)                        ## Plot the tree of clf.
```

Listing 3.10. Decision tree.

weighted average of these two would give a variance that is lower than the original box but still relatively high.

At this point, you can probably see which deciding rule is most effective. It is $X1 > b$. All the samples on the left subset are yellow (variance = 0) and the majority of the samples in the right subset are green (variance ≈ 0). So the average would give (variance ≈ 0). This means that this deciding rule has the largest variance reduction between the four conditions.

The idea of training a decision tree is finding and optimizing deciding rules that maximize the variance reduction. For more details about the mechanics of training a decision tree, see [23, 24].

Similar to the other techniques that we have discussed so far, scikit-learn provides an effective implementation of the decision tree technique. In listing 3.10, you can also see that its syntax is the same as the other techniques that we have covered.

Similar to KNN, decisions can be used for regression tasks as well.

Question: Design an algorithm that uses the idea of a decision tree as discussed here to make a model for regression.

3.2.2.8 Ensemble techniques

Thus far we have discussed different approaches to adding complexity and non-linearity to our models. We started with polynomial models and then went through two techniques that are inherently non-linear.

In this section we will review some of the most powerful ideas in traditional ML. These are known as 'ensemble techniques' [25–27]. Ensemble techniques combine an ensemble of simpler models to make more powerful ones. For years, these techniques have enabled some of the most successful practical applications of ML. In some cases, they have been going toe to toe with NNs. You can also see that many of the winning models in Kaggle competitions are based on these techniques.

Let us go back to the simplest model that we talked about, the linear model. Consider the data in figure 3.30. This is not a linearly separable dataset, so a linear model cannot capture the complexity of the data on its own. In figure 3.30 you can see that for linear models, each of them is good at classifying a subset of samples or a part of the feature space but not all of it. However, by just looking at it, you can see that if we combine the four of them we may obtain a really good classifier.

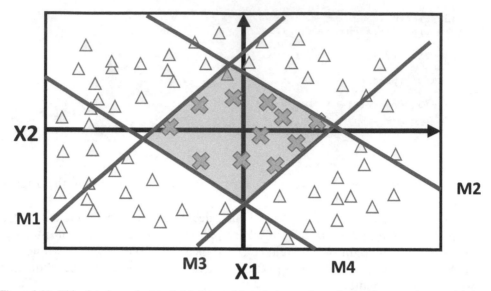

Figure 3.30. This plot shows the idea behind ensemble techniques schematically. There are four models here, each of which can capture some of the instances correctly and most of them incorrectly. We can then build a model that combines these four and classify almost all of the samples correctly. Each model, on its own, is far from perfect, however, the overall model can have a high performance.

Question: How would you combine the linear classifiers? (*Hint*: For instance, you can use AND and OR functions on the results of each linear model which return 0 or 1.)

There are different ways to combine models and make more powerful ones. Here are three major ensemble techniques,

- Bagging (bootstrap aggregating).
- Boosting.
- Stacking.

For bagging we train *m* homogeneous models. By homogeneous, we mean that they are all of the same types. For instance, they are all decision trees. Figure 3.31 gives a schematic depiction of bagging.

If we use the same data for training the models, the resulting ensemble may not be diverse enough. Thus we do not use the same data for training them. We bootstrap the data [28]. This means that for each model, we take a random subset of the original dataset. These subsets are not exclusive and may overlap. Training models on these subsets will lead to different models, each of which is good at predicting some of the samples and not necessarily the others. Once the ensemble of the models is created, we aggregate them. The aggregation can be taking the majority votes for a classification problem. In other words, for a new sample, we obtain the predictions of all the *m* models. We then use the majority of the *m* predictions as the final prediction of the model.

Bagging is particularly good when the building models are really good at a specific subset but do not generalize well. One of the most popular implementations

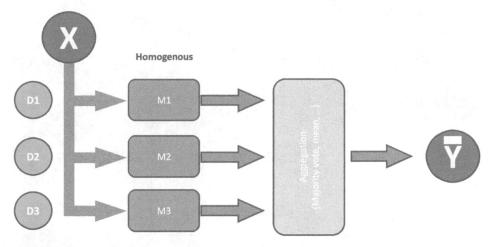

Figure 3.31. Schematic depiction of bagging. Several models, all of the same type, are trained. Each one is trained on a subset of the data. These subsets are sampled randomly from the dataset and may overlap (i.e. bootstrapping). Since each model is trained on a different subset, they are different. We then aggregate the results and make the final prediction.

```
1 from sklearn.ensemble import RandomForestClassifier
2 clf = RandomForestClassifier()                     ## Cunstruct an object of
3                                                     ## RandomForest.
4 clf.fit(x_train, y_train)                           ## Train the parameters of
5                                                     ## the object
6 y_pred=clf.predict(x_test)                          ## Use the object to make
7                                                     ## predication.
```

Listing 3.11. Random forest.

of bagging combines decision trees and is called 'random forest' [29]. Random forests are one of the most effective supervised learning techniques and in many cases their results can compete with complex NNs.

Scikit-learn provides an implementation for random forest. The code in listing 3.11 shows how is should be used.

Stacking is a similar idea to bagging, but the ensemble is made of heterogeneous models, i.e. different types of models [26]. All the models are trained on half (or a portion of the data). The rest of the data are used to train a meta-model that decides how to combine the predictions from different models in the ensemble. Figure 3.32 shows the schematic design of a stacking model.

This can also be implemented in scikit-learn. The code in listing 3.12 shows an example that combines classifications from an SVM classifier, a KNN model, and a decision tree. Finally, for the meta-model it uses a random forest.

Boosting is another ensemble technique [26]. In contrast to bagging and stacking, it trains the models in series. Imagine that you start with some initial model that is trained on all the data and while it performs well on some samples, there are others that it misclassifies. To improve the result of the model we can put more focus on the samples that are misclassified. So, next, we train a new model that puts the emphasis

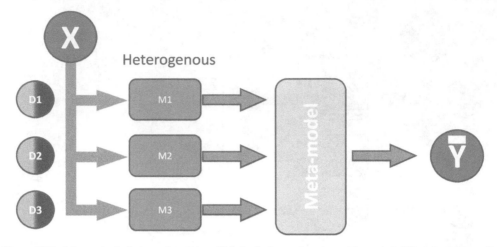

Figure 3.32. Schematic depiction of stacking. This is similar to bagging with several differences. First, the models are not of the same type. Second, instead of aggregation, a meta-model is trained to combine the outcomes of the different models. Part of the data are used to train the inside models and the rest is used to train the meta-model.

```
1  from sklearn.ensemble import StackingClassifier
2  from sklearn.svm import SVC
3  from sklearn.neighbors import KNeighborsClassifier
4  from sklearn.tree import DecisionTreeClassifier
5  from sklearn.ensemble import RandomForestClassifier
6
7  ## List of estimators that we are using for stacking
8  estimators = [ ('svr', SVC() ), ('knn', KNeighborsClassifier()), ('dt'
       , DecisionTreeClassifier() )]
9
10 clf = StackingClassifier(estimators=estimators, final_estimator=
       RandomForestClassifier() )
11
12 clf.fit(x_train, y_train)                    ## Train the parameters of
13                                              ## the object
14 y_pred=clf.predict(x_test)                   ## Use the object to make
15                                              ## predication.
```

Listing 3.12. Stacking.

on mislabeled samples. In this way, we can build a sequence of models and as we go deeper and apply more sequential models, the performance of the predictions improves.

There are different implementations of boosting, including adaptive boosting (i.e. AdaBoost), gradient boosting, and XGBoost (although this is a more efficient implementation of gradient boosting).

Scikit-learn includes an implementation of boosting, but we are going to use a different library for this one. This library is called 'XGBoost' and provides a more thorough and efficient implementation for gradient boosting algorithms. Fortunately, the syntax is fairly similar to the one for scikit-learn, see listing 3.13.

```
1  from xgboost import XGBClassifier
2
3  clf  = XGBClassifier()
4
5  clf.fit(x_train, y_train)        ## Train the parameters of
6                                   ## the object
7  y_pred=clf.predict(x_test)       ## Use the object to make
8                                   ## predication.
```

Listing 3.13. Boosting.

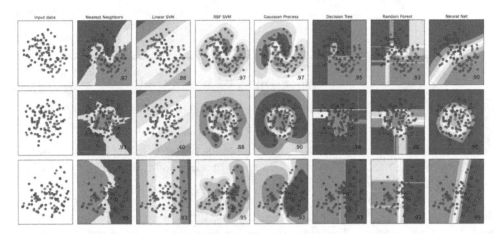

Figure 3.33. Comparison of different classification techniques for different types of data. The rows correspond to three types of data. The samples with their labels are indicated in the first column. Different columns correspond to different classification techniques. The accuracy of each classification is indicated in the plots. We do not cover all of these methods in this book. (Image credit: scikit-learn library [33].)

This section only scratches the surface of ensemble techniques. For a more thorough review of the ensemble techniques, see [26].

Also, traditional supervised learning techniques are not limited to the ones that we described here. For example, we did not cover the naive Bayes models [30]. However, the models that we reviewed briefly here should give you a taste of the diverse techniques that have been developed for supervised learning problems. For a more comprehensive list of supervised learning models, see [31, 32]. The reader is also encouraged to see the documentation of the scikit-learn library [33]. It provides a list of different techniques that are implemented in the library which is relatively comprehensive.

Exercise: Which model is better?

This is one of the common questions that people ask when they learn about all the different techniques. The answer is that it depends. They have different performances for different problems.

Figure 3.33 is from the scikit-learn library and provides an interesting comparison between different classification techniques for three different sets of data. Visually, you can see that the best model changes for each dataset. For example, while for the

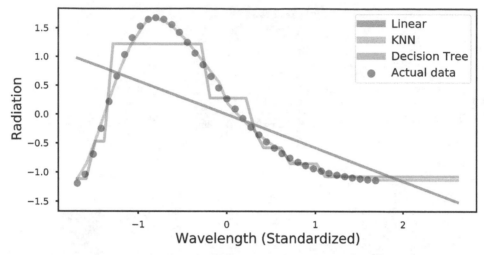

Figure 3.34. Three models fitted to the black body radiation data.

first row the SVM with an RBF kernel seems to be offering a better decision boundary, for the second row, the Gaussian Process technique seems to do better (although the RBF SVM is still doing well).

Performance is not the only factor that should be considered for comparing different techniques. The training and prediction times are other factors that need to be taken into account. For instance, as we mentioned, sometimes we are also interested in the explainability of the classification. If this is the case, KNN is not a great choice even if it provides an accurate classification. The choice of the model is often driven by a combination of performance and other requirements that may be specific to the application for which we are training a model.

Note that for the implementation, the codes that are provided so far are fairly basic and are only meant to give you a sense of how to use the models that we introduce practically for different problems. The objects that were created for each of the models can have a variety of inputs that can significantly change the model. For example, for the decision tree you can specify the maximum depth of the tree, or for the SVM classifier, the kernel can be specified as well as a large range of parameters.

To avoid confusion, we refer to these as 'hyper-parameters' (HPs). In contrast to the free parameters of the model, HPs are not trained. Later, we will discuss how we fine-tune the models by tuning the HPs.

As we have mentioned, the same models can be used for regression.

Exercise: Take the black body radiation data and train a linear model, a KNN model, and a decision tree for it.

The result should look like figure 3.34.

You can find the helping code for the example above in listing 3.14. You can use it to reproduce the plot in figure 3.34.

```
1
2  from sklearn.linear_model import LinearRegression
3  from sklearn.svm import SVR
4  from sklearn.neighbors import KNeighborsRegressor
5  from sklearn.tree import DecisionTreeRegressor
6  from sklearn.ensemble import RandomForestRegressor
7
8  lm = LinearRegression()
9  lm.fit(X, Y)
10
11
12 svm = SVR()
13 svm.fit(X, Y)
14
15 knn = KNeighborsRegressor()
16 knn.fit(X, Y)
17
18 dt = DecisionTreeRegressor()
19 dt.fit(X, Y)
```

Listing 3.14. Regression.

So far we have introduced some of the common traditional supervised learning models, but how do we train a model?

For training a model, we need to first quantify the performance of the model. This defines the objective for which we are training. In the next section we will learn how to quantify the performance of a model.

3.2.3 Loss functions

The performance of a supervised learning model is characterized by the difference between the predicted labels and the ground truth values.

Consider the regression example in figure 3.35. Two models are included in the plot, a KNN model and a linear model.

Exercise: Which model is better? Why? Try to describe your intuition mathematically.

You probably answered the KNN model. But what makes the KNN a better model?

In order to answer this question we need a measure that quantifies how close the predictions of a model are to the actual labels. We refer to this as the 'loss function' [34]. A loss function can be described as a distance function between the actual labels and the predictions of the model, i.e.

$$\mathcal{L} = d(Y, f_w(X)). \tag{3.33}$$

Question: For the example in figure 3.35, what can we use for the loss function?

Note that, from a mathematical point of view, a loss function does not need to be a distance function. A distance should be symmetric and satisfy the triangle inequality. However, one can make loss functions that violate these two conditions. However, in general, the most common loss functions are distance functions too.

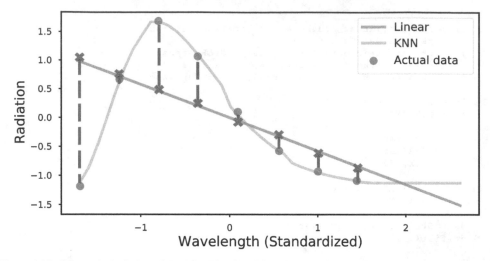

Figure 3.35. Schematic depiction of the loss. The plot shows the black body radiation data with a linear fit. The gray crosses indicate the prediction of the linear model and the dashed red line shows the difference between the predicted values and the actual values that are indicated in blue. A KNN model is also included which gives a closer fit to the data.

In this section we will review some of the more common loss functions. Here are some of the more common loss functions that you may be familiar with:

- Mean-squared error.
- Mean absolute error.
- Root-mean-squared error.

The first and probably the most common loss function that we use is the mean-squared error (MSE). MSE can be used for both regression and classification. Mathematically that is

$$\mathcal{L}_{\text{MSE}}(Y, \bar{Y}) = \frac{1}{n_s} \sqrt{\sum_{i}^{n_s} |Y_i - \bar{Y}_i|^2}. \tag{3.34}$$

In the case of the models in figure 3.35, each of the blue dots indicates the ground truth radiation for the specific wavelength. The red dashed lines indicate the differences between the predictions and the ground truth for the linear fit. We refer to them as 'errors'. For the MSE we take the average of the square of errors.

For a good fit like the KNN, the errors for all of these points are close to zero. So the loss is small and the fit is good. On the other hand, for the linear fit, as indicated by the red dashed lines, the errors are relatively large and the MSE is not negligible.

A good model is expected to have a small loss value. This means that the predictions of the model are close to the ground truth values.

The choice of the loss function can significantly influence the final model. In fact, this is where we can enforce different attributes that we want for the model. Here, we review some of the popular loss functions.

MSE is one of the most common loss functions, but there are other loss functions as well. For example, we could use the average of absolute values of the errors, i.e.

$$\mathcal{L}_{\mathrm{MAE}}(Y, \bar{Y}) = \frac{1}{n_s}\sqrt{\sum_i^{n_s}|Y_i - \bar{Y}_i|}. \tag{3.35}$$

This is known as the mean absolute error (MAE).

Another common choice that is equivalent to MSE is root-mean-squared error (RMSE) which is $\sqrt{\mathrm{MSE}}$.

We can also build loss functions based on l-norms mathematically, that is

$$\mathcal{L}_l(Y, \bar{Y}) = \left(\sum_i |Y_i - \bar{Y}_i|^l\right)^{1/l}. \tag{3.36}$$

The value of l can be any positive integer. Probably the most common values are $l = 1, 2, \infty$ which give:

- L_1: $\mathcal{L}_1(Y, \bar{Y}) = \sum_i |Y_i - \bar{Y}_i|$, which is equivalent to MAE.
- L_2: $\mathcal{L}_2(Y, \bar{Y}) = \sum_i |Y_i - \bar{Y}_i|$, which is equivalent to RMSE.
- L_∞: $\max_i |Y_i - \bar{Y}_i|$, which gives the maximum errors is also known as the 'max error'.

These loss functions have different properties and are useful for different applications. For instance, max error is used when we want to make sure that none of the individual errors are large. In other words, if the max error of a model is ϵ, this sets a bound on all the errors. This is particularly useful for dealing with worst-case scenarios.

Another example is that the MSE penalizes large errors, but is less sensitive to small errors (less than one). On the other hand, MAE is better at handling smaller errors. So if we have error values that are smaller than one, the MAE might be a better choice. Figure 3.36 compares different l-norms for errors above and below one. It shows how different loss functions penalize errors for the two different ranges.

There are also some loss functions that are used specifically for classification tasks. Two such examples are the cross-entropy and the hinge loss functions.

Cross-entropy is defined as

$$\mathcal{L}_{\mathrm{CE}}(Y, \bar{Y}) = -\sum_i^{n_s}(Y_i \log(\bar{Y}_i) + (1 - Y_i)\log(1 - \bar{Y}_i)). \tag{3.37}$$

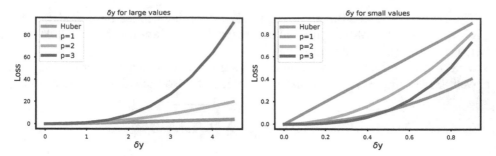

Figure 3.36. l-norm for $p = 1, 2, 3$. We consider two regimes, one where the difference between the predicted and the actual label is less than one and one where it is more than one. The y-axis shows the loss and the x-axis shows the error, i.e. $\delta y = |y - \bar{y}|$. The Huber loss function is also included.

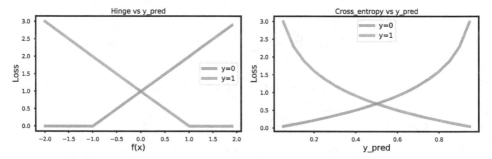

Figure 3.37. The cross-entropy and the hinge loss functions. These two loss functions are often used for classification problems where the actual label is either 0 or 1 (binary classification).

This is a popular choice for logistic regression models and models that return the probability of belonging to a class for a binary representation. In particular, if there are two classes 0 and 1 and the model returns the probability of class 1, (i.e. $\bar{Y} = P(y = 1)$), then the cross-entropy loss can simplify and speed up the training.

Note that Y is either 0 or 1 for a binary classification problem. In this case, the first term penalizes when the ground truth is one and the model returns a small probability. In the extreme case of $\bar{Y} = 0$ it diverges to infinity. Note that the second term is zero for $Y = 1$. Similarly, the second term penalizes when $Y = 0$ and the model returns a high probability. For $\bar{Y} = 1$ the first term vanishes, but the second term diverges.

The right panel of figure 3.37 plots the cross-entropy loss for the two cases of $Y = 0$ and $Y = 1$.

Another interesting loss that is used for classification is the hinge function. This is particularly used for SVMs and penalizes the samples in the margin in the vicinity of the decision boundary. Mathematically, the hinge function is defined as

$$\mathcal{L}_{\text{Hinge}}(Y, f(X)) = \max(0, 1 - Y*f(X)), \tag{3.38}$$

where $f(X)$ is what the classification model returns. Note that this is not the same as $\bar{Y}$. For instance, for a linear classification the labels are extracted by $\bar{Y} = \text{sign}(f(X))$.

The hinge function works directly with the model, $f(X)$. The left panel of figure 3.37 depicts the hinge function for $Y = 0$ and for $Y = 1$. It shows that the loss function penalizes the samples where $|f(X)| \leq 1$ even when they are classified correctly. As we discussed for the SVM mode, this pushes the model to leave as much margin from the decision boundary as possible.

We can also incorporate other properties in which we are interested in the loss function. This means that if in addition to a good fit, we want our model to have some other properties, we can adjust the loss function to account for that as well.

One example is the SVM model. Recall the classification problem in figure 3.23. One can fit different linear models that predict all the samples accurately. As we discussed, we can use the hinge loss function to build a model with the largest margin, see figure 3.22. Of the three models, although they all predict the labels almost perfectly, the middle one is preferred because it leaves the largest margin between the two classes and the decision boundary. With MSE or MAE, all three models give approximately the same loss (0). However, if the loss is hinge, the first and the last one will be penalized for the samples that fall in close proximity to the decision boundary.

Question: Verify that the hinge loss function maximizes the margins.

There is one more factor that could play a role in the choice of the loss function. We prefer loss functions that are easier to optimize. Ideally, we want the loss function to be strictly convex which means that it has only one minimum point. Some loss functions may have multiple local minima for a specific class of problems or models. This complicates optimizing the parameters of the model and training it.

We also do not want the loss function to be computationally complex. If the loss function is hard to compute or takes a long time, the training process will slow down. If we are using gradient-based optimization techniques (as we will see in the next section), we also want the gradient of the loss function to be easy to calculate.

For a more comprehensive review of the loss functions, see [34].

Once the loss function is specified, it characterizes the similarity of the predictions of the model and the ground truth values and quantifies the performance of the model. Changing the free parameters of the model would change the predictions. The goal of a supervised training task is to find the parameters that minimize the loss function. The next section will provide more details about the optimization part.

3.2.4 Optimization techniques

Consider the example in figure 3.35. Assume that we want to find a linear model and we are using MSE for the loss function. If we plot the loss function with respect to the slope of the linear fit, we get a plot similar to the blue plot in figure 3.38. Here we are taking the intercept to be zero.

Exercise: What is the best value of the free parameter of the model? How can we use the plot in figure 3.38 to find that best model?

As you have probably guessed, the best value is the red point where the loss is minimized. This means that for this value, the predictions of the model have minimum deviation from the actual label values.

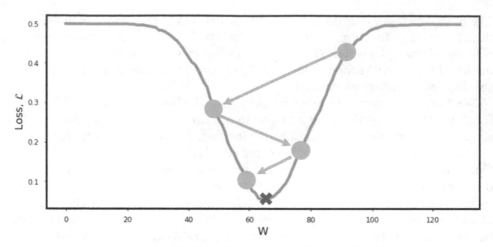

Figure 3.38. Schematic idea of the GD loss and the GD for finding the minimum.

This transforms the problem of training the model to find the set of values of the free parameters that minimize the loss function.

Question: In figure 3.38, why does the loss function become flat for the large and small values of w?

Exercise: How can we find the minimum point?

One way is to calculate the loss for all possible values of the free parameters (i.e. make the loss landscape as we did in figure 3.38) and find the minimum value and its corresponding free parameters. However, this could be extremely expensive. For a simple example with one free parameter, it is even easy to visualize this and find the minimum. However, it is not always this easy. Some of the models that we will work with in this book have a few million parameters. We need a systematic and efficient way to find the minimum.

Fortunately, this topic has been studied extensively in mathematics [35] and a variety of techniques have been developed for optimizing such functions [36–38]. Here we focus on gradient-based optimization techniques and, specifically, a technique known as 'gradient descent' (GD) [39]. This is one of the most commonly used optimization techniques. We first review the basics of GD and then study some of the extensions and variations that are commonly used in the field of ML.

3.2.4.1 Gradient descent

Imagine that you are hiking on a mountain and you want to get back down to the base. What would you do?

You probably would follow the slope. More specifically, at each point, you will move in the direction that goes down. This is the idea behind GD. Recall that the slope is in fact the gradient.

For the GD optimization, we start with a random starting point for the free parameters. We then use the gradient to decide how we should change the parameters. A positive gradient tells us that the loss would increase if we increase the parameter (going uphill). So to find the minimum, we have to reduce the parameter (going downhill). Similarly, if the gradient is negative it means that increasing the parameter reduces the loss and, therefore, we need to increase the parameter.

This makes an iterative algorithm that takes a small step at each iteration in the opposite direction to the gradient. This iterative process can gradually move the parameters toward the minimum. Figure 3.38 illustrates schematically what happens when GD is used to find the minimum. Mathematically that is

$$w \rightarrow w - \text{Sign}\left(\frac{d\mathcal{L}}{dw}\right)\Delta W, \tag{3.39}$$

where w is the free parameter and ΔW is the step size. This determines how far we move in each iteration. In figure 3.38, if our step size is too big, we may pass the minimum and increase the loss again, maybe even more than the initial value. We can choose a small value for the step size. However, the drawback is that this slows the convergence to the minimum. This is because if we are taking smaller steps, we would need to take more steps (iterations) to reach the minimum.

We need to adjust the step size such that it is not too big to miss the minimum and it is not too small that would take forever to find the minimum. For this, we may adopt the step size to where we are with respect to the loss landscape. If we are close to the minimum, the step size should be small. And if we are far from the minimum, the step size should be large.

Exercise: How can we adopt the step size, without knowing where the minimum is?

We can use the value of the gradient to adjust the step size. For a parabola, the magnitude of the gradient increases as we go away from the minimum and it approaches zero when we get close to the minimum. Let us set the step size to be

$$\Delta W = \eta \left| \frac{d\mathcal{L}}{dw} \right|. \tag{3.40}$$

We refer to η as the 'learning rate' and it adjusts how big the step size is with respect to the gradient. The step size in equation (3.40) leads to the following update rule for the optimization process

$$w \rightarrow w - \eta\frac{d\mathcal{L}}{dw}. \tag{3.41}$$

Note that we have combined the sign of gradient from equation (3.39) and the magnitude from equation (3.40) which gives the gradient.

The parameter η is another hyper-parameter of which we need to keep track. This is in fact one of the most important hyper-parameters which can significantly affect the training speed as well as the final performance of the model. If η is too big, the model is likely not to converge. On the other hand, if it is too small, the training would be slow too and it may not converge in the time specified for training.

The update rule in equation (3.41) defines the GD algorithm for minimization. The pseudo-code below (algorithm 2) shows how this iterative process works.

Algorithm 2: Gradient descent algorithm.

$$\textbf{Data: } \mathcal{L}(w), \eta, N$$

1 Pick a random w;
2 **for** $n_{itr} = 1..N$ **do**
3 $\quad$ Calculate $\frac{d\mathcal{L}}{dw}$.;
4 $\quad$ $w \to w - \eta \frac{d\mathcal{L}}{dw}$.;
end

Note that here we take the number of iterations as the input. We can also define a convergence condition and iterate until w converges.

Question: Implement this algorithm in Python.

For the question above, you may realize that there is still one more piece missing from using GD for optimization. Equation (3.41) gives the update rule for GD, but we still need to calculate the $\frac{d\mathcal{L}}{dw}$.

To better understand the issue, let us do this for the MSE loss. The derivative is given by

$$
\begin{aligned}
\frac{d\mathcal{L}}{dw} &= \frac{d}{dw}\left(\frac{1}{n_s}\sum_i^{n_s}(Y_i - f_w(X_i))^2\right) \\
&= \frac{1}{n_s}\sum_i^{n_s}\frac{d}{dw}\left((Y_i - f_w(X_i))^2\right) \\
&= \frac{2}{n_s}\sum_i^{n_s}\left[(f_w(X_i) - Y_i)\frac{df_w}{dw}(X_i)\right].
\end{aligned}
\tag{3.42}
$$

The key point here is that the derivative depends on the feature vector and the label of each sample. In other words, each sample may be affecting the loss function in a different way. For a specific sample, the predicted value may be close to the actual label and for another one, it may be too different. For GD with the MSE, we average over the derivative for all the samples. Because the loss is averaged over all samples too, this guarantees that the loss will decrease (or stay the same).

The calculation above can be repeated for other loss functions as well and it always depends on the feature vectors and the labels of the samples.

Equation (3.42) also indicates that for the training we need to be able to calculate the derivative of the loss function. This, as we mentioned, is one of the key considerations that need to be factored in for choosing the loss function. Not only the loss function but also its derivative should be efficiently calculable. Note that we need to evaluate the derivative of the loss function in each iteration. If it is a computationally complex function, it could slow down the training.

Question: Implement the GD algorithm with the MSE in Python. Assume that you are doing this for a dataset with two features and a linear hypothesis.

Re-do it for MAE.

Question: Try your algorithms on a simple classification dataset with a linear hypothesis.

Question: Try different values of the learning rate. Try $\eta \in \{0.001, 0.1, 0.3, 1, 3, 10\}$.

- Plot the number of steps that it takes to get to the minimum (within $w_{\min} \pm .1$) versus the values of the learning rate η.
- Plot w through the optimization process. Do it for the different values of the learning rate η.
- Plot the variance of w through the optimization process, versus the learning rate η.
- What happens if the learning rate is too big?
- What happens if the learning rate is too small?

Figure 3.39 shows a typical optimization with GD. Here we are assuming that we have two free parameters and that the loss landscape has a minimum at the red dot. The left panel shows a color map of the loss, the darker the color, the lower the loss. The values corresponding to each color are shown on the color bar. Here we are starting at a random point on the top right of the plot. The white points show the values of the free parameters in each iteration You can see that it moves towards the minimum.

The middle panel shows how the loss function drops as we do more iterations. This plot is extremely helpful for troubleshooting optimization algorithms and even training algorithms. Ideally, we want the loss to go down as we do more iterations. If it goes up or does not drop, it is usually an indication of an issue.

The panel on the right shows how the two parameters change with more iterations. This plot could be helpful and informative about the convergence process. The following questions will help you better understand how this plot changes under different circumstances.

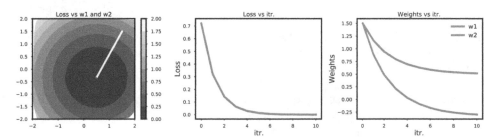

Figure 3.39. An example of the application of GD.

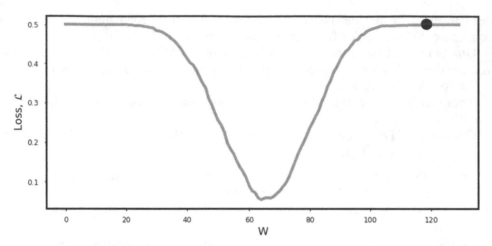

Figure 3.40. What does GD do if we start from the black dot?

Question: What happens if the learning rate is too big? Describe what happened for each of the plots.

Question: What happens if the learning rate is too small? Describe what happened for each of the plots.

From a physical point of view, one can see the loss $\mathcal{L}(w)$ as a potential function. Then the updated term of the GD algorithm can be described as force (scaled by the learning rate). Remember that for an object in a potential function, $\phi(x)$, we obtain

$$F = -\frac{d\phi(x)}{dx},$$

with x the displacement of the object from the minimum of the potential function. In other words, GD can be described as an algorithm that follows the force. It just needs the learning rate η to control the step size.

Exercise: In figure 3.40, imagine that the starting point is the black dot. What does the GD do? Can it converge?

Starting from the black dot, you can see that the derivative is close to zero. This means that the update rule is not going to be able to change the free parameters.

Question: What can we do if we are stuck in the condition in figure 3.40?

Question: Local minimum: consider the landscape in figure 3.41.

- What happens if we start from 1?
- What happens if we start from 2?
- What happens if we start from 3?
- Does GD always converge to the actual minimum?

As can be seen from these two questions, GD is not always the best approach and does not always converge to the global minimum.

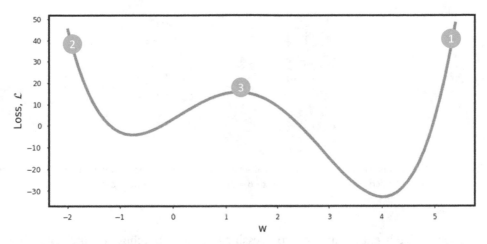

Figure 3.41. What does GD converge to starting from any of the three initial conditions?

We recommend playing with some of the interactive demos on the Internet to gain a better intuition. Here is a nice webpage with interesting interactive examples: https://fa.bianp.net/teaching/2018/COMP-652/.

Next, we will discuss some variations of the GD algorithm that resolve some of these issues. Specifically, these ideas help with the performance and the speed of the training process.

3.2.4.2 Stochastic gradient descent: batch optimization

Consider the particle identification dataset, i.e. DST-PI see (table 1.2). This dataset has about 10^6 samples. In each iteration of the GD we need to process all the samples to calculate the derivative. Remember that the derivative of the loss depends on the samples and we take the average of the derivative over all the samples to update the free parameters.

In the case of the dataset of particle identification, for each iteration, we need to calculate the derivative for all the samples for the GD algorithm. But do we need to do that?

If the samples are drawn from the same distribution and are shuffled randomly, one would expect that a large enough subset of the data would give a good enough approximation of the gradients.

In other words, in each iteration of the algorithm, we can use a subset of the data instead of all the samples. This reduces the computational complexity of the algorithms and makes them more efficient.

This idea is known as 'batch optimization' [36]. Instead of calculating the derivative over all the samples, a batch is used to calculate the derivative.

The batch optimization can speed up the convergence of the algorithm. This is because instead of using all the samples to take one step, we use a smaller subset. This way, processing all the samples, we take more than just one step. This is called

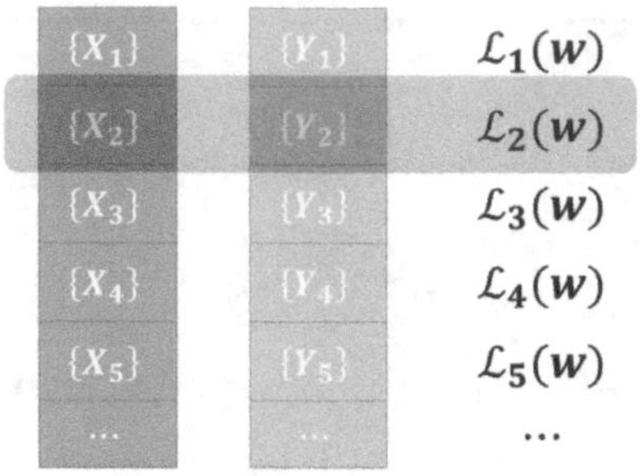

Figure 3.42. A schematic picture of splitting the dataset into batches. Each batch would give a different value for the loss and for the derivative of the loss. For the optimization, the loss value and its derivative are used on each batch to take one step of GD.

an 'epoch'. Each epoch includes processing multiple batches. Figure 3.42 shows schematically how this works.

The smaller the batch, the more steps we take in each epoch. This can be a more efficient way of using the data, but this is only true up to a point.

Let us go through this with the following questions.

Question:

- For the particle identification problem, implement the GD with a linear model.
- How long do 100 iterations of the algorithm take?
- How long does it take for GD to converge?

Question:

- Repeat the previous question with batch optimization. Do this for batch sizes of {1000, 100, 10, 1}.
- How long do 100 iterations of the algorithm take for each of the batch sizes?
- How long does it take for the algorithm to converge? Do this for all the batch sizes.
- Plot the time versus batch size.

What typically happens is that as the batch size becomes smaller and smaller, the process becomes more stochastic. This means that the loss may no longer reduce monotonically as we saw in figure 3.39. Similarly, if we look at the trajectory of the free parameters in the parameter space (left panel), for a small batch the trajectory would be stochastic. This is because for a small batch the derivative may not be aligned with the derivative over the whole set. This means that for that iteration the gradient descent follows the loss for that batch and may even move in a direction that increases the loss for the whole set.

To obtain a better intuition, assume that the batch size is one. This means that we take the data sample by sample, calculate the derivative for that specific sample and move to the next sample for the next iteration. For some samples and some values of the free parameters, the derivative is not going to be the same as the average over the whole set. They may even have a different sign which would indicate that the corresponding free parameter will be updated in the opposite direction which reduces the loss.

Although individual batches may push the parameters in the wrong direction, the overall process that includes processing all the data would usually converge toward the minimum.

The batch size is also a hyper-parameter that can significantly influence the training process. In particular, the speed of the training process depends on the batch size and it is important to fine-tune the batch size for long training tasks.

The stochasticity that comes with batch optimization could have an advantage. Namely, if the loss landscape has local minima other than the global minimum (figure 3.41), the GD optimization may get stuck in one of the local minima. The stochasticity of batch optimization can help escape the local minimum.

3.2.4.3 Adaptive learning rate

One of the typical issues with GD is setting up the learning rate, η. Typically, we want to start with a large learning rate when we are far from the minimum. However, as we approach the minimum, it becomes difficult to converge with a large learning rate.

Figure 3.43 shows schematically what sometimes happens when we are using GD to find the minimum. At first, the loss decreases relatively fast, but as we approach the local minimum, we get stuck and keep jumping over the minimum. The top panel shows a situation where after the second iteration, the parameter jumps over the optimal value and takes a value that has almost the same loss as point two. If the loss function is symmetric, it may even get stuck there and jump back and forth between 2 and three. Another situation that may be difficult for GD to converge is illustrated in the second panel of figure 3.43. Here, after two, the parameter is updated to a new value that has an even higher loss and after that, since the derivative has a greater value for point three (compared to two), after the update it may jump over the minimum and increase the loss again. After four, it may come down and up again.

Exercise: How can we resolve this issue and avoid the situation shown in figure 3.43?

One solution is reducing the learning rate. In fact, finding the right value for the learning rate is essential to the convergence of the algorithm. Note that this depends on the loss function. If the loss function has a deep minimum (large derivatives), we would need to pick a smaller value.

However, this solution leads to two new possible issues. The first problem is that starting from a small learning rate could significantly slow down the training process. In figure 3.43, imagine that we are starting from a point on the left plateau, where the derivatives are close to zero. With a small learning rate, it would require too many steps to get out of the plateau.

The second issue is that the loss function may have two distinct scales and one learning rate, although effective for part of the optimization process, it may be

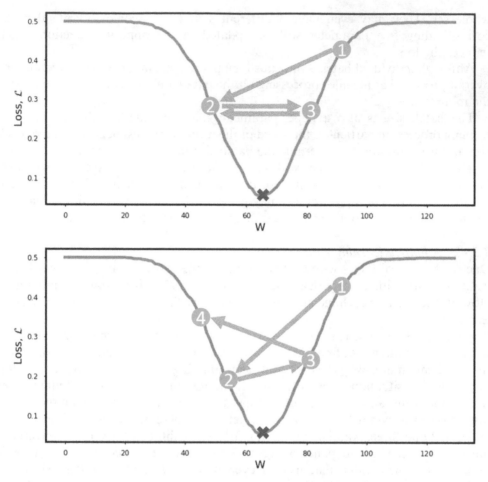

Figure 3.43. Examples of what could happen if the learning rate is too large. As the optimization approaches the minimum, it may become stuck at a certain distance from the minimum or even end up increasing the loss for a few steps. This usually leads to the loss fluctuating.

ineffective for the other parts. Figure 3.44 shows one such situation schematically. As you can see, there is a central dip inside the outer dip.

Question: Make such a function in Python and try to see what happens as you approach the central dip during the optimization.

Exercise: How can we resolve the issues? What solutions can you think of?

We can change the learning rate through the optimization process. For instance, in the case of figure 3.44 we can use a rate up to the central dip and reduce the dip after that. Unfortunately, it is not always this easy, because we do not know the structure of an unknown loss function.

Question: Assuming that the loss is as shown in figure 3.44, find a way to figure out when to change the learning rate. *Hint*: Use the loss function.

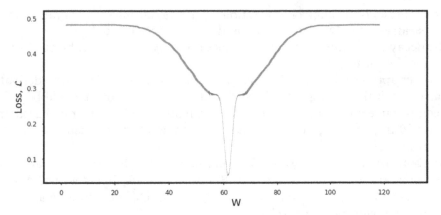

Figure 3.44. An example of a loss function that has features on two distinct scales. GD with a single learning rate cannot effectively converge the minimum.

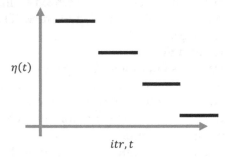

Figure 3.45. An example of decaying rate learning rate. The *x*-axis (*t*) indicates the iteration. We start with some value for the learning rate, then reduce the learning rate after a certain number of iterations. We repeat this a few times. The idea is that as we approach the minimum, we will need a smaller learning rate to converge.

Techniques that change the learning rate through the optimization process are known as 'adaptive learning rates' [36, 40]. In this section, we will review some of the popular adaptive learning rate techniques.

Decaying learning rate
One of the simplest adaptive learning rate approaches is to use a time-decaying learning rate [36, 40]. Figure 3.45 shows an example of such a learning rate. As the optimization algorithm takes more and more steps, the learning rate is reduced. The idea is that as we approach the minimum, the learning rate reduces. This approach is particularly helpful for situations such as the ones in 3.43. This approach could help prevent the oscillations around the minimum.

Some of the popular choices for the decaying learning rate functions are

$$\eta(t) = e^{-\beta t}\eta_0,$$
$$\eta(t) = \frac{\eta_0}{\sqrt{t}}, \tag{3.43}$$

3-59

where t represents the number of iterations, η_0 is the starting learning rate, and β is a hyper-parameter that we can adjust based on the specific problem.

The decaying learning rate approach does not fully solve the problem. It still may decay too fast or too slowly.

Another approach is to use the changes in gradients, i.e. higher-order derivatives. For instance, if the process is stuck as in figure 3.43, the gradient would be jumping between positive and negative values. We can reduce the learning rate based on the variance in the gradient, or we can use the average of the gradient instead of the gradient in each step.

For both of these ideas we need to consider not only the latest value of the gradient but also the values before that. But how far back should we go? Also, how do we incorporate the sequence of the gradients? Do we consider all of them uniformly, i.e. with the same weight?

Exercise: Propose a technique for using the sequence of gradients to adaptively change the learning rate.

To introduce the next adaptive techniques, we need to introduce the concept of the moving average and exponentially weighted average. The next part will review the concept of moving averages.

Moving average or weighted average

The left panel in figure 3.46 shows some data (blue dots) that follow a sinusoidal trend with some fluctuations and noise. Imagine that these represent the gradients in different iterations. We would like for the averaging to capture the general trend of the data without being too susceptible to fluctuations in each iteration. We also want to put more emphasis on the more recent gradients.

If we use the normal average, we obtain the black curve. For this, at each point we calculate the average of all the gradients up to that point. As can be seen, the black curve does not really capture the trend of the data. This is partly because, for each iteration, we are considering all the history with the same emphasis. In other words, at each iteration, the gradient in that iteration contributes to the average the same way that the gradient in the first iteration or any other iteration does.

A better approach would be to put more emphasis on the more recent iterations. This means that instead of using a uniform average of the points, we can assign

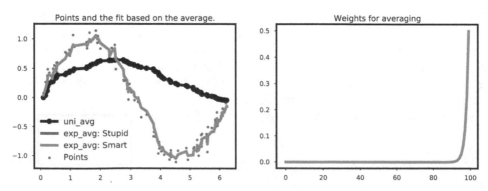

Figure 3.46. Weighted average.

weights to them such that the more recent history has a larger weight compared to the rest of the points.

The plot in the right panel of figure 3.46 shows one such weighting. This is an exponentially decaying distribution. To calculate the weighted average using this distribution, at each point, we multiply the values by the weights from this plot. Here we are only considering the last 100 points. This can be adjusted based on the number of iterations in the optimization. Mathematically this can be described as

$$\left(\frac{\partial \mathcal{L}}{\partial w}\right)_{avg}^{j} = \sum_{i=1}^{j} w_{(N-j+i)} \left(\frac{\partial \mathcal{L}}{\partial w}\right)^{i},$$

$$(3.44)$$

where $\left(\frac{\partial \mathcal{L}}{\partial w}\right)_{avg}^{j}$ represents the average of the derivative at iteration j, w are the weights, and N is the total number of iterations. Note that the indices of w are tuned such that they go from $N - j$ to N, i.e. the last j values of the weight function.

Question: Implement the weighted average in Python.

Use your implementation to reproduce the green curve in figure 3.46. Note that you can easily generate the data for the sinusoidal function.

The calculation of the weighted average as was described above (equation (3.45)) can be costly. This is because for each iteration of the optimization we would need to re-do the whole averaging. Fortunately, there is a nice trick that we can use to calculate the exponentially weighted average. We will describe this trick here. Also for simplicity, we will refer to the derivatives as v.

We use a recursive algorithm for the calculation of the average in each iteration. Assume that we have the average from the previous iteration. Then to calculate the average for the current iteration we can use

$$\bar{v}_{i+1} = \beta \bar{v}_i + (1 - \beta) v_{i+1},$$

$$(3.45)$$

where β is a parameter that sets the exponent of the exponential distribution.

We leave it to the reader to verify that equation (3.45) leads to an exponentially decaying averaging.

Question: Show that the recursive relation in equation (3.45) leads to an exponentially decaying averaging.

For the starting point, we take $\bar{v}_0 = 0$. This could introduce some bias for the first few averages. To compensate for that, we can normalize the equation (3.45). For instance, we can use

$$\bar{v}_{i+1} = \frac{\beta \bar{v}_i + (1 - \beta) v_{i+1}}{1 - \beta^{i+1}}.$$

$$(3.46)$$

Question: Implement the exponential weighted average according to equation (3.45).

Try different values for β. How does it affect the distribution?

Does increasing β increase or decrease the history that is taken into account?

Next, we will discuss how we can make adaptive optimization techniques using a moving average.

Momentum

One way to avoid fluctuations around the minimum is to use the moving average of the gradients. The red plot in figure 3.47 shows schematically a fixed number of iterations for optimization. As you can see, while $W1$ is decreasing, $W2$ is oscillating around $W2 \approx -0.3$.

In this situation we want the update rule to continue for $W1$ but slow down for $W2$. But how can we do this? Remember that for GD we use one learning rate for all the parameters.

The intuition behind the momentum approach is to use the momentum of the update rule to make the process more efficient. In the example of figure 3.47 the updates for $W1$ are consistent and moving in the negative direction, so it should continue in that direction. However, for $W2$ it is oscillating around $W2 \approx -0.3$. These oscillations indicate that the process cannot build momentum and would slow down.

The blue curve in figure 3.47 uses the moving average of the gradients to update the parameters $W1$ and $W2$. For $W2$, the average dampens the oscillation. However, the update of $W1$ is not significantly affected by the average because it was not oscillating. Vaguely speaking, using the average of the gradient instead of the gradient itself can help smoothen the trajectory of the parameters and reduce oscillations around the minimum. This technique is called momentum [36, 40].

Specifically, the update rule for GD with momentum is

$$\left(\frac{\partial \mathcal{L}}{\partial w}\right)^{t+1}_{avg} = \beta\left(\frac{\partial \mathcal{L}}{\partial w}\right)^{t}_{avg} + (1-\beta)*\left(\frac{\partial \mathcal{L}}{\partial w}\right)^{t+1},$$

$$w \rightarrow w - \eta*\left(\frac{\partial \mathcal{L}}{\partial w}\right)^{t+1}_{avg}.$$

(3.47)

The superscript t indicates the iteration index. Note that when we implement this, we use the same variable for both $(\partial \mathcal{L}w)^{t+1}_{avg}$ and $(\partial \mathcal{L}w)^{t}_{avg}$, since this is a recursive algorithm.

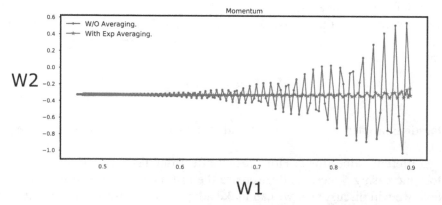

Figure 3.47. An example of the application of the momentum technique.

Question: Implement the GD with momentum technique in Python. Also test it for dataset DST-ED (see table 1.2).

RMSProp

Another approach to reducing the fluctuations is to use the variance. Consider the schematic example in figure 3.48 which is similar to the one we considered for figure 3.47. The red curve shows a process where $W2$ oscillates around $W2 \approx -30$. In such a situation, we would need to reduce the learning rate. Similarly, for $W1$ it seems that it is moving consistently in the right direction as there is oscillation. This indicates that we can increase the learning rate for $W1$.

One approach is to rescale the learning rate based on the variance in the derivative. For instance, imagine that the variances for $W1$ and $W2$ are 0.1 and 10, respectively. If we rescale the learning rates based on the variance we will obtain

$$
\begin{aligned}
W1 &\to W1 - \frac{\eta}{0.1}\partial \mathcal{L}W1 \\
W2 &\to W2 - \frac{\eta}{10}\partial \mathcal{L}W2.
\end{aligned}
\tag{3.48}
$$

This leads to reducing the step size for $W2$ while increasing it for $W1$. The blue curve in figure 3.48 uses this approach to update the free parameters. As is evident in figure 3.48, the blue curve that uses the variance, with the same number of steps, manages to go further in $W1$ while reducing the oscillations in $W2$.

Exercise: How do we calculate the variance?

As you can guess, we should put more emphasis on the more recent iterations. So we use the moving average again. Instead of the variance, we will use the moving average of the mean-squared of the gradient. This choice is mostly motivated by computational simplicity.

Using the moving average of the mean-squared of the gradient, we obtain the following update rule

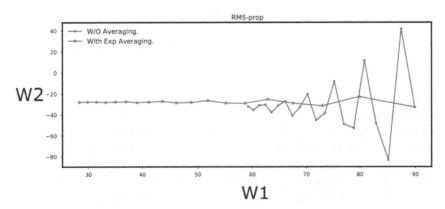

Figure 3.48. An example of the application of RMSProp.

$$ms = \beta * ms + (1 - \beta) * \left(\frac{\partial \mathcal{L}}{\partial w}\right)^2,$$

$$w \rightarrow w - \frac{\eta}{\sqrt{ms + \epsilon}} * \partial \mathcal{L} w. \tag{3.49}$$

Note that we introduced two new hyper-parameters, the first is β, which sets the exponent of the weighted averaging, and the second hyper-parameter is ϵ. If $ms \rightarrow 0$, then ϵ prevents the denominator from becoming zero or the step size from diverging. Also, we assume that the ms is initially set to zero and in each iteration the value is updated. This technique is known as 'RMSProp' [36, 40].

Question Show that the first line of equation (3.49) gives the weighted average of the mean-squared of the derivatives.

Adam
You probably are wondering which one to choose, momentum or RMSProp. The good news is that you do not need to choose. It is possible to combine the two techniques.

Exercise: How would you combine the two techniques?

$$\left(\frac{\partial \mathcal{L}}{\partial w}\right)_{\text{avg}} = \beta_1 \left(\frac{\partial \mathcal{L}}{\partial w}\right)_{\text{avg}} + (1 - \beta_1) * \left(\frac{\partial \mathcal{L}}{\partial w}\right)^{t+1},$$

$$ms = \beta_2 ms + (1 - \beta_2) * \left(\frac{\partial \mathcal{L}}{\partial w}\right)^2, \tag{3.50}$$

$$w \rightarrow w - \frac{\eta}{\sqrt{ms + \epsilon}} * \left(\frac{\partial \mathcal{L}}{\partial w}\right)_{\text{avg}}.$$

This leads to four hyper-parameters, η, β_1, β_2 and ϵ. Different ranges have been tested for these hyper-parameters and the following values are commonly used in the community for the starting points of these hyper-parameters [41].

$$\beta_1 = 0.9,$$
$$\beta_2 = 0.99,$$
$$\epsilon_1 = 10^{-8}. \tag{3.51}$$

3.2.4.4 Comparison
Figure 3.49 compares four techniques for optimization for some sample data. The left panel shows how the two free parameters change in the feature space. The right panel shows the loss versus iterations. The red curves correspond to when we only use GD without any additional tricks.

For the black one, we start using batch optimization. Note that for each iteration, only a small subset of the data are used and, as a result, each iteration of GD with

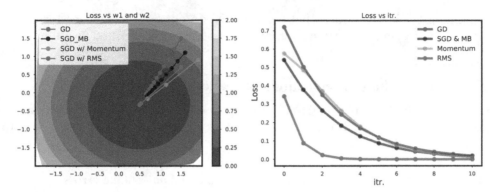

Figure 3.49. Comparison of different techniques.

mini-batches is much faster. It is also evident that in this case it converges faster, i.e. in fewer iterations.

The green and the blue curves correspond to using momentum and RMSProp, respectively. Note that this may not be the best example to see the effect of these techniques. This is because, as can be seen from the feature space, there is no oscillation. However, it still shows that the RMSProp can significantly outperform the other techniques in this example.

This, however, may not always be the case. The possibilities for the loss function are really diverse and there may be situations in which any of these techniques perform better than the others. Different optimization techniques have been studied and benchmarked extensively. For more details on this subject see [36, 40].

Question: Use the identical particle identification data, i.e. DST-GSE (table 1.2), and assume a linear model. Make plots like the ones in figure 3.49. You can also include a panel for the plot of the free parameters versus iteration. Answer the following questions for normal GD, momentum, and RMSProp techniques:

- How does changing the initial values of the free parameters affect the optimization?
- How does the batch size affect the training process?
- Try different values for the learning rates. How does the learning affect the training?

Before we move to the next section, let us review what we have covered so far. We reviewed the main ingredients of a supervised learning task. We start with the data which comprises the feature vectors of the samples and the labels of the samples. We then choose a hypothesis or model. We initiate the model using a random set of free parameters. We then introduced the loss function which characterizes and quantifies the difference between the predictions of the model and the actual labels. Finally, we use one of the optimization techniques introduced in this section to tune the free parameters to minimize the loss.

But finding the optimal values of the free parameters does not mean that we have a good model. In fact, you probably have noticed that for some of the questions in this section the linear models that were trained do not have a good performance. Next, we are going to see how we evaluate a trained model and fine-tune it, if necessary.

3.3 Model evaluation and model selection

Before we get to the metrics and scores that are used for the evaluation of supervised learning models, we need to review some basics of evaluation. The first step is to understand the difference between in-sample and out-sample errors [42, 43].

3.3.1 A good fit versus a good predictor: in-sample and out-sample errors

You may have noticed that from the start, we introduced the training set and the test set, we used the training set for training the model and finding the optimized values of the free parameters. But we never used the test set for the training part.

Exercise: Why do we separate the test and not use it for training?

We use the test set to check the predictions of the model. In fact, we often characterize the quality of a model by its performance on the test set.

Note that a good model is expected to generalize well over unseen data. In other words, we expect a good model to be predictive. Without this requirement, we can always build a model by memorizing all the samples and their labels in our dataset. The loss for such a model would be zero by definition, but this is clearly not a useful model. This is because it does not know what to predict for samples that are not in the dataset. In other words, it has no predictive power.

How can we check for the predictive power of a model? After all, we only have access to the samples in the dataset and have no knowledge of any new sample that is not in the set.

Exercise: How would check for the predictive power of a model after training it?

The solution is to not reveal all the data to the model for training. This is why we split the data into the training and test subsets. The training set is used to train the model. After the model is trained, we test its performance on the test set. The performance of the model on the test set mimics its performance on the data that are not given to the model and characterizes its prediction power [42, 43].

The performance on the training set and test set are referred to as 'in-sample' and 'out-sample', respectively. For instance, the loss on the training set (which is used for training the model) is referred to as the in-sample error. Similarly, the loss on the test sample is known as the out-sample error.

Implicitly, we are making some assumptions here. The first one is that the training and the test sets are coming from the same distribution. To assure that this condition is met, it is critical to pick the two sets at random. We normally shuffle the data randomly before picking the training and the test samples.

Another assumption is that the test set is representative of unseen samples. Recall that we use the performance of the model on the test set as a measure of its predictive power. We need to be really careful about this assumption. This assumption imposes a restriction on the generalizability of the model. Specifically, the performance measured on the test set only guarantees the predictive power on samples that are similar to the ones in the test set. By similar, we mean samples that are generated with the same process or drawn from the same probability distribution.

For instance, imagine that we want to build a weather prediction model and assume that we only have access to the climate data of Beijing. We split the data into a training and a test set and train the model on the training set and evaluate it on the test set. Imagine that the model can predict the weather (i.e. temperature, precipitation, etc) with 99% accuracy for the samples in the test set. What does that tell us? How well do we expect the model to work for predicting the weather for next Sunday in Beijing? It should work well, as was evaluated on the test set. But how about predicting the weather in Sydney or Toronto? Can we generalize and expect 99% accuracy for those other cities? There is no reason why this model should perform as well in other cities. This does not mean that the model is not going to perform well in other cities. It only means that we have not tested the model for those other cities and we need to be careful about what our 'test score' represents.

Question: What determines the predictive power of a model? How can we make models that generalize well? (Think about this question, we will get to it soon.)

3.3.2 Over-fitting and under-fitting

Let us start this section with two exercises.

Exercise: Consider the data in figure 3.50. This is a regression task where each sample has one feature. Each sample is indicated with a red point. Figure 3.50 includes three polynomial fits with degrees $d = 1, 3, 9$. Which model do you think is a better model and why?

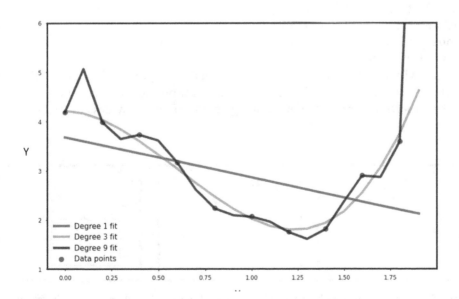

Figure 3.50. Overfitting: the plot shows three different fits to the same data. All models are polynomial models. The degree of each polynomial model is shown in the legend of the plot.

If you only take the loss into account, then the black plot ($d = 9$) is the best since it passes all the red points and has a loss of zero. However, it is evident from the plot that $d = 9$ does not follow the general trend of the data between the data samples. For instance, between the first two samples, it goes up and then comes down. Our intuition suggests that if there were a new sample between the two points, the $d = 9$ model would not be able to generalize well for that.

On the other hand, $d = 1$ has a relatively large loss and cannot capture most of the samples.

The model $d = 3$ seems to have the right balance. It has a relatively low loss, although not as low as $d = 9$, it seems more consistent and generalizable.

Let us also look at a classification example.

Exercise: Consider the classification task in figure 3.51. The three plots show the feature space. Each point represents a sample and the color and shape of the samples illustrate the category of the samples. The tree panels show three different decision boundaries for this classification task. Which one do you think is a better model and why?

The model in figure 3.51(a) has a high loss since it misclassifies a lot of samples. This is referred to as 'under-fitting' [43]. On the other hand, panel (c) in 3.51 has the lowest value of loss. This is because it is correctly classifying all the samples in the training set. But does this make the model in (c) the best model? The decision boundary in (c) is specifically tailored to the data that it is trained with. This is referred to as 'over-fitting' [43]. Specifically, the model in (c) classifies all the samples, including the red sample that is to the right of the panel. This sample may be an outlier or even a mislabeled sample. Because the model in (c) is over-fitting, it tries too hard to classify all the samples in the training set and loses its predictive power. In figure 3.51(c) all the regions between the red sample at the right of the panel and the mass of red samples fall in the red zone (the left side of the decision boundary). This means that if the model is extended to new samples in that region it will misclassify them.

This is why we are usually interested in models like figure 3.51(b), where the loss is relatively low and the general trend of the data is captured, yet it is not over-fitting to all the micro-features of the training data. This provides a high-accuracy

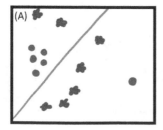 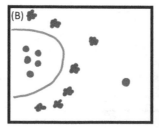 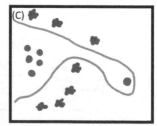

Figure 3.51. Overfitting: here we have a classification task. The plots show the samples in the feature space. The label of each sample is identified by its colors and shapes. Each panel shows a different decision boundary for this classification task.

classification, although it sacrifices some of the samples for the general trend. The model in figure 3.51(b) is expected to generalize and perform well on new data samples.

We can use the loss on the training and test sets to characterize if a model is under-fitting, over-fitting, or if it is a good fit.

Exercise: If a model is under-fitting, how would the training and test loss be affected?

For a model that is under-fitting we expect both the training and test losses to be high. The high loss value on the training data indicates that the model cannot even capture the training data well.

Exercise: If a model is over-fitting, how would the training and test loss be affected?

If the model is over-fitting we would expect it to have a low loss on the training set. However, since it is over-fitting to the samples in the training set, it would not do well on the test set and would have a high test loss. A significant difference between the training and the test loss usually indicates over-fitting.

Exercise: How can we build models that are not under-fitting or over-fitting?

In the next section, we will break down the loss into two parts and explain how they are related to over-fitting and under-fitting. We will provide some tools and guidelines for finding the right model.

3.3.3 Bias and variance trade-off

For the predictive power of a model, we can break the loss into two parts. The first part is the loss that we obtain on the training set. This is a measure of how well the model can fit the data. But, as we saw in the last section, this is not enough for a good prediction. The second part is the variance between the training loss and the test loss. Typically, the loss on the test set is more than the loss on the training set. In this context, the loss on the training set is referred to as the 'bias' and the difference between the test and training losses is referred to as 'variance'. For more rigorous and mathematical definitions see [43].

Bias indicates the capability of the model for capturing the complexity of the data. Usually, complex models have lower biases (i.e. better performance). For instance, in figure 3.50 the $d = 9$ polynomial has a higher complexity and lower bias. As the complexity is reduced, the bias increases. The linear model ($d = 1$) has the highest bias).

Variance on the other hand is an indication of how much the model can be generalized beyond the training set. High variance is an indication of over-fitting. As we will see, the more complex the model, the higher the variance. We saw this in figures 3.50 and 3.51 in the last section.

The prediction loss is usually the sum of the bias and variance. Although there may be additional contributions from noise and other sources of variance.

Exercise: For a model that is under-fitting, what can you tell about the bias and variance? How about a model that is over-fitting?

For an under-fitting model, the bias is high. Under-fitting means that even for the training set, the loss is high. However, usually models that under-fit have low variance, because the difference between the training and test losses is small.

For a model that is over-fitting, usually, the loss on the training set is low which means that it has a low bias. However, since it is over-fitting, the difference between the training and test losses is high, i.e. the variance is high.

Exercise: How can we reduce the bias?

Remember that bias is the performance on the training set. In principle, it is possible to reduce the bias to zero by memorizing all the labels, but as we mentioned before, this would not make a good model.

For this exercise, let us limit ourselves to polynomial hypotheses. As we increase the degree of the polynomial, the loss would decrease. In fact, for n_s samples, it is possible to find a polynomial of degree $n_s - 1$ that would pass through all the points. This would give a zero loss. However, as you can guess, this would be a high-degree polynomial. What do you think would happen to the variance?

Exercise: How would you reduce the variance?

For the polynomial models you can see that as the degree of the polynomial increases, the models start to overfit. In other words, the lower the polynomial degree, the smaller the variance. So to make the variance small, we need to simplify the model.

Exercise: Can we do both? More specifically, can we change the degree such that both the variance and bias would decrease?

Ideally, we want to reduce both variance and bias to zero. However, as we saw, increasing the polynomial degree decreases the bias but increases the variance. In other words, bias and variance are competing against each other.

Since the full prediction loss is the sum of the two, we need to find the trade-off, i.e. the right amount of complexity for which the bias is relatively small and the variance is not too big. Figure 3.52 shows schematically what this looks like. This takes us to our next topic which provides a powerful tool for tuning the complexity of our models.

Validation curve

The plot in figure 3.52 is not limited to polynomial models and is a trend that is generally observed for the complexity of models. This plot is known as the 'validation curve' and helps identify the right amount of complexity for the model [43, 44]. Here we review this tool and how it is used.

Imagine that you have a family of hypotheses with a hyper-parameter that characterizes their complexity.

Exercise: What is the hyper-parameter that characterizes the complexity for KNN, decision trees, and polynomial models?

For polynomial models, it is the degree of the polynomial. The higher the degree the more complex the model is.

For KNN it is the number of neighbors. If we consider more neighbors, the decision boundaries would become more smooth and less complex. So the smaller the number of neighbors, the more complex a KNN model gets.

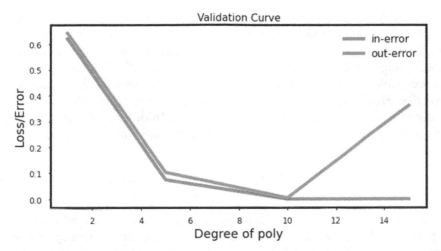

Figure 3.52. Validation curve: the in-sample and out-sample errors are plotted against the model complexity. Here we are focusing on polynomial models for which the complexity is characterized by the degree of the polynomial. Usually, initially (less complexity) the bias is high. As we increase the complexity of the model, the bias reduces. However, gradually, the model starts to overfit, and the variance increases which leads to increasing the out-sample error.

Finally, for the decision tree it is the depth of the tree. The deeper the tree, the more complex it is.

We encourage the reader to pick one of the datasets in this book (e.g. elementary particle identification) and try training the models with different values for these parameters and see how that affects the decision boundary. For instance, try KNN with $k = 1, 3, 10, 20$.

Exercise: How can we set the complexity?

Using models with high complexity leads to high variance. On the other hand, models with low complexity would have high bias and under-fit. How can we tune the complexity of a model?

In order to tune the complexity hyper-parameter of the model, we can use the validation curve. It is similar to the plot in figure 3.52. This plot shows the loss or a metric of performance versus the complexity of the model or the hyper-parameter that represents the complexity of the model [43]. Usually, the bias is expected to decrease with increasing complexity and the variance to increase with increasing complexity. We are interested in the point where the sum of the two is minimized.

This is the general idea that is used for tuning other hyper-parameters of the model too. For instance, a similar idea is used for setting the learning rate. For this, one may use the loss or training time or both to find the optimal value.

Exercise: How can we tune the complexity of a model without the tunable hyper-parameter for the complexity?

For instance, imagine that you have a polynomial model, and based on some domain knowledge, the degree is set to $d = 4$. Can we still control the complexity of this model?

It is possible to control the complexity of such models by penalizing large values of the free parameters. You can check that for a polynomial of fixed degree, you can force the model to be less complex by limiting the range of the free parameters. For instance, imagine that the coefficient corresponding to X^d is limited to $[-1, 1]$. This has less complexity compared to when the coefficient takes a large value.

Exercise: How can we turn this into a controllable parameter?

There is a technique called 'regularization' [45]. In order to penalize large values for the free parameters, we can include them in the loss function. More specifically, that is

$$\mathcal{L}_R = \mathcal{L} + \lambda \sum_i |w_i|, \tag{3.52}$$

where $\mathcal{L}_R$ is the regularized loss function, $|w_i|$ represents the magnitude of the free parameters, and λ is a parameter that determines how much the large value of the parameters is penalized. For $\lambda = 0$, we retrieve the non-regularized loss function. But as we increase λ, the contribution from the second term in equation (3.52) grows. This means that the optimization cannot reduce the loss at the cost of using wildly large values for the free parameters. Large values of the parameters would increase the second term of equation (3.52). So, the optimization will be forced to find a compromise where the loss is fairly small and the free parameters are not too big.

The plots in figure 3.53 show regularized models. For reference, compare them with the $d = 9$ polynomial model in figure 3.50. The regularized plots are smoother and less complex. Also, the larger the lambda, the less complex they become.

The regularized loss used in equation (3.52) is known as 'L1' regularization [45]. Alternatively, we can use

$$\mathcal{L}_R = \mathcal{L} + \lambda \sum_i (w_i)^2, \tag{3.53}$$

which is known as the 'L2' loss [45]. The L1 regularization is usually used for sparse models. It penalizes $|w_i| < 1$ more than L2 regularization and pushes the small free parameters to vanish which leads to more sparse models. Figure 3.53 compares L1 and L2 regularized models. The top panel shows an L1 regularized plots and the bottom one shows an L2 regularized plot.

Question: Add regularization to your implementation of GD. Use the GD optimizer that you built in the optimization section and add regularization to it. For simplicity, you can do this for MSE.

Question: Take the black body radiation dataset, i.e. DST-GSE (table 1.2), and use your regularized implementation of GD to train a polynomial model of degree $d = 7$ for the data.

Question: For the last question, change the λ and plot the validation curve.

For implementing regularization in scikit-learn, most models have a hyper-parameter. You need to read the documentation of the model. For instance, for the SVM there is a parameter called 'C' that sets the regularization. C is inversely

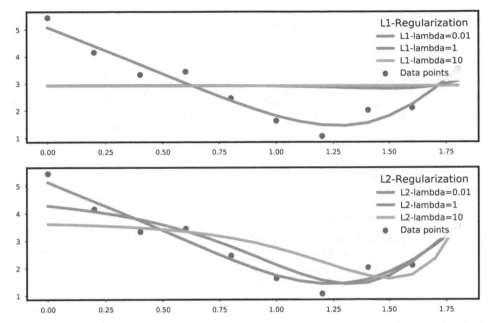

Figure 3.53. Regularization. The two plot shows regularized polynomial models of degree $d = 9$. For comparison, see figure 3.50. The $d = 9$ polynomial is over-fitting to minor fluctuations in the data. The regularized versions, however, are more effective at capturing the main trend without over-fitting. The top plot shows the results for L1 regularization. The bottom plot shows the results for L2 regularization. Lambda characterizes the strength of regularization (λ in equations (3.52) and (3.53)). The large the lambda, the less complex the models become and beyond some point they become almost linear.

```
1 from sklearn.svm import SVC
2 lambda = .1
3 model = SVC(C=1/lambda )
4 model.fit(X_train, Y_train)
5 Y_precited = model.predict(X_test)
```

Listing 3.15. Regularization-SVM.

proportional to λ. The code in listing 3.15 shows how you can make a model with more regularization in scikit-learn.

Question: Take the black body radiation dataset. Train an SVM with an RBF kernel. Tune the regularization to obtain a good fit.

The result would look like the plots in the figure 3.54.

You can use the scikit-learn library to plot the validation curve. The code in listing 3.16 gives an example.

For more information, see the documentation for the validation curve.

Learning curve

The complexity of the model is not the only parameter that affects the bias and variance. The size of the dataset also plays an important role. To see this, let us do an exercise.

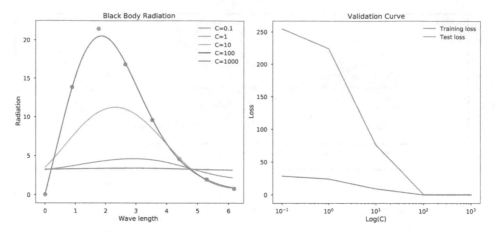

Figure 3.54. Tuning the complexity using the regularization parameter of the SVM model, *C*. The plot on the left shows the results of the trained models. It shows that for higher values of *C* (complexity) the SMV starts to train more accurate models. The plot on the left shows the in-sample and out-sample errors for different values of *C*.

```
1  from sklearn.model_selection import validation_curve
2  from sklearn.neighbors import KNeighborsClassifier
3
4  # Number of neigbours to try for KNN.
5  # Note that this represents the complexity for KNN.
6  k_list = [1,3,5,7,10, 15, 20, 25, 30, 40, 50 , 75,  100, 125, 150,
       175, 200]
7
8  train_scores, valid_scores = validation_curve(KNeighborsClassifier(),
9                                         X_train, Y_train,
10                                         param_name="n_neighbors"
       ,
11                                         param_range=k_list ,
12                                         )
```

Listing 3.16. Validation curve.

Exercise: Re-do the validation curve in figure 3.52 once with half the data and once with all the data.

Exercise: How does increasing the number of samples change the learning curve and the loss value for the optimal model?

Figure 3.55 shows the validation curve, once for five samples and once for 19 samples. For both of them we are using a polynomial fit, and for the complexity we change the degree of the polynomial.

In other words, the optimal complexity is pushed up when we use more data.

If you go back to the example in figure 3.50 you can see how this happens. With more samples, the higher-order polynomial will see data for the samples for the gaps between the current samples and would try to fit them too.

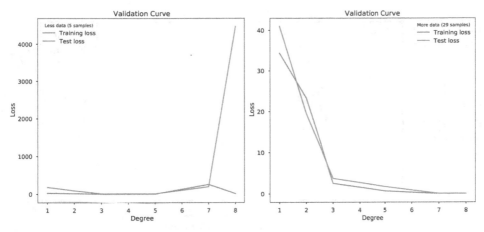

Figure 3.55. The two plots show validation curves for two different numbers of samples. They are both for the black body radiation dataset. Polynomial models are trained for them. The plots show the validation curves. The one on the left has only five samples and it is evident that for high-degree polynomials, the variance is too high. However, the plot on the right shows that increasing the number of samples to 19 can help reduce the variance even for the more complex models (higher degrees). If we push the degree even higher, the variance starts to grow, even for the right panel. The plot shows that with more data, we can use more complex models.

Generally, one way to improve the performance of the model is to use more data. However, based on what we have covered so far, you can see that more data only helps with reducing the variance. It cannot improve the bias. For instance, the linear model in figure 3.50 would not improve much by adding more data.

It is important to understand if the performance of a model is affected by bias or variance. There have been cases where ML practitioners spent a lot of time and money on collecting more data without realizing that the performance of their models was affected by the model and more data would not help them.

Exercise: How can we check if we have enough data?

The next tool that we want to introduce is called the 'learning curve' and is designed to answer this question. The learning curve is a plot of the in- and out-sample errors/losses versus the size of the dataset. As the number of data points increases, the variance should reduce and converge to the in-sample [43]. It usually looks like the plot in figure 3.56.

Note that for the size, we take different numbers of samples from the dataset and the size of the dataset is not really changing.

Using more data can increase the bias because there are more samples and for a fixed complexity, it becomes more challenging to fit all the points.

The variance, however, decreases with more samples. Remember that the gap between the training and test losses is the variance of the model. This is because, for a fixed level of complexity, it would be more challenging to overfit all the points and it is often a better strategy to find the general trend.

Generally, more data are better and make more robust data. However, data are usually not cheap. Whether it is coming from a data collection process or a physical simulation, it may be expensive and time-consuming to gather more data. Thus,

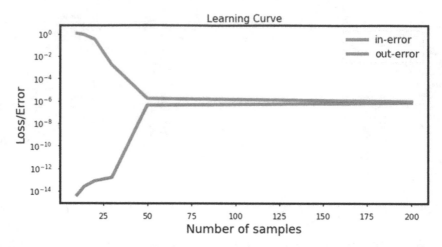

Figure 3.56. Learning curve: the in-sample and out-sample errors are plotted against the size of the dataset. This represents the typical situation. As we include more samples, the variance (the difference between the in and out-sample error) decreases and ideally, they converge to the sample level.

```
1  from sklearn.model_selection import learning_curve
2  from sklearn.svm import SVC
3
4  # Number of samples to try for the Learning Curve
5  ns_list = np.array([ 3, 5, 10, 20 , 30 , 50, 76, 200])
6
7  ns_list, train_scores, validation_scores = learning_curve(
8                                        estimator = SVC( ),
9                                        X = X_train, y =
   Y_train,
10                                       train_sizes =
   ns_list,
11                                       )
```

Listing 3.17. Learning curve.

before you decide to spend your resources on obtaining more data, you need to check if the lack of performance is coming from high variance and can be reduced with more data.

Ideally, we need enough data that minimizes or even closes the gap between the training and test loss. At this point, our main limitation is the bias of the model, and adding more does not really help. This is how the learning curve provides a visual tool to see if we have enough data or if we need to get more.

You can use scikit-learn to plot the validation curve. The codes in listing 3.17 provide an example.

For more information, see the documentation for the learning curve.

3.3.4 Model tuning

Up to this point, we have talked about the training process which optimizes the free parameters of the model and optimizes the approximation that the model gives for the target function that connects the input features and labels. As we have mentioned, besides the main parameters of the models, there are also hyper-parameters. In this section, we will discuss fine-tuning the hyper-parameters of the models which enhance the performance.

Before we start, let us review some of the hyper-parameters that we have seen so far:

- Poly degree in polynomial models.
- k in KNN.
- Depth in decision trees.

Question: Check the documentation for SVM classifiers on scikit-learn and identify its hyper-parameters.

We have also had some other hyper-parameters such as the ones for optimization. Some of the more important ones are:

- The learning rate η.
- Regularization coefficient.
- The batch size.
- β_1 and β_2 for Adam optimization algorithm.

As you can see, training a model could involve a lot of hyper-parameters and without the right values, the performance of the training might be too low.

Question: Take the black body radiation and train an SVM regressor for it. Use the default values of the SVR object and do not tune any of the hyper-parameters. How is the performance of the model?

Tuning the hyper-parameters is an important part of developing a good model. In this section, we will review some of the basic approaches and best practices of hyper-parameter tuning.

The first approach is to make a grid for the possible values of the hyper-parameters and find the values that work best. For instance, consider a model with two hyper-parameters, $hp1$ and $hp2$, and imagine that we are trying to find the best values for $hp1$ and $hp2$.

The first approach is to make a 2D grid for $hp1$ and $hp2$ and test out the values on the grid. Figure 3.57 shows a schematic grid for this these hyper-parameters.

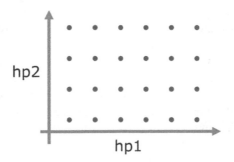

Figure 3.57. Grid search for hyper-parameter tuning.

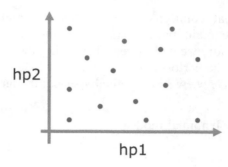

Figure 3.58. Random search for hyper-parameter tuning.

This is sometimes referred to as the 'grid search' approach [33]. The downside of doing the grid search is that the number of points grows exponentially with the number of hyper-parameters that need to be tuned. For instance, if the grid involves ten values for $hp1$ and ten values for $hp2$, the total number of points to try would be $10^2 = 100$. But if we have a third hyper-parameter, then the number of points would be $10^3 = 1000$.

A better approach might be to pick some random points for the values of the hyper-parameters. This is sometimes referred to as 'random search' [33]. Figure 3.58 shows the random alternative to the grid search.

The points may be picked based on a uniform distribution, a normal distribution, or other kinds of distributions that might be relevant to the distribution of the hyper-parameter. For instance, we may expect that the value of $hp1$ should be around 1 and its probability decreases exponentially as we go away from 1.

Exercise: Apply the grid search for the black body radiation problem using an SVM regressor.

It is possible to manually implement the grid or random search, however, but these are efficiently implemented in scikit-learn, see listing 3.18.

Another approach is to use the values from the grid search or the random search and train a secondary model that would predict the performance for other values of the hyper-parameters.

There are more sophisticated approaches used for model tuning that are beyond the scope of this book. For more information see [46, 47]

One of the important practices for model tuning is not to use the test set for measuring the performance of different values of the hyper-parameters. The problem is that if we use the test set for evaluation, we will pick the hyper-parameters that would give the best performance on the test set, but this may not generalize. This is sometimes referred to as data 'leakage'. Remember that the purpose of making a test set was to set aside part of the data that would represent unseen data. For model fine-tuning, the test set cannot be used because then we optimize for models that give better performance on the test set (i.e. optimizing for the test set).

```
1  from sklearn.svm import SVR
2  model = SVR()
3
4
5  from sklearn.model_selection import RandomizedSearchCV, GridSearchCV
6  ### This is randomly sample values of the
7  ### hyperparameters based on an exponential PDF
8  from scipy.stats import expon
9
10
11 #----------------Random Search----------------------
12 ### Here we fine-tume C (the regularization) and
13 ### gamma, the Kernel coefficient.
14 ### For more details, see the documentatio of SVR
15 params_dist = {'C': expon(scale=10), 'gamma':expon(scale=10)}
16
17 ### Build
18 opt_clf = RandomizedSearchCV(estimator = model,
19                              param_distributions=params_dist)
20
21 opt_clf.fit(X_train,Y_train)
22
23
24
25 #----------------Grid Search----------------------
26 params = {'C':[1,3,5], 'kernel':['rbf', 'poly']}
27
28
29 clf_opt = GridSearchCV(estimator = model,
30                        param_grid=params
31                        )
32
33 clf_opt.fit(X_train, Y_train)
```

Listing 3.18. Random search for hyper-parameter tuning.

Exercise: How can we evaluate the performance of the model for model tuning? Remember that we cannot use the test set. We also cannot use the performance of the data that are used for training.

The solution is to make another split. Specifically, we break the data into three subsets, the training set, the test set, and a 'validation' set. We use the training set to train the models. We then use the validation set for model tuning. Once we find the best values of the hyper-parameters, we use the test set to estimate the performance of the model over any new data that the model has never seen. Figure 3.59 shows a schematic picture of the splitting of the data.

3.3.5 Metrics

We have talked about the performance of the model, but we have not clearly specified what that means. One approach is to use the loss, i.e. models with a low loss would have high performance. However, this is not always what we perceive as performance.

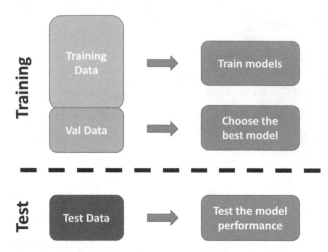

Figure 3.59. A schematic illustration of the training, validation, and test data.

For instance, imagine that we are doing a classification problem and we obtain a value of 0.02 for the loss and imagine that we are using mean-squared-error for the loss. What does that tell us about the performance of the classification? Is this a good model? A more direct measure of performance for this case may be the accuracy, i.e. the ratio of the samples that the model classifies correctly. A model with 99% accuracy probably has a good performance and a model with 50% accuracy for binary classification is extremely bad (completely random).

We use metrics to measure the performance of models. Metrics are usually determined by the specific application. For instance, for classification tasks, accuracy is usually a popular metric.

We can also design metrics to evaluate specific properties of the model. For instance, there are metrics that check for performance with regard to a specific class. We will see some examples.

There are some common metrics that we will review here. However, the choice of the metric is usually dictated by the problem. In other words, what counts as a good measure of performance greatly depends on the problem and the specific application. This will become more clear through some of the examples.

We start with metrics for regression. Often the loss functions could give a good measure of performance for regression tasks. For instance, we can use the mean-squared error or the max error (i.e. $\max_i(Y_i - \bar{Y}_i)$) as a measure of performance. One issue with these two metrics could be that the absolute numbers may not mean much on their own.

Some of the popular regression metrics are variations of regression loss functions that are easier to interpret or use. Let is review an example of such metrics.

Imagine that the max error for a model is 1. Is this a good model? We would need a scale to which to compare this. For instance, if the model is to predict the age of an adult, this probably would represent a high-performance model. If the model is trying to predict the age of a child, the performance of the model may not be acceptable. We may be interested in having a model with max error of 0.01 (days) or 0.1 (months).

Exercise: How can we solve the issue above?

We need to rescale the loss to turn it into an interpretable metric. Sometimes this scale is dictated by the physics of the problem. For example, if we are making a model to estimate the wavelength of a beam of light in the visible range, then the scale is a few hundred nanometers.

Another way to set the scale is to use the variance of the Y values. This is particularly helpful if we do not have much domain knowledge or intuition about the problem or the relevant scales. One example of such metrics is the R^2 metric which is defined as

$$R^2(Y, \bar{Y}) = 1 - \frac{\sum_i (Y_i - \bar{Y}_i)^2}{\sum_i (Y_i - Y_{avg})^2}, \tag{3.54}$$

where Y_{avg} represents the average of the labels Y.

Typically metrics are increasing functions in terms of performance. In other words, the higher the performance, the higher the metric value. For the R^2 metric the value 1 represents the best possible performance. Note that if the mean-squared error of the model is small compared to the variance of the labels, Y, the model would have a high score. On the other hand, if the mean-squared error is large, then the metric decreases and can even become negative.

Next, we will review the metrics for classification tasks.

The most obvious metric for classification is accuracy, i.e. the ratio of the samples that are predicted correctly by the model. But there are other metrics that, depending on the specific application and problem, might be more relevant than the accuracy. Let us perform the following exercises first.

Exercise: For the particle identification problem, there are four types of particles that are labeled as {0, 1, 2, 3}. The population of these classes is

$$1: 1118, 3: 788, 2: 88, 0: 6.$$

Take classes 0 and 1.

- Train a model and measure the accuracy.
- Let us use a dummy classifier that classifies all the input samples as 1. What is the accuracy of this model?
- What does this tell you about the accuracy?

If you do the exercise above, you will see that both models have accuracies of about 99.5%. This is because there is a large imbalance between the two classes and even if we ignore the second class completely, we still can obtain high performance. Imbalanced classification problems are one of the situations where accuracy may not be a good performance metric.

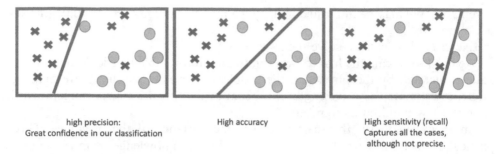

high precision:
Great confidence in our classification

High accuracy

High sensitivity (recall)
Captures all the cases,
although not precise.

Figure 3.60. An example of an asymmetric classification where the class of purple crosses is more important. The three plots show different classifiers which have different properties with respect to the reference class.

Another point that needs to be taken into account is that sometimes the errors that a model makes are not equivalent. For a binary classification task, misclassification of samples from class 0 for samples from class 1 may not be the same as mistaking 1s for 0s. Let us see this in some examples.

Exercise: Imagine that you are building a security check at the airport to flag suspicious bags.

- Turn this into a classification problem.
- What are the possible misclassifications?
- Are they equivalent?

The task is classifying bags as safe (0) or suspicious (1).

If the test flags a bag as suspicious, it would go through some further inspections. So if a safe bag is misclassified as suspicious, the cost is only a few minutes of time for the additional investigation.

The other error is that the bag contains a dangerous item and is misclassified as safe. In this case, this could risk passengers' lives and the cost is much more significant.

This is an example where the two classes and their corresponding misclassifications are not symmetric.

As is evident from these exercises, accuracy may not be the best metric. When data are imbalanced or the two classes are not symmetric, we need to use metrics other than accuracy.

To better understand this, see the example in figure 3.60. It shows an example of a binary classification where class (the purple crosses) is more important. This could be the class of suspicious bags in the example above. Usually, the class of normal samples is referred to as the negative class and the class of interest is referred to as the positive class.

Question: Imaging that you are building a Covid test kit (not a machine learning example). Which class is the more important class? What is the positive case?

Figure 3.60 shows three types of classification for the same data. Each of them has its own advantage. The one in the middle has the highest accuracy, but it misclassifies positive samples for negative ones and vice versa. The first one on the left has perfect precision when it comes to the positive samples. In other words, every sample that is classified as positive (purple cross) is in fact a positive sample. However, it is not sensitive and it misses some of the positive samples. The classifier in the right panel on the hand, catches all the positive samples, although it is not precise, i.e. many of the samples that are classified as positive are negative. You can see that the precision and sensitivity are not symmetric and are defined with respect to a specific class.

Exercise: For the case of flagging suspicious bags, do we want a classifier with high precision or high sensitivity for the positive class?

In this case, the classifier needs to be sensitive (similar to the one in the right panel). This is because it is ok if some normal bags are labeled as suspicious, the cost is only a few minutes of inspection. However, if the sensitivity was low (as the one on the left), then the test is missing some of the suspicious bags which could be dangerous.

Question: Make an example where we want a high precision test.

For the evaluation of classification models, we start with a tool instead of a metric. One of the powerful tools that are extremely helpful for understanding the performance of a model and its errors is the 'confusion matrix' [33, 48]. Figure 3.61 shows the confusion matrix for a binary classification problem.

For a binary classification problem, there are four possibilities. The sample is:

- positive and classified as positive, i.e. True Pos (TP);
- negative and classified as negative, i.e. True Neg (TN);
- negative and classified as positive, i.e. False Pos (FP);
- positive and classified as negative, i.e. False Neg (FN).

The confusion matrix shows the number of samples that fall in each of these categories in a matrix like the one in figure 3.61. This matrix gives a full overview of how the model is performing as well as the different types of mistakes that it makes.

Question: Find the confusion matrix for each of the classifiers in figure 3.60.

The confusion matrix is not limited to binary classification tasks and can be used for multi-class classification problems too. For the multi-class case, there are more types of error and the confusion matrix can show each type of mistake.

The confusion matrix can be used to extract different metrics for the evaluation of a classifier. Here are some of the more popular classification metrics that are commonly used.

		Predicted Label	
		Positive	Negative
Real label	Positive	True Pos	False Neg
	Negative	False Pos	True Neg

Figure 3.61. Confusion matrix for a binary classification problem.

Recall: Specifies the sensitivity with respect to a class of interest [33, 48]. For the recall of the positive cases, this is the ratio of the detected positive cases to all the positive ones. Mathematically that is

$$R = \frac{TP}{TP + FN}. \tag{3.55}$$

Recall can be defined for all the classes.

Precision: This is the precision of a classifier with respect to its prediction for a specific class [33, 48]. For positive samples, this is the ratio of the samples that actually positive to all the samples that are classified/predicted to be positive. Mathematically, that is

$$P = \frac{TP}{TP + FP}. \tag{3.56}$$

Precision can be defined for each class as well.

Ideally, a classifier should have high recall and precision. But if we want to find a balance between the two, we can use the 'f1-score' which tries to find a balance between precision and recall.

f1-score: This is a geometrical average of the recall and precision [33, 48]. A high f1-score guarantees that the classifier has both high recall and precision. Mathematically, it is defined as

$$f1 = \frac{2 \times P \times R}{R + P}. \tag{3.57}$$

The scikit-learn library implements all of these metrics. You can use the code in listing 3.19 to implement them.

```
1  from sklearn.svm import SVC
2  model = SVC()
3  model.fit(X_train,Y_train)
4  Y_predicted = model.predict(X_test)
5
6  #--------Confusion Matrix-------
7  from sklearn.metrics import confusion_matrix, plot_confusion_matrix
8  print('The confusion matrix is: \n {}\n'.format(confusion_matrix(
       Y_test, Y_predicted) ) )
9  ## or
10 plot_confusion_matrix( model, X_test, Y_test)
11
12 #--------Precision and Recall-------
13 from sklearn.metrics import recall_score, precision_score, f1_score
14
15 print(f"The recall for the classifier: \n {recall_score(Y_test,
       Y_predicted, pos_label=1)}" )
16 print(f"The precision for the classifier: \n {precision_score(Y_test,
       Y_predicted, pos_label = 1)}" )
17
18 ### You guess the one for f1-score
```

Listing 3.19. Evaluation of classification models.

For more information on metrics in the scikit-learn library see [33].

Exercise: How can we enhance the recall or precision of a model?

In the next section, we will discuss how precision or recall can be improved.

Tuning the threshold of a classifier

Imagine that we are interested in a classifier with a high precision value for a specific class. One approach is to implement this in our loss function. For instance, if we are interested in a model with a low FP, we can make the loss such that the FP errors would have a larger contribution to the loss compared to FN cases.

However, for a large range of classifiers there is an alternative way to improve the recall or precision. This can even be done after the model is trained with a normal loss function.

Imagine that we have trained a logistic regression model for a binary classification task. The model returns the probability of being positive, i.e. $P(Y = 1)$. For logistic regression, the model normally makes predictions based on $P(Y = 1) \geqslant 1/2$. This is illustrated schematically in figure 3.62(A). Samples above the halfway point (the purple region) are classified as positive.

If we were to increase the precision for the positive predictions, we can increase the threshold and use $P(Y = 1) \geqslant 1/2 + \delta$ as the condition. The higher the δ, the more confidence we have in the positive predictions. For instance, take $\delta = 0.25$. This means that only samples with probabilities above 75% are classified as positive.

This is illustrated schematically in figure 3.62(B). This shows that the expected probability of classifying a sample as positive is much higher.

The drawback is that the sensitivity decreases as we increase the threshold. In fact, if we want to be sure to catch all or at least most of the positive samples, we would need to reduce the threshold. In other words, the condition for classification should be $P(Y = 1) \geqslant 1/2 - \delta$. This is illustrated schematically in figure 3.62(C).

For specific applications where high recall or high precision values are required, this trick can be used to tune the model into a classifier that meets the required expectations.

In some cases, increasing the precision with this approach can significantly reduce the recall. Ideally, there should be a value of the threshold that while precision is as high as is needed for the application, the recall is also relatively acceptable. Similarly, if the threshold is tuned for enhancing the recall, the precision should not be too low.

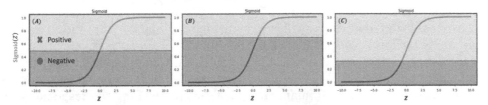

Figure 3.62. Schematic image of a logistic regression model with three classification thresholds. Increasing the threshold increases the precision of the classification. In contrast, reducing the threshold improves the sensitivity of the classification.

The 'precision–recall curve' is a tool that helps evaluate a model in different regimes of the threshold [33, 48]. The threshold is changed and for each value, both the precision and recall are calculated and put on a plot (precision on the Y-axis and recall on the X-axis).

For an ideal classifier there should be a point where both the precision and recall get to one. In other words, one of the points in the plot should be (1, 1). In practice, this rarely happens, but a good model can get close to the ideal point.

Question: See how you can implement the precision–recall curve in the scikit-learn library.

Some other popular tools that are used for the characterization of the performance of a classifier are the ROC curve and AUC curve' [33, 48].

Question: Research what the AUC curve is and use the scikit-learn library to implement it.

Before we finish this section, we need to discuss one of the common practices for model evaluation. You may have noticed when you calculate the loss or a metric for example, if the test set changes, the numbers may change slightly. If the training and test sets are big enough and if they are chosen randomly from the same distribution, then the deviations in the loss or metrics values should be small when the test set changes.

However, although unlikely, there may be cases where the loss or metric deviates too much for a test set. For example, it may be that by chance all the samples in the test set are classified correctly. In such situations, the reported loss or score values are too specific for the test set that was used and would not generalize well.

Exercise: How can we resolve this issue?

The next section provides a solution for this issue.

3.3.6 Cross-validation

The test and training sets are usually sampled randomly from the data. But imagine that for a specific instance, the distribution of the samples in the test set is different from the ones in the training set. This could happen in particular if the dataset is small.

Exercise: How can we make the performance less susceptible to the random choice of the test set?

One popular solution is to try different sub-samples for the test set and average the performance over the different choices of the test set. This is known as 'cross-validation' [33, 44].

There are different cross-validation methods. One of the most popular approaches for this is to split the whole data into k-folds and pick one of them as the test set each time. More specifically, we train k different models, each time we would take one of the k-folds as the test set and use the rest for training the model. In the end, we calculate the performance metric of each model for its corresponding test set. The overall performance would be the average of all the calculated metrics. Figure 3.63 shows the k-folds schematically.

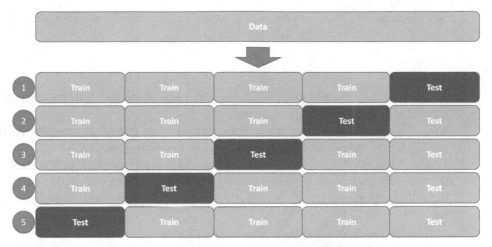

Figure 3.63. Schematic picture of k-fold cross-validation. Here $k = 5$.

3.4 Summary

In this chapter we covered the basics of supervised learning models. We started with data. Data are one of the most important building blocks for building a good model. Next is the model. We explained that we usually work with models that have some trainable parameters. The goal is to find the set of parameters that would give a good approximation to the actual process that has generated the data. To quantify the difference between the results of the model and real labels, we introduced the loss functions. We then introduced optimization techniques to use the loss function to optimize the parameters of the model.

It was also explained that it is not enough for a good model to have a good performance (low loss) on the data that it is being trained with. We also need the model to have good prediction power. To this end, we split the data into a training and a test set. The test set represents the new and unseen data and the performance of the model on the test set shows how well the model can handle new data that have not been presented to the model during the training process.

We also discussed the model selection and fine-tuning of the model. We reviewed different techniques and practices for tuning the complexity of the models as well as the hyper-parameters of the model.

Last, we discussed in detail what it means for the model to have high performance and investigated different metrics as well as different practices for evaluating the performance of a model.

These concepts and tools provide the foundations of supervised learning. In the next chapter we will introduce NNs. As you will see, all the elements that we discussed in this chapter will extend to supervised learning with NNs. In other words, an NN is a model with a lot of trainable parameters. As for any supervised learning task, we choose a loss function and optimization technique and try to find the set of parameters that minimizes the loss, i.e. the difference between the predictions of the model and the actual labels.

3.5 Questions

1. *Regression with KNN*: How can we use the ideas described for classification with KNN to build a regression model?
2. *Regression with a decision tree*: How can we use the ideas described for classification with a decision tree to build a regression model?
3. *Feature importance*: Often, some features are more important to the model than others and play a more crucial role in the predictions. How can we introduce an ordering that characterizes the importance of different features in:
   - a linear model?
   - a decision tree?
   - KNN?
4. *Benchmarking models*: Imagine that you have two models. What metrics would you use to compare them? How do you decide which model is better?
5. *Asymmetric loss function*: Consider a binary classification problem. The model can make two types of mistakes: mislabeling samples from class 1 as 0 and vice versa. Imagine that for some reason the cost of mistakes of the first type is twice as expensive as the second type. Build a loss function that captures this.

Exercise: Try to make the tree for the data in figure 3.1.

References

[1] Dincer B Star type classification/NASA *kaggle* https://www.kaggle.com/datasets/brsdincer/star-type-classification (Accessed 2023)
[2] Abdollahi M, Torabi N, Raeisi S and Rahvar S 2023 Hierarchical classification of variable stars using deep convolutional neural networks arXiv preprint (arXiv:2301.08497)
[3] Aguirre C, Pichara K and Becker I 2019 Deep multi-survey classification of variable stars *Mon. Not. R. Astron. Soc.* **482** 5078–92
[4] Schatzki L, Arrasmith A, Coles P J and Cerezo M 2021 Entangled datasets for quantum machine learning arXiv preprint (arXiv:2109.03400)
[5] Yosefpor M, Mostaan M R and Raeisi S 2020 Finding semi-optimal measurements for entanglement detection using autoencoder neural networks *Quantum Sci. Technol.* **5** 045006
[6] Reza F M 1994 *An Introduction to Information Theory* (North Chelmsford, MA: Courier) https://store.doverpublications.com/0486682102.html
[7] Pierce J R 2012 *An Introduction to Information Theory: Symbols, Signals and Noise* (North Chelmsford, MA: Courier) https://store.doverpublications.com/0486240614.html
[8] Jolliffe I T and Cadima J 2016 Principal component analysis: a review and recent developments *Phil. Trans. R. Soc.* A**374** 20150202
[9] Huang X, Wu L and Ye Y 2019 A review on dimensionality reduction techniques *Int. J. Pattern Recognit. Artif. Intell.* **33** 1950017

[10] Mohammed Salih Hasan B and Abdulazeez A M 2021 A review of principal component analysis algorithm for dimensionality reduction *J. Soft Comput. Data Min.* **2** 20–30

[11] Izenman A J 2012 Introduction to manifold learning *Wiley Interdiscip. Rev. Comput. Stat.* **4** 439–46

[12] Lin B, He X and Ye J 2015 A geometric viewpoint of manifold learning *Appl. Inform.* **2** 1–12

[13] Jakkula V 2006 Tutorial on support vector machine (SVM) *School of EECS, Washington State University* **37** 3

[14] Smola A J and Schölkopf B 2004 A tutorial on support vector regression *Stat. Comput.* **14** 199–222

[15] Kleinbaum D G, Klein M, Kleinbaum D G and Klein M 2010 Introduction to logistic regression *Logistic Regression: A Self-Learning Text* (New York: Springer) pp 1–39

[16] Hofmann M 2006 Support vector machines—kernels and the kernel trick *Hauptseminar "Reading Club : Support Vector Machines"* pp 1–16

[17] Hofmann T, Schölkopf B and Smola A J 2008 Kernel methods in machine learning *Ann. Stat.* **36** 1171–220

[18] Kim E 2013 Everything you wanted to know about the kernel trick http://www.eric-kim.net/eric-kim-net/posts/1/kernel_trick.html (Accessed in 2023)

[19] Dummit D S and Foote R M 2004 *Abstract Algebra* vol 3 (Hoboken, NJ: Wiley) https://www.wiley.com/en-us/Abstract+Algebra%2C+3rd+Edition-p-9780471433347

[20] Gupta A R 2018 Simple and in depth introduction of kNN (*K*-nearest neighbor) *Medium* https://medium.com/@guptaalokraj/simple-and-in-depth-introduction-of-knn-k-nearest-neighbor-168a6077946e (Accessed 2023)

[21] Kodratoff Y 2014 *Introduction to Machine Learning* (Amsterdam: Elsevier)

[22] Grootendorst M 2021 9 distance measures in data science *Medium* https://towardsdatascience.com/9-distance-measures-in-data-science-918109d069fa (Accessed 2023)

[23] Kotsiantis S B 2013 Decision trees: a recent overview *Artif. Intell. Rev.* **39** 261–83

[24] Suthaharan S and Suthaharan S 2016 Decision tree learning *Machine Learning Models and Algorithms for Big Data Classification: Thinking with Examples for Effective Learning* pp 237–69

[25] Dieterich T G 2000 Ensemble methods in machine learning *Multiple Classifier Systems: 1st Int. Workshop, MCS 2000 Cagliari, Italy, June 21–23, 2000 Proc. 1* (Berlin: Springer) pp 1–15

[26] Zhang C and Ma Y 2012 *Ensemble Machine Learning: Methods and Applications* (Berlin: Springer) https://doi.org/10.1007/978-1-4419-9326-7

[27] Sagi O and Rokach L 2018 Ensemble learning: a survey *Wiley Interdiscip. Rev. Data Min. Knowl. Discov.* **8** e1249

[28] Johnson R W 2001 An introduction to the bootstrap *Teach. Stat.* **23** 49–54

[29] Breiman L 2001 Random forests *Mach. Learn.* **45** 5–32

[30] Lowd D and Domingos P 2005 Naive Bayes models for probability estimation *Proc. 22nd Int. Conf. on Machine Learning* pp 529–36

[31] Kotsiantis S B, Zaharakis I and Pintelas P *et al* 2007 Supervised machine learning: a review of classification techniques *Proc. 2007 Conf. on Emerging Artificial Intelligence Applications in Computer Engineering* vol 160 pp 3–24

[32] Nasteski V 2017 An overview of the supervised machine learning methods *Horizons B* **4** 51–62

[33] User guide *scikit-learn* https://scikit-learn/stable/user_guide.html (Accessed 2023)

[34] Wang Q, Ma Y, Zhao K and Tian Y 2022 A comprehensive survey of loss functions in machine learning *Ann. Data Sci.* **9** 187–212

[35] Bellman R 1963 *Mathematical Optimization Techniques* (Oakland, CA: University of California Press)

[36] Henrichs E, Lesch V, Straesser M, Kounev S and Krupitzer C 2022 A literature review on optimization techniques for adaptation planning in adaptive systems: state of the art and research directions *Inf. Softw. Technol.* **149** 106940

[37] Venter G 2010 *Review of Optimization Techniques* (New York: Wiley) https://doi.org/10.1002/9780470686652.eae495

[38] Foulds L R 2012 *Optimization Techniques: An Introduction* (Berlin: Springer) https://doi.org/10.1007/978-1-4613-9458-7

[39] Ruder S 2016 An overview of gradient descent optimization algorithms arXiv preprint (arXiv:1609.04747)

[40] Sun S, Cao Z, Zhu H and Zhao J 2019 A survey of optimization methods from a machine learning perspective *IEEE Trans. Cybern.* **50** 3668–81

[41] Kingma D P and Ba J 2014 Adam: a method for stochastic optimization arXiv preprint (arXiv:1412.6980)

[42] Emmert-Streib F and Dehmer M 2019 Understanding statistical hypothesis testing: the logic of statistical inference *Mach. Learn. Knowl. Extr.* **1** 945–62

[43] Mehta P, Bukov M, Wang C-H, Day A G R, Richardson C, Fisher C K and Schwab D J 2019 A high-bias, low-variance introduction to machine learning for physicists *Phys. Rep.* **810** 1–124

[44] Bartlett P L, Boucheron S and Lugosi G 2002 Model selection and error estimation *Mach. Learn.* **48** 85–113

[45] Tian Y and Zhang Y 2022 A comprehensive survey on regularization strategies in machine learning *Inf. Fusion* **80** 146–66

[46] Yu T and Zhu H 2020 Hyper-parameter optimization: a review of algorithms and applications arXiv preprint (arXiv:2003.05689)

[47] Yang L and Shami A 2020 On hyperparameter optimization of machine learning algorithms: theory and practice *Neurocomputing* **415** 295–316

[48] Fawcett T 2006 An introduction to ROC analysis *Pattern Recognit. Lett.* **27** 861–74

IOP Publishing

Machine Learning for Physicists
A hands-on approach
Sadegh Raeisi and Sedighe Raeisi

Chapter 4

Neural networks

Over the past two decades, neural networks have become the gold standard of machine learning and have led to unprecedented growth of machine learning and its applications [1]. From self-driving cars [2] to natural language processing [3–6], deep learning with neural networks has enabled applications of machine learning in a wide range of fields. In this chapter, we will review the basics of neural network models and discuss why neural networks are so interesting and powerful. We also provide practical tools for using neural networks.

4.1 Introduction to neural networks

Neural networks are a class of supervised models similar to the ones we reviewed in chapter 3. Here we will review the inner mechanics of a neural network model.

We start this chapter with an introduction to neural networks and their properties. We then describe how neural networks are trained. We will review some of the most common libraries that are used for training neural networks. After that, we will review some of the most well-known architectures of neural networks, including convolutional neural networks and recurrent neural networks.

We skip the historical discussion. If you are interested to know more about the historical development of neural networks see [7–10].

4.1.1 What is a neural network?

We start this section with the schematic picture of a neural network in figure 4.1 and explain how the model works. We will then introduce the notation that we will use for neural networks in this book.

The circles in figure 4.1 are referred to as 'nodes'. As can be seen, the nodes in the model cluster into layers. The yellow layers represent the input and output of the

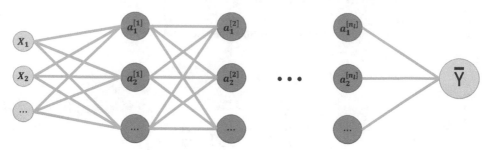

Figure 4.1. Schematic picture of a neural network.

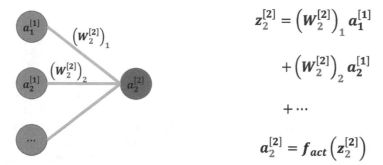

$$z_2^{[2]} = \left(W_2^{[2]}\right)_1 a_1^{[1]}$$

$$+ \left(W_2^{[2]}\right)_2 a_2^{[1]}$$

$$+ \cdots$$

$$a_2^{[2]} = f_{act}\left(z_2^{[2]}\right)$$

Figure 4.2. Schematic picture of the operation for a node in the neural network.

model. The layers in blue are referred to as the 'hidden layers' and represent middle processes that are carried out to get to the output.

Each node can be seen as a logistic regression model on its own. It takes the values of the nodes from the previous layer as inputs and generates an output which is the value of that node.

Figure 4.2 illustrates a node in the neural network. We use a for the values of the nodes. The superscripts ([.]) indicate the layer index and the subscript indicates the index of the node in the layer. For instance, in the example of figure 4.2, $a_2^{[1]}$ means that the node is the second node of the first layer.

Figure 4.2 also shows how the value of a typical node depends on the nodes from the preceding layer. The function can be broken down into two parts. The first part calculates a linear combination of the nodes in the preceding layer. We refer to this as $z_i^{[l]}$. The coefficients of the linear part of the functions are referred to as weights $w_{i,j}^{[l]}$. The weights are specified with two indices, i, j, the first one, i refers to the index of the output node, and the second one, j, refers to the index of the input node. The linear part can also have a constant term which is referred to as the bias, $b_i^{[l]}$. In figure 4.2 the lines that are connecting the nodes from the first layer to the red node represent the weights corresponding to the red node.

The second part of the function is a non-linear function that acts on the linear part, $z_i^{[l]}$. This function is referred to as the 'activation function'. This is similar to the logistic regression model in chapter 3. In fact, the sigmoid function is one of the popular choices for the activation function. The activation functions are an essential part of a neural network [11]. In the following subsection we briefly review the basics of activation functions.

Activation functions

If we only use the linear part of the function without the non-linear activation function, the whole network reduces to a linear function and the hidden layers lose their functionality.

Question: Show that without the activation functions the output node reduces to a linear combination of the input features and a constant bias. Try to find a closed form for the linear coefficients in terms of the weights and biases in the neural network.

Here we will review some of the more commonly used activation functions. Figure 4.3 shows these functions.

Sigmoid

The sigmoid function is given by

$$\text{Sig}(z) = \frac{1}{1 + e^{-z}}. \tag{4.1}$$

It returns a value between 0 and 1.

You may remember this function from your statistical physics course. This is similar to the Gibbs distribution function [12]. In fact, if you calculate the probability of the ground state for a two-level system, you can derive equation (4.1) from the Boltzmann distribution.

Question: What should be the energy gap in the system to give exactly the probability in equation (4.1) for the ground state? *Hint*: express the energy in terms of the Boltzmann constant k_B and the temperature T.

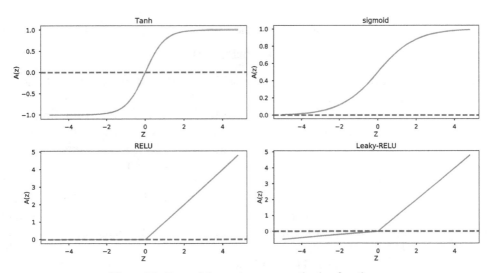

Figure 4.3. Four of the most common activation functions.

The sigmoid function is particularly suitable for representing probabilities. For instance, for a binary classification problem, the sigmoid function may be used for the output node. Then the output value could be trained to return the probability of a sample belonging to the class 1, i.e. $P(Y = 1)$. But this does not mean that the applications of the sigmoid are limited to the output node of binary classification problems and in many cases it is used for the hidden layers as well.

Softmax

You may be wondering if there is an extension of the sigmoid function for a multi-class classification problem.

Exercise: Use the idea of the Gibbs distribution to extend the sigmoid function for a multi-class problem.

As you probably guessed, it is going to be

$$\text{Softmax}(z_i) = \frac{e^{-z_i}}{\sum_j e^{-z_j}},$$

(4.2)

where z_i is the linear function in figure 4.2 which is calculated for each node. The probabilities in equation (4.2) are normalized and add up to one.

For an m-class classification problem, the last layer would consist of m nodes with a softmax activation function. After the activation, each node returns the probability corresponding to its associated class. We will cover some examples later in this chapter and this will become more clear.

The softmax is usually only used for the output layer of a multi-class classification and not the hidden layers.

Tanh

Tanh is another activation function that is similar to sigmoid but ranges between −1 and 1. Tanh is particularly used for recurrent neural networks.

ReLU

Another popular choice for activation functions is ReLU [11]. ReLU is defined as

$$\text{ReLU}(z) = \max(0, z).$$

(4.3)

The function is plotted in figure 4.3. For positive inputs it returns the input and for negative values it returns zero.

One of the advantages of ReLU compared to sigmoid and tanh is that in certain cases it can help speed up the training of the neural network. This is related to the fact that for functions such as sigmoid and tanh, the derivatives vanish for large values of their input. However, for ReLU the derivate remains constant for large values of the input. We will later see that the derivative of the loss function with respect to the trainable parameters depends on the derivative of the activation function. If the derivative of the activation function vanishes it could slow down or even stop the optimization of the trainable parameters of the neural network.

Leaky ReLU: For the ReLU activation function, if the input is negative, the derivative would be negative. This could lead to the same issue that we described above. Although in practice it usually works fine, there is a variation of ReLU that has a non-zero gradient for both positive and negative values. This is known as the 'leaky ReLU' [11] and is defined as

$$\text{Relu}(z) = \max(0, z) + a \min(0, z), \tag{4.4}$$

where a is some constant between 0 and 1. Note that as a approaches 1, the function becomes more and more linear.

We will later play with the choice of activation functions and explore how activation functions can affect the performance and speed of training.

4.1.2 Notation

Before we get to the details of neural networks, we need to establish our notation.

We are going to use some linear algebra to simplify and compress our notation.

We start with the weights. As we discussed, $w_{i,j}^{[l]}$ represents the weights of the node i in the $l-1$ layer for the calculation of the node j in the following layer. All of these weights can be compressed in a matrix $W^{[l]}$. Similarly, we use a vector $B^{[l]}$ for the biases of the nodes in layer $[l]$. Also, we use vectors $a^{[l]}$ for the values of the nodes. From each layer to the next, to calculate the values of the nodes we first need to calculate the linear part, for which we use another vector $z^{[l]}$ and is given by

$$z^{[l]} = W^{[l]} \cdot z^{[l-1]} + B^{[l]}. \tag{4.5}$$

Here $\cdot$ represents a matrix multiplication. Next, the values of the new nodes can be calculated by applying the activation function on the $z^{[l]}$. This is done element-wise, i.e. on each element.

Question: Calculate the dimensions of the matrices corresponding to $W^{[l]}$, $B^{[l]}$, $z^{[l]}$, $a^{[l]}$ in terms of the number of the nodes in each layer (i.e. n_l).

Vectorization

The notation $a^{[l]}$ shows the values of the nodes for each sample. However, if you recall, our data consist of n_s samples. We compress this into $A^{[l]}$ where A is a two-dimensional tensor (matrix) where the rows correspond to different samples and the columns correspond to different nodes in the layer. This is similar to the notation that we use for the input feature matrix with the nodes representing different features.

Similarly, we use $Z^{[l]}$ for the linear part of each node, i.e. the rows correspond to the linear part of the values of the nodes, before the activation function, for different samples and each column corresponds to a different sample.

This notation also helps with performance. This is because matrix multiplication can be done more efficiently than looping over the samples individually [13].

Question: Generate two random matrices with dimensions of $d = 1000$. Implement the matrix multiplication, once using the np.dot function in Python and once by manually looping over the elements. Compare the speed. (*Remark*: to compare the speed between the two, you need to repeat them multiple times and report the average.)

Figure 4.4 summarizes our notation for neural networks.

$n^{[l]}$: #nodes in layer l

$W^{[l]}$: Weights in layer l $\qquad\qquad W^{[l]}: \left(n^{[l]}, n^{[l-1]}\right)$

$B^{[l]}$: Bias in layer l $\qquad\qquad\qquad B^{[l]}: \left(n^{[l]}\right)$

$Z^{[l]}$: Linear outcome in layer l $\qquad Z^{[l]}: \left(n^{[l]}, n_s\right)$

$f_{act}^{[l]}$: Activation func. in layer l

$A^{[l]}$: Full outcome in layer l $\qquad\quad A^{[l]}: \left(n^{[l]}, n_s\right)$

$$Z^{[l]} = W^{[l]} . A^{[l-1]} + B^{[l]}$$
$$A^{[l]} = f_{act}^{[l]}(Z^{[l]})$$

Figure 4.4. Summary of the notation that we will be using in this chapter for neural networks. It also shows the dimensions of the tensors.

4.1.3 Intuition

In this section we will try to understand the intuition behind neural networks. This helps us better understand how neural networks operate and why they can be effective at solving complex problems.

Let us start by reviewing how we normally solve problems. We often use 'reductionism' for solving complex problems [14, 15]. Loosely speaking, this means that we break a complex problem into smaller and simpler problems and then solve those simpler problems. If those problems are still challenging, we break them even further into simpler problems. We continue this up to the point that it becomes easy to solve the resultant problems. Then, layer by layer, we can find the answer to the more challenging problems all the way to the original problem.

Exercise: Take some random problem in one of your courses and map out your chain of thought. Try to identify the layers and smaller problems that you break a problem into at each layer.

The process of a neural network can be interpreted in the same way. If you think about it, each node in the network can be seen as a logistic regression unit (if sigmoid is used for the activation). However, we know from chapter 3 that logistic regression models are linear. This means that each node provides a simple function of its inputs and is not going to be complex enough to capture the solution to a complex problem.

However, we can break a complex problem into simpler problems and continue doing this up to the point that the problems are not too complex anymore. In that sense, the output node of the neural network represents the answer to the main (complex) problem. The further you go back into the network, the easier it gets. In other words, the complexity can increase as you add more and more layers. Neural networks provide the possibility to incorporate more complexity into your model by adding more layers and more nodes. In fact, in the next section, we will review the 'universality' which indicates that this framework is capable of modeling almost any function.

4.1.4 Universality of neural networks

In chapter 3 we reviewed different types of supervised models. It is natural to wonder which one is better. But what makes a good model? What do we expect from a good model? As you may recall, we want our models to have low bias and low variance.

Sometimes a model works well for one problem and not for another one. An ideal model should be able to achieve low bias and low variance for all problems or at least as wide and large of a set of problems as possible. In other words, we are interested in a model that is flexible enough to capture any kind of complexity in any given data.

Most models cannot do this. Usually, with traditional machine learning techniques, on some level you need to rely on some domain knowledge and any given hypothesis is good for some problems/datasets and not for others.

In contrast, for neural networks it is possible to show that they can universally model a large class of problems [16–21]. This is one of the main reasons why neural networks are so interesting for supervised learning tasks. They have the capability to capture the complexity of a wide range of problems. This means that without any domain knowledge, neural networks provide a framework to model the relation between the input and output in almost any dataset.

Mathematically, universality means that a neural network can approximate the function that connects the feature matrix X and the labels Y in the dataset, with arbitrary precision. In other words, you can get as close as you want to the unknown function that connects the input and outputs in the dataset.

To be more rigorous, there are some conditions for the function to be approximated by the neural network. But it usually covers most situations that we encounter. To see some examples of the universality theorems for neural networks see [16–21]. We do not cover them here because the language used for these theorems is relatively technical and we would need to cover concepts such as Bochner–Lebesgue p-integrable functions. Instead, we try to provide an insight into how these universality theorems work.

To this end, let us look at a 1D example. Consider the function in figure 4.5(A). Imagine that you want to build a neural network that would approximate this function. Based on how precise we need the approximation to be, we can discretize

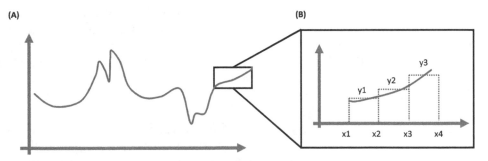

Figure 4.5. Approximation of a schematic 1D function. Panel (A) shows the full function and panel (B) shows a small window of the function that will be used to show how a neural network will approximate the function.

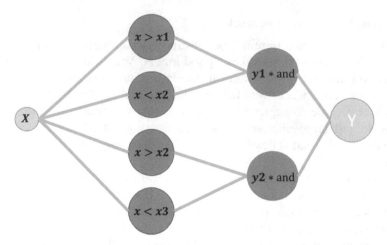

Figure 4.6. A neural network that gives two of the segments of the discretized function in figure 4.5(B).

the function (figure 4.5(B)). Let us first build a neural network for one element of the discretized function and then will extend that to cover the whole function.

Exercise: Design a neural network that can approximate the part of the function in figure 4.5(B) (the part of the function that falls in the black window).

Take the segments of the discretized function in figure 4.5(B). The neural network in figure 4.6 provides an approximation to the function. Each segment can be described as a piecewise function that is zero outside its range of approximation and non-zero and equal to the function for its specific range. For instance, for the first segment the approximation is a function that is zero outside $[x1, x2]$ and is equal to $y1$ in that range. The full approximation is the sum of all of the segments. So we first need to make a network that implements the segments.

To make a neural network for approximating one segment, we first need to identify the range over which the function is non-zero. For this, we need two conditions, one specifies the upper end of the range and one for the lower end. Then the AND of the two conditions would specify the points, i.e. it is one for the points in the range and zero for the points outside the range. As the last step the AND is multiplied by the value of the function over that range.

Figure 4.6 shows the network for two segments of the discretized function in figure 4.5(B). In the first layer the two upper nodes specify the range for the first segment, i.e. $[X1, x2]$. The AND of the output of these two nodes is one for input values $x \in [x1, x2]$. Thus in the second layer the upper node represents the function corresponding to the first segment in figure 4.5(B).

Similarly, for the second segment, i.e. $[X2, x3]$, we need two nodes in the first layer and then the AND in the second layer.

With this approach, for every element of the discretized function we need two nodes in the first hidden layer. Then in the second hidden layer the pair of the two nodes are fed to an AND function and multiplied by the value of the function over the corresponding range. In the end, the results of the nodes in the second hidden layer are summed to make the output layer. This gives an approximation of the function.

Question: How can we improve the precision of approximation (i.e. how can we reduce the difference between the actual function and approximation by the neural network function)?

This approach is not focused on efficiency. In other words, this may not be the most efficient way for approximating the function. However, it provides an easy illustration of how a neural network can approximate a function.

Question: Can you think of a better (more efficient) neural network for approximating the function in the example above?

Also note that the illustration above is for a 1D function, i.e. an input with only one feature. The same idea can be extended for functions with more input features.

Exercise: How does it scale with the dimension?

For multi-dimensional inputs we can discretize the function for every dimension (i.e. input feature). For instance, for a 2D function each element of the discretized function is specified by two ranges, one for each dimension. As you can guess, four nodes are needed in the first layer to specify the range. The rest is similar to the 1D case.

Question: How does the complexity (number of nodes) scale with the dimension?

Question: Can increasing the depth reduce the complexity (*Hint*: With a different approach)? If so, how does increasing the depth of the neural network reduce the complexity?

If you look at the example above, you can see that to improve the approximation we need to make the discretization finer which leads to more nodes (width) and/or more depth for the neural network. It indicates that a neural network needs enough depth and width to be able to approximate a target function with arbitrary precision. But is that enough?

It is also important to pay attention to the role of the activation function in the universality of neural networks. In the example above the nodes in the first hidden layer are using a step function for activation. This is a highly non-linear function. What if we limit our activation functions to linear functions? Or polynomial functions?

It is shown that with only polynomial activation functions, neural networks lose the universality power [19]. This indicates that the non-linearity of the activation function plays an important role in the power of neural networks for modeling complex datasets.

Exercise: Is universality enough for building a good model? How is universality connected to bias and variance?

The universality only means that we can lower the bias as much as we want (i.e. a great fit). However, it does not guarantee a low variance and, in fact, from the examples above you can see that increasing the precision of the approximation leads to increasing the complexity of the network. With increasing complexity, the model is more likely to overfit (i.e. high variance). In other words, the universality on its own does not guarantee that neural networks are going to make a good model.

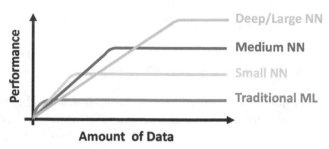

Figure 4.7. A schematic picture of how the performance of neural networks and traditional ML models is affected by the size of the dataset. For small datasets, usually, traditional ML models can outperform neural networks. However, as the problem becomes more complex and as we get access to more data, neural networks start to outperform traditional ML models or shallow neural networks. Note that here small, medium, and large NN refer to the width and depth of the neural networks. The larger it gets, the more data it needs to outperform smaller/simpler models. However, given enough data, the larger neural network often performs better.

Exercise: Considering that the universality of neural networks makes them susceptible to overfitting, how can we lower the variance?

As you may remember from the last chapter, to reduce the variance we need more data. This is why training neural networks often requires large datasets.

This is one of the reasons why neural networks have only recently become popular, although the concept and even the universality properties can be traced back to the twentieth century [22–24].

This also indicates that neural networks are not always helpful. For simple problems with small datasets, neural networks are likely to not perform well. However, as problems become more complex and if we have enough data, neural networks start to outperform traditional ML approaches.

Figure 4.7 illustrates schematically how we usually expect neural networks to perform and how their performance changes with more depth and width. As you can see, for small data, traditional ML techniques are expected to perform better. This indicates that blindly using neural networks is not always a good idea.

However, with more data the variance of neural networks decreases and since they could achieve lower bias compared to traditional ML techniques, they would outperform traditional ML techniques.

This also explains one of the main reasons why neural networks have become popular only recently [25]. Over the past two decades, the amount of data that we have collected has increased significantly. There is one more reason for the recent surge in interest in neural networks, which is tied to the complexity of the neural network. Deployment and training of neural networks are often computationally expensive, compared to traditional ML techniques. Two decades ago, the computation power required for training neural networks was lacking. However, recently advances in high-performance GPUs have made it possible to build large neural network models in a relatively short amount of time. Training these models with the large data required would not have been possible with computers two decades ago.

4.2 Training neural networks

Thus far we have become familiar with a neural network model as a function that takes the input and passes them layer by layer to generate the outcomes. We also learned that such functions are universal and have the capability to approximate a large class of functions. But how do we train a neural network?

Exercise: Based on what we learned in chapter 3, try to find a way to train a neural network.

In this section, we briefly explain how a neural network is trained. The principles are exactly the same as those explained in chapter 3.

Figure 4.8 shows the training process schematically. We use a loss function to quantify the difference between the predictions of the model and the ground truth labels of the samples. Loss functions have been discussed extensively in chapter 3. Training the model is equivalent to finding the set of parameters $W_{i,j}^{[l]}$ and $B_i^{[l]}$ that minimizes the loss function, i.e. the difference between the ground truth and predicted labels. In chapter 3 we also introduced several optimization techniques such as Adam that can be used to optimize the free parameters of the neural network and train the model.

Exercise: Imagine a neural network with one hidden layer, with two input features, five hidden nodes, and one output node. Assume that we want to use MSE for the loss and simple GD for the optimization.

- Find the update rule for the weights that connect the input features to the hidden layer.
- How would this generalize to more complex neural networks with more layers?

The challenge is that a neural network often has too many parameters. What makes it worse is that they cannot be optimized independently. The optimization process as we explained before could be extremely inefficient and slow. However, the training process can be simplified using the structure of the neural network. At a

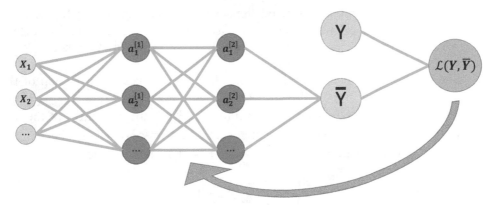

Figure 4.8. Schematic illustration of the training process. It starts with the loss functions which quantify the difference between the ground truth Y and the results from the model $\bar{Y}$. The free parameters of the neural network need to be tuned to minimize the loss function.

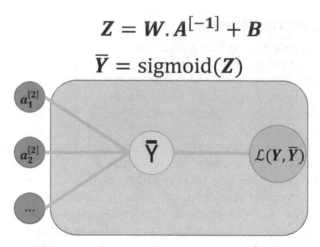

Figure 4.9. Schematic picture of the last layer of a neural network model. For simplicity, we assumed that the activation for the output layer is sigmoid. The equations show how the output is calculated from the values of the last hidden layer and the weights of the last layer.

high level, we use the chain rule for calculating the derivatives of the loss function with respect to parameters in the inner layers of the neural network.

To better understand this, let us start with the last layer of the neural network. Figure 4.9 shows this schematically. For the derivative of the loss function with respect to the weights in the last layer, we can use the chain rule. We express the derivative in terms of the product of three derivatives, the derivative of the loss function with respect to the outputs $\frac{d\mathcal{L}}{d\bar{Y}}$, then the derivative of the output the linear part of the output $\frac{d\bar{Y}}{dZ}$, and finally, the derivative of the linear part to the free parameters $\frac{dZ}{dW}$. Mathematically, that is

$$\frac{d\mathcal{L}}{dW} = \frac{d\mathcal{L}}{d\bar{Y}} \times \frac{d\bar{Y}}{dZ} \times \frac{dZ}{dW}. \tag{4.6}$$

Here, for simplicity, we have dropped the superscript corresponding to the layer index. Also, let us assume that all the hidden layers have only one node. This means that in each layer there is only one weight, $W^{[l]}$, and one $B^{[l]}$ that needs to be optimized. This can be generalized easily.

It could still be inefficient to calculate all these derivatives for each step of the training. So we go one step further and simplify these derivatives.

The first, $\frac{d\mathcal{L}}{d\bar{Y}}$, only depends on the loss function. So, if the derivative of the loss functions is specified for the training algorithm, the process will be faster. For instance, if the loss function is MSE, i.e. $\frac{1}{n_s}\sum_i(\bar{Y}_i - Y_i)^2$, then the derivative is

$$\frac{d\mathcal{L}}{d\bar{Y}} = \frac{2}{n_s}\sum_i(\bar{Y}_i - Y_i).$$

Next, we need $\frac{d\bar{Y}}{dZ}$. This only depends on the activation function. Thus similarly to the loss function, the derivative of the activation functions should be specified for the training algorithm. For instance, for the sigmoid function $\sigma(z)$ we obtain

$$\frac{d}{dZ}\sigma(z) = \sigma(z)(1 - \sigma(z)).$$

Question: Derive the equation above.

This means that if sigmoid is used for the activation, the second term of the derivative in equation (4.6) is $\bar{Y}(1 - \bar{Y})$.

The last term, i.e. $\frac{dZ}{dW}$, is more straightforward. Remember that

$$Z = W. \, A^{[-1]} + B,$$

where $A^{[-1]}$ refers to the nodes of the last hidden layer. So the derivative with respect to W is $A^{[-1]}$. But remember that $A^{[-1]}$ is a 2D matrix where each row corresponds to a different sample. For the derivative, we need to average over the values for all the different samples. That is

$$\frac{d\mathcal{L}}{dW} = \frac{1}{n_s}\sum_i \left(\frac{d\mathcal{L}}{d\bar{Y}} \times \frac{d\bar{Y}}{dZ} \times A \right)_i, \tag{4.7}$$

where the index i refers to the index of the samples.

Question: Follow the same steps and find the derivatives for the biases, $\frac{\mathcal{L}}{B}$.

Question: Calculate $\frac{d\mathcal{L}}{dW}$ for when MSE is used for the loss function and sigmoid for the activation.

Try this for other loss functions and activation functions.

For the case where there is more than one node in the hidden and output layer, it is possible to express the derivative as

$$\frac{d\mathcal{L}}{dW_{1,k}} = \frac{1}{n_s}\sum_i \left(\frac{d\mathcal{L}}{d\bar{Z}_1} \cdot A_k^{T} \right)_i, \tag{4.8}$$

where A_k^{T} represent the kth element of the transposition of A.

Question: Verify the relation in equation (4.8).

This enables optimizing the weights and biases in the last layer. But what about the layer before that? Or all the other layers inside the network.

To find the derivative for other hidden layers we use

$$Z^{[l]} = W^{[l]}. \, A^{[l-1]} + B^{[l]},$$

and build a recursive algorithm. This means that

$$\frac{d\mathcal{L}}{dW^{[l]}} = \frac{1}{n_s}\sum_i \left(\frac{d\mathcal{L}}{dZ^{[l]}} \times \frac{dZ^{[l]}}{dW^{[l]}} \right)_i. \tag{4.9}$$

In the equation, the last can be simplified as

$$\frac{\mathrm{d}Z^{[l]}}{\mathrm{d}W^{[l]}} = A^{[l-1]}.$$

This indicates that for calculating the derivative of the loss with respect to the weights in that layer, we only need to calculate the $\frac{\mathrm{d}\mathcal{L}}{\mathrm{d}Z^{[l]}}$.

This leads to a recursive algorithm. Assume that we have $\frac{\mathrm{d}\mathcal{L}}{\mathrm{d}Z^{[l+1]}}$, i.e. the derivative for the following layer. We can use that to calculate the $\frac{\mathrm{d}\mathcal{L}}{\mathrm{d}Z^{[l]}}$. Specifically, we have

$$\frac{\mathrm{d}\mathcal{L}}{\mathrm{d}Z^{[l]}} = \frac{\mathrm{d}\mathcal{L}}{\mathrm{d}Z^{[l+1]}} \times \frac{\mathrm{d}Z^{[l+1]}}{\mathrm{d}A^{[l]}} \times \frac{\mathrm{d}A^{[l]}}{\mathrm{d}Z^{[l]}}. \qquad (4.10)$$

The last term, $\frac{\mathrm{d}A^{[l]}}{\mathrm{d}Z^{[l]}}$, is determined by the activation function. And the second last term is

$$\frac{\mathrm{d}Z^{[l+1]}}{\mathrm{d}A^{[l]}} = W^{[l+1]}.$$

This indicates that we can use a recursive algorithm to calculate the derivative for each layer. We start with the derivative of the last layer which gives $\frac{\mathrm{d}\mathcal{L}}{\mathrm{d}Z^{[n]}}$, $\frac{\mathrm{d}\mathcal{L}}{\mathrm{d}W^{[n]}}$, $\frac{\mathrm{d}\mathcal{L}}{\mathrm{d}B^{[n]}}$. We then use the $\frac{\mathrm{d}\mathcal{L}}{\mathrm{d}Z^{[n]}}$ to calculate $\frac{\mathrm{d}\mathcal{L}}{\mathrm{d}Z^{[n-1]}}$ and $\frac{\mathrm{d}\mathcal{L}}{\mathrm{d}W^{[n]}}$, $\frac{\mathrm{d}\mathcal{L}}{\mathrm{d}B^{[n]}}$ from there. This is called the 'back-propagation' algorithm [26]. In a sense, we are back-propagating the derivatives.

We did not cover all the details of the back-propagation technique. This section is only meant to provide some intuition and some high-level understanding of how a neural network is trained. For more details on the back-propagation technique see [26].

To get a sense of how this process works in action, see the interactive demonstration at https://playground.tensorflow.org/.

This helps provide some intuition about the training process of a neural network. The width and the color of the edges between the nodes represent the value of corresponding weights. The larger the weight, the thicker the edge. Also, the color indicates the positivity or negativity of the weight. Play around with the parameters and the activation functions to see how each of them can affect the speed and performance of the training.

4.3 Libraries for working with neural networks

There are several libraries that implement neural networks and the training algorithm. Two of the most popular libraries are PyTorch [27, 28] and TensorFlow [29, 30], both of which are Python libraries.

The implementation of the neural networks in these libraries is slightly different from what was described here. For example, some of them build a computation

```
1 from tensorflow import keras as ks
              ## Import the library
2
3 model = ks.Sequential()
              ## Make   sequential object
4 model.add(ks.layers.Dense(10, activation=ks.activations.relu, input_dim =
      2)  ) ## Add a dense layer with 10 neuron
5 model.add(ks.layers.Dense(10, activation=ks.activations.relu)  )
              ## Add a dense layer with 10 neuron
6 model.add(ks.layers.Dense(1, activation=ks.activations.sigmoid)  )
              ## Add a dense layer with 1 neuron
7 model.summary()
              ## Display a summary of neural network
8 model.compile( loss=ks.losses.binary_crossentropy  ,
              ## Define the loss of neural network
9             optimizer = ks.optimizers.SGD() ,
              ## Define the optimizer of neural network
10            metrics = ks.metrics.binary_accuracy )
              ## Define the metic to evaluate the predictions
11 history = model.fit(X_train, Y_train,
              ## Train the network for 50 epochs
12                    epochs=50
13                    )
```

Listing 4.1. A simple neural network with Keras.

graph from the neural network and then use that to generate the inverse graph for back-propagation. Or in the case of PyTorch, every variable has an attribute that can be used to keep track of the gradient for gradient-based optimization tools. More specifically, if a variable a is used in calculating a variable b, the variable a has an attribute that keeps track of $\frac{db}{da}$. This is referred to as the 'auto-grad' in PyTorch. For more details see [27]. These ideas provide more powerful and efficient algorithms for training neural networks.

We will use both PyTorch and TensorFlow in this book. The code in listing 4.1 is for building a simple neural network and training it.

Similarly, with PyTorch you can use the code in listing 4.2.

4.4 Summary

In this chapter we introduced neural networks. We reviewed the inner mechanics of these models and learned how to train them and how to implement them in Python using libraries such as PyTorch and TensorFlow. We also discussed the universality of neural networks and why neural networks are so powerful.

It is important to practice using neural networks for different applications. This will help you obtain some intuition and become more fluent in building deep learning models.

```
1
2
3 import torch
4 X_train=torch.from_numpy(np.array(x_train,dtype='float')).to(torch.
     float32)      ## Convert features and targets into torch tensor
5 X_test=torch.from_numpy(np.array(x_test,dtype='float')).to(torch.float32)
6
7 Y_train=torch.from_numpy(np.array(y_train,dtype='float')).to(torch.
     float32)
8 Y_test=torch.from_numpy(np.array(y_test,dtype='float')).to(torch.float32)
9
10 class NeuralNetwork(torch.nn.Module):
              ## Make the class of neural network
11   def __init__(self,n_features):
12     super(NeuralNetwork,self).__init__()
13     self.fc1=torch.nn.Linear(n_features,10)
14     self.fc2=torch.nn.Linear(10,10)
15     self.fc3=torch.nn.Linear(10,1)
16
17   def forward(self,x):
18     x=torch.relu(self.fc1(x))
19     x=torch.relu(self.fc2(x))
20     x=torch.sigmoid(self.fc3(x))
21     return x
22
23 criterion=torch.nn.MSELoss()
              ## Define the loss
24 model=NeuralNetwork(n_features=X_train.shape[1])
              ## Make an object of the model
25 optimizer=torch.optim.Adam(model.parameters(),lr=0.001)
              ## Define the optimizer
26
27 for epochs in range(50):
              ## Train the model
28   y_pred=model(X_train)
              ## Get the predictions
29   y_pred=torch.squeeze(y_pred)
30   train_loss=criterion(y_pred, Y_train)
              ## Compute the loss
31   print('------------')
32   print(f"epochs={epochs},train_loss={train_loss}")
33   optimizer.zero_grad()
              ## Clear the gradian history.
34   train_loss.backward()
              ## Make the back propagation
35   optimizer.step()
              ## Update weights.
```

Listing 4.2. A simple neural network with PyTorch.

References

[1] Balas V E, Roy S S, Sharma D and Samui P 2019 *Handbook of Deep Learning Applications* (Berlin: Springer) **136**

[2] Ni J, Chen Y, Chen Y, Zhu J, Ali D and Cao W 2020 A survey on theories and applications for self-driving cars based on deep learning methods *Appl. Sci.* **10** 2749

[3] Xie Y, Le L, Zhou Y and Raghavan V V 2018 Deep learning for natural language processing *Handbook of Statistics* vol 38 (Amsterdam: Elsevier) pp 317–28

[4] Torfi A, Shirvani R A, Keneshloo Y, Tavaf N and Fox E A 2020 Natural language processing advancements by deep learning: a survey arXiv preprint (arXiv:2003.01200)

[5] Lauriola I, Lavelli A and Aiolli F 2022 An introduction to deep learning in natural language processing: models, techniques, and tools *Neurocomputing* **470** 443–56

[6] Zhao W X *et al* 2023 A survey of large language models arXiv preprint (arXiv:2303.18223)

[7] Wang H and Raj B 2017 On the origin of deep learning arXiv preprint (arXiv:1702.07800)

[8] Wikipedia contributors 2023 History of artificial neural networks *Wikipedia* https://en.wikipedia.org/wiki/History_of_artificial_neural_networks (Accessed 9 April 2023)

[9] Vidhya A 2019 Brief history of neural networks *Medium* https://medium.com/analytics-vidhya/brief-history-of-neural-networks-44c2bf72eec (Accessed 9 April 2023)

[10] Alexander D 2020 *Neural Networks: History and Applications* (New York: NOVA Science)

[11] Nwankpa C, Ijomah W, Gachagan A and Marshall S 2018 Activation functions: comparison of trends in practice and research for deep learning arXiv preprint (arXiv:1811.03378)

[12] Kardar M 2007 *Statistical Physics of Particles* (Cambridge: Cambridge University Press) https://doi.org/10.1017/CBO9780511815898

[13] Vidhya A 2020 Mathematics and vectorization behind neural network *Medium* https://medium.com/analytics-vidhya/mathematics-and-vectorization-behind-neural-network-b6d491fa617d (Accessed 9 April 2023)

[14] Sachse C 2017 *Reductionism in the Philosophy of Science* (Berlin: Springer) https://doi.org/10.1515/9783110323320

[15] Wikipedia 2023 Reductionism *Wikipedia* https://en.wikipedia.org/wiki/Reductionism (Accessed 9 April 2023)

[16] Cybenko G 1989 Approximation by superpositions of a sigmoidal function *Math. Control Signals Syst.* **2** 303–14

[17] Hornik K, Stinchcombe M and White H 1989 Multilayer feedforward networks are universal approximators *Neural Netw.* **2** 359–66

[18] Hornik K 1991 Approximation capabilities of multilayer feedforward networks *Neural Netw.* **4** 251–7

[19] Leshno M, Lin V Y, Pinkus A and Schocken S 1993 Multilayer feedforward networks with a nonpolynomial activation function can approximate any function *Neural Netw.* **6** 861–7

[20] Pinkus A 1999 Approximation theory of the MLP model in neural networks *Acta Numer.* **8** 143–95

[21] Zhou D-X 2020 Universality of deep convolutional neural networks *Appl. Comput. Harmon. Anal.* **48** 787–94

[22] McCulloch W S and Pitts W 1943 A logical calculus of the ideas immanent in nervous activity *Bull. Math. Biophys.* **5** 115–33

[23] Rosenblatt F 1958 The perceptron: a probabilistic model for information storage and organization in the brain *Psychol. Rev.* **65** 386

[24] Minsky M and Papert S 1969 *Perceptrons; An Introduction to Computational Geometry* (Cambridge, MA: MIT Press)

[25] Lee T B 2019 How neural networks work–and why they've become a big business *Ars Technica* https://arstechnica.com/science/2019/12/how-neural-networks-work-and-why-theyve-become-a-big-business/ (Accessed 2023)

[26] Hecht-Nielsen R 1992 Theory of the backpropagation neural network *Neural Networks for Perception* (Amsterdam: Elsevier) pp 65–93

[27] PyTorch 2023 https://pytorch.org/ (Accessed 2023)

[28] Imambi S, Prakash K B and Kanagachidambaresan G R 2021 PyTorch *Programming with TensorFlow: Solution for Edge Computing Applications* (London: Springer Nature) pp 87–104

[29] TensorFlow 2023 https://www.tensorflow.org/ (Accessed 2023)

[30] Shukla N and Fricklas K 2018 *Machine Learning with TensorFlow* (Greenwich, CT: Manning)

Chapter 5

Special neural networks

In this chapter we will review special types of problems and applications in machine learning. These applications include structured data such as images, time series, and graphs. Due to their importance, special machine-learning techniques have been developed for these applications. Through these applications you will learn more about some of the most powerful and practical use cases of machine learning. The main focus of this chapter will be on deep learning and neural networks (NNs). In particular, we will introduce new network architectures such as convolutional neural networks (CNNs), recurrent neural networks (RNNs), and graph neural networks (GNNs).

Thus far, we have discussed the basics of machine learning and neural networks. However, there are different variations of supervised problems and as a result different types of NNs with different properties. In this section, we will review some of the more practical applications and their corresponding applications.

5.1 Convolutional neural network (CNN)

Let us first look into one of the main challenges with ordinary neural networks (NNs).

Exercise: Imagine an NN with n_1 hidden layers. For simplicity, assume that this is a binary classification problem. Also assume that all the hidden layers have the same number of nodes, N. How does the number of parameters in the NN scale with the number of hidden layers, n_1?

You can see that for each layer the number of parameters is $N(N + 1)$. Considering that there are N hidden layers, we obtain $O(N^3)$. This indicates that the number of parameters grows fast with the number of layers and nodes.

For instance, for an input image of 100×100 pixels, the input has 10^4 features and this still does not count as a large input for a lot of applications. For such an input, with even a modest hidden layer of 100 nodes, we obtain 10^6 parameters for only the first layer. Ordinary NNs can easily become too large in size. This makes them difficult to train and susceptible to over-fitting.

To better understand this, let us go through an example. For most of this section, we use the Galaxy Zoo dataset, i.e. DST-GSE (see table 1.2). The samples in this dataset are images.

Exercise: What are the features of each sample and what does the feature matrix look like?

The pixels of the images can be treated as features. Here the features do not automatically make a feature vector and have a 2D shape. One way to work with such features is to flatten the matrix into a vector.

Question: Try this with Keras or PyTorch. Assume a network with one hidden layer with 100 nodes.

- How many parameters does the model have?
- What is the performance (accuracy) of the model?
- How long does each epoch take? Specify your batch size and learning rate.

You can see that for such a simple task we need to train a relatively large network with too many parameters. This gets worse as we add more layers to improve the performance.

Exercise: Is there a better way to add layers to an NN? Do we need all the edges in a fully connected NN?

The input features, in their original image form, have some patterns that can be used to simplify the structure of the network.

Convolutional NNs provide a smart way to exploit the pattern or structure in the input data to reduce the number of parameters in the network and make robust models [1–3].

Next, we will discuss the two main ideas that are used to reduce the number of parameters in CNNs. For this section, we assume that the input samples are 2D data. Note that CNNs may be not effective if the input data are unstructured. It will become clear when it is expected to work well.

Locality

Take the first layer of the NN. With a normal NN every node is linked to and is affected by every pixel of the input image. This helps take into account all the connections and correlations between input pixels.

For unstructured input data, all the features may have some correlation or relation and all the connections should be taken into account.

However, for an image we expect the features to be local. This means that we expect the dependence between the pixels to decay and drop as the distance between them increases. Figure 5.1 illustrates this schematically for a 1D example.

This suggests that it may be redundant to have every hidden node connected to every pixel. Instead, for every pixel we can keep a neighborhood around it and ignore the rest of the pixel.

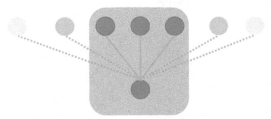

Figure 5.1. Schematic picture of a hidden node that is not fully connected to the inputs. The first row is the input layer and the second row is the hidden layer. The circles illustrate the nodes. Here the node in the hidden layer is connected to all the nodes in the input. However, if the input features are locally related, the dashed links would be small or even zero.

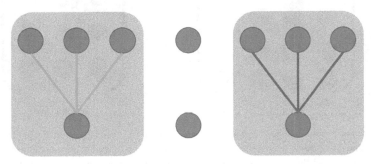

Figure 5.2. Schematic picture of a hidden layer that is not fully connected to the inputs. The first row is the input layer and the second row is the hidden layer. The circles illustrate the nodes. Here, we are assuming locality and as a result, each node in the hidden layer is only connected with a local neighborhood in the input layer. The gray boxes identify the neighborhoods. The weights for the first box are indicated in green and may be different from the right node (indicated in red).

To preserve the structure of the input it is easier to use hidden layers with the same structure as the inputs, in this case, a 2D array. Every pixel and its neighbors are connected to the corresponding node in the hidden layer, but all the other weights are set to zero and ignored. This implies that each node in the hidden layer will only be affected by a local region in the input image. Figure 5.2 shows a 1D depiction of this.

Exercise: In figure 5.2, identify the nodes in the input layer that are connected to the central node of the hidden layer.

Exercise: How does the scaling of the parameters change if we use locality (i.e. instead of a fully connected network)?

It is important to note that if the input features are not structured, this will not work. For example, without locality, pixels anywhere in the figure could be correlated. In this case, for the hidden model to capture the pattern of the input, they need to be connected to all nodes.

Symmetry and parameter sharing
If you look at the figure 5.2 you can see each hidden node has a different set of weights (indicated in different colors). However, if you think about it, for an image

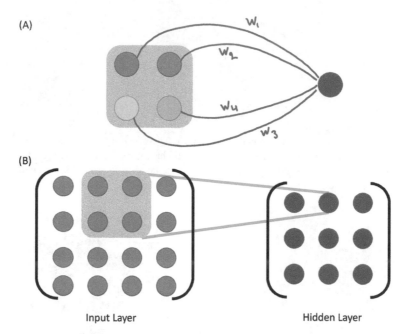

Figure 5.3. Schematic picture of convolution. Panel (A) shows how a single node of the hidden layer is built. Panel (B) shows how this moves over all the blocks of the input to build the different nodes of the hidden layer. The gray block starts from the first block and moves to evaluate the nodes in the hidden layer from the input.

we expect the process to be translationally invariant. In other words, it should not matter where an object is located in the image. It should be processed in the same way. For instance, if we are looking for a disk object in an image, we should be able to identify it no matter where in the image it is located.

If the weights for each hidden node are different, then depending on where an object is located in the image, it may go through a different process. If we incorporate the translational invariance, the weights for different hidden nodes should be the same.

In the context of deep learning, this is also known as 'parameter sharing', since different nodes share the same weights and biases.

Putting all of these together, we get to the schematic picture in figure 5.3. Each block in the matrix representing the 2D input is mapped to a node in the first hidden layer. As you can see, for a whole layer a constant number of parameters are used which simplifies the model and makes it less susceptible to over-fitting. This means that we can build deep models with few parameters. In a way, we are using the structure and symmetries of the input to reduce the number of parameters.

The operation in figure 5.3 is known as 'convolution' [4, 5]. In the next section, we will explain how convolution works and provide some examples to show why it can be so effective in processing complex input data.

5.1.1 Convolution

The convolution operation was known before machine learning and has extensive applications in a wide range of fields from mathematics to signal processing [4, 5]. Here we are going to review the convolution operation in the context of CNNs. This means that we will not cover the mathematical foundations of convolution and focus on how it is used to build hidden layers in a neural network. If you are interested to learn more about the foundations and history of convolution see [4, 5]. Also for a graphic demonstration of the convolution operation see https://mathworld.wolfram. com/Convolution.html.

The convolution operation takes an input and a filter. For the context of this section, we take both the input and the filter to be 2D tensors. The convolution operation maps the input to a new 2D tensor. Let us refer to the input, the filter, and the output of the layer as I, F, and O, respectively.

Figure 5.4 shows the convolution operation schematically. The * indicates the convolution operation.

Each element of the output is calculated as follows

$$O_{i,j} = \sum_{m,n=0} I_{m+i,n+j} \times F_{m,n},$$ (5.1)

with i, j starting from zero. For the example in figure 5.4, I is a 5 by 5 tensor and the filter is a 3 by 3 tensor. You can see that the first element of the output is the sum of the element-wise product of the filter and the first block in the input tensor. To obtain the rest of the elements, we move the filter over the input and cover all the possible blocks.

Question: Implement this operation in Python. You will be able to test it shortly.

But how does this operation help with building effectively hidden layers? Historically, convolution has been used for extracting features from inputs, in particularly in the field of image processing [6, 7].

Let us look at a simple example. The images in figure 5.5 show three kinds of borders—horizontal, vertical, and diagonal. Detecting the borders of an object

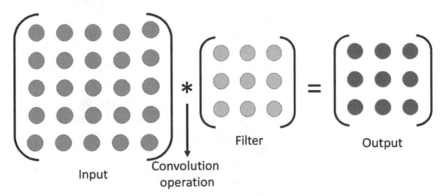

Figure 5.4. Schematic illustration of the convolution operation.

Figure 5.5. Three types of border. Borders are one of the fundamental features of an image. Their detection helps with tasks such as object detection.

could provide important information for a variety of computer vision tasks (e.g. object detection) [8, 9].

Exercise: Design a convolution operation that would detect the borders in the images in figure 5.5.

There are different convolution operations that can identify the borders in these images. Here we review some of the simplest ones.

Consider the following filter:

$$F_v = \begin{pmatrix} 1 & 0 & -1 \\ 1 & 0 & -1 \\ 1 & 0 & -1 \end{pmatrix}. \tag{5.2}$$

Exercise: Apply this convolution using your code from the previous question. (For the input, make a 2D array of zeros and set the appropriate elements to one. Refer to the code on GitHub.)

The result should look like the first column of figure 5.6. As you can see, this convolution operation is identifying the vertical borders in the images. Note that the second image does not have any vertical image and as a result, the convoluted output does not show any border.

Exercise: Design the appropriate filters for horizontal and diagonal borders. Verify that they generate the second and the third column of figure 5.6.

There are more sophisticated convolution operations for edge detection (e.g. Laplacian, Sobelx, Sobely). For more information see [8, 9].

This should help clarify why convolution operation can help with our machine learning tasks. The convolution layers extract different features from their inputs. The goal is to use different convolution filters to extract features that can help with the machine learning task.

Note that we usually apply multiple convolution operations in each layer to extract different features. For example, we probably need to extract both horizontal and vertical borders. In this case, we will apply two convolution operations in parallel and the output will be two 2D tensors.

At this point you may be wondering about the filters and how we should identify the right filters. One of the smart ideas in convolutional NNs is that we do not specify the filters. Instead, we set them as trainable parameters and let the model

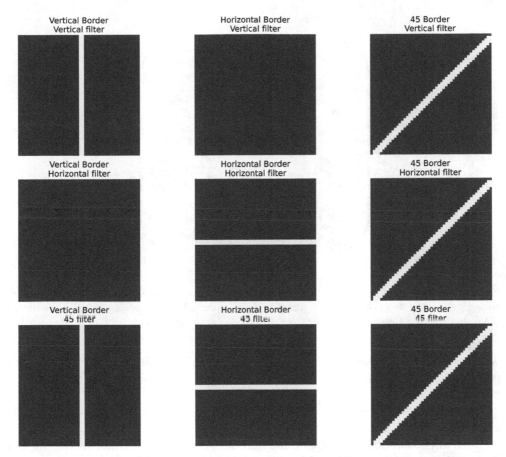

Figure 5.6. The result of applying convolution with three different types of filters to the three types of border in figure 5.5.

learn them. In a way, through the training process, the filters are optimized to extract features that are the most informative with respect to the task that the model is being trained for. These may be edge extraction or more complex operations.

Exercise: How many learnable parameters does a convolution layer have?

To answer this question, we need to characterize the convolution layer and define some new notations. Let us use n_w and n_h for the dimensions of the input of the convolution layer. Also, assume that we have n_c filters all of which are $f_s \times f_s$. The assumptions about the filters can be relaxed. For instance, there are examples where the filters do not share the same size. For the convolution layer specified here, there will be n_c outputs, and each of them is a $(n_h - f_s + 1) \times (n_w - f_s + 1)$.

Question: Verify the size of the output.

Each output is referred to as a channel. As we explained, they represent different extracted features from the input.

The input may have multiple channels as well. For instance, the input may be an RGB image, i.e. three tensors, one for each color. Another common example is

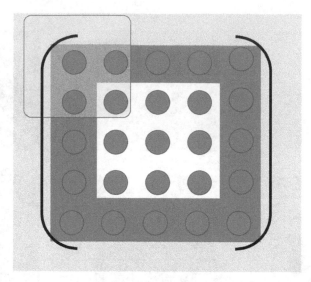

Figure 5.7. A schematic depiction of padding. The blue circles indicate the pixels of the input image. The green rectangle shows the filter. The red ribbon identifies the edge pixels. Without padding, the pixels on the red ribbon have less contribution to the output compared to the rest of the pixels.

when there is a sequence of convolution layers. In such situations, each layer of convolution generates multiple channels that provide the input to the following convolution layer.

Exercise: How can we adapt the convolution operation for inputs with multiple channels?

One simple solution is to expand the filter to more layers. In other words, we can use a 3D tensor for the filter with $f_s \times f_s \times n_c^{[l-1]}$ for the dimensions. Here we are using $n_c^{[l-1]}$ to show the number of channels in the input layer or previous layer. Note that we use $n_c^{[l]}$ with a superscript denoting the layer to avoid confusion. You can check that such a filter takes the input and generate one output.

Up to this point, for each layer we have $n_c^{[l]}$ filters. Each filter has $f_s \times f_s \times n_c^{[l-1]} + 1$ learnable parameters. Note that we also considered a bias for each filter. This means that for each convolution layer, the total number of learnable parameters is

$$f_s \times f_s \times n_c^{[l-1]} \times n_c^{[l]} + n_c^{[l]}.$$

This does not depend on the n_w or n_h, as expected, which means that we can add more nodes and layers and the number of parameters grows linearly with the depth.

Padding

In some cases, we may consider padding for the convolution. Padding means that we add rows and columns of zeros around the input image.

Figure 5.7 shows how padding works. We use 'pad size, p_s' to indicate the number of rows and columns that we add for padding.

Normally, nodes on the edges of the image have less contribution to the output. Padding can help with the balance of the contribution.

Question: For an input of 5×5 and with a filter of $f_s = 3$, calculate the number of nodes in the output that each node from the input contributes to. For instance, in figure 5.4 the node in the center of the input ([3,3]), contributes to all the nine nodes in the output.

Do all the input nodes have the same contribution toward the output?

Question: Repeat the previous question, but this time, add paddings with a pad size of 1, i.e. add a row to the top and bottom and a column to the left and right of the input image and set them to zero.

Stride

You may be wondering why we only move the convolution window in steps of size 1. The answer is that we do not have to. This introduces another hyper-parameter which is known as the stride, s.

See the online resources 'CNN Explainer: Learn Convolutional Neural Network (CNN)' at https://poloclub.github.io/cnn-explainer/ and 'Animations of Convolution and Deconvolution' at https://hannibunny.github.io/mlbook/neural-networks/convolutionDemos.html.

Question: Show that the size of the output of the convolution has the following dimensions:

$$\left(\frac{\left[n_h - fs + 2p_s \right]}{s} + 1 \right) \times \left(\frac{\left[n_w - fs + 2p_s \right]}{s} + 1 \right).$$

Exercise: Identify the hyper-parameters of a convolution layer.

The main two hyper-parameters are the number of channels and filter sizes. But we also have the padding size, p_s, and the stride s.

This completes our discussion about a convolutional layer. However, this is only one element of a CNN. A CNN usually has three types of layers: convolutional layers, pooling layers, and fully connected layers.

A pooling layer can be seen as a coarse-graining operation in the network. Similar to the convolution operation, imagine a window that moves over the input. However, instead of multiplying them by a filter, we take the average (average pooling) or the maximum (maximum pooling) of the values in that window. This often helps map large inputs to smaller ones while preserving important information in each block of the input.

Similar to the convolution layer, a pooling layer can have different pooling sizes as well as different padding sizes and strides.

Often a convolution layer or blocks of convolution layers are followed by a pooling layer. These units extract features from the input and pass them to the next block.

Once enough features are extracted from the input, it is time to get to the main task of the model, e.g. classification. For this part, the extracted features are flattened to vectors and then fully connected layers are used to map the extracted features of each sample to their corresponding labels.

In a way, the convolution units are trained to extract the most relevant features from the inputs and the fully connected layers are trained to make predictions based on those extracted features.

Often the structure of a CNN is designed in such a way that the width and height of the layers reduce with the depth of the network and at the same time the number of channels increases. This allows for reducing the number of parameters of the CNN while extracting large numbers of features from the input.

Exercise: Identify the hyper-parameter of a convolution unit.

For each convolution layer, here are the hyper-parameters with some of the most common choices for them:

- Filter size, f_s: 3, 5, 7.
- Padding size, p_s: same or valid (no padding).
- Stride, s: 1.

Similarly, for the pooling, we have
- Type: max pooling or average pooling.
- Size: 2, 3.
- Padding: 0.

This covers the basics of CNNs. However, there are many variations and extensions of these ideas that we did not cover here. Different architectures of CNNs have been explored and benchmarked for different applications. For more information about some of these variations and architectures see [10–12].

Both PyTorch and TensorFlow provide efficient implementations of CNNs. The code in listings 5.1 and 5.2 shows how you can use these libraries to build a CNN and train it in a few lines of code.

5.2 Time-series and recurrent neural networks (RNNs)

In this section we will focus on time series datasets. This is a common form of data, particularly in physics.

Imagine a time-dependent quantity, $\nu(t)$. The measurements of this quantity over time would give a sequence of values which is referred to as a 'time series' [13].

The different elements of a time series are not independent of each other and have a temporal connection. This means that their order plays an important role in the analysis of the sequence.

Here are some examples of time series datasets:

- Earthquakes and earth vibrations over time [14].
- Historical measurements of sunspots, i.e. DST-SS (table 1.2).
- Air pollution over time.
- Weather conditions over time.
- Traffic condition over time.

```
 1 from keras.models import Sequential
 2 from keras.layers import Dense, Conv2D, MaxPooling2D, Flatten
 3
 4 train_images.shape
 5
 6 X_train=train_images.reshape((-1,28,28,1))                        ##
       Reshape data into 3D
 7 X_test=test_images.reshape((-1,28,28,1))
 8
 9 from tensorflow.keras.utils import to_categorical
10
11 Y_train=to_categorical(train_labels)                             ##
       Convert the labels into one-hot vectors
12 Y_test=to_categorical(test_labels)
13
14 model=Sequential()
            ## Make an object of sequential
15
16 model.add(Conv2D(filters=32,kernel_size=(3,3),activation='relu',
            ## Add a CNN layer
17             input_shape=(28,28,1)))
18 model.add(Conv2D(filters=64,kernel_size=(3,3),activation='relu'))
            ## Add the second CNN layer
19 model.add(MaxPooling2D(pool_size=(2,2)))
            ## Add a maxpooling layer
20 model.add(Conv2D(filters=32,kernel_size=(3,3),activation='relu'))
            ## Add the third CNN layer
21
22 model.add(Flatten())
            ## Convert the input into a vector
23 model.add(Dense(units=64,activation='relu'))
            ## Add a dense hidden layer
24 model.add(Dense(units=10,activation='softmax'))
            ## Add an out-put layer
25
26 model.summary()
            ## Display the summary of the model
27
28 model.compile(optimizer='adam',
            ## Define the optimizer
29             loss='categorical_crossentropy',
            ## , the loss of the model
30             metrics='categorical_accuracy')
            ## and the metric.
31
32 model_hist=model.fit(X_train,Y_train,epochs=1,validation_split=.2)
            ## Train the model
```

Listing 5.1. CNN with Keras.

Time series can be univariate or multivariate. A univariate series has only one variable over time. The sunspot time series, i.e. DST-SS (table 1.2), is a univariate series. However, there are also time series that include multiple variables over time. For instance, most weather datasets involve temperature, precipitation, and wind speed over time. This makes a multivariate time series. We use the superscript $\langle t \rangle$ to refer to the time index. For instance, $Y^{\langle t \rangle}$ indicates the Y variable at the tth step of the time series. We also keep using the subscript and superscript to refer to the features and sample index.

```
1  #CNN with Pytorch
2
3  from tensorflow.keras.utils import to_categorical
4  train_labels=to_categorical(train_labels)
            ## Convert the labels into one-hot vetors
5  test_labels=to_categorical(test_labels)
6
7  import torch
8  X_train=torch.from_numpy(np.array(train_images,
            ## Convert the data into tensor
9                              dtype='float32').reshape
   ((-1,1,28,28)))
10 Y_train=torch.from_numpy(np.array(train_labels,dtype='float32'))
11
12 X_test=torch.from_numpy(np.array(test_images,
13                             dtype='float32').reshape((-1,1,28,28)
   ))
14 Y_test=torch.from_numpy(np.array(test_labels,dtype='float32'))
15
16
17 from torch.nn import LogSoftmax
18 import torch.nn as nn
19 import torch.nn.functional as F
20 import torch.optim as optim
21
22
23 class CNN_Net(nn.Module):
            ## Define the class of the model
24     def __init__(self):
25         super(CNN_Net, self).__init__()
26         self.conv1 = nn.Conv2d(in_channels=1,
            ## Define the first conv layer
27                            out_channels=8,
28                            kernel_size=3,
29                            stride=1,
30                            padding=1)
31
32         self.conv2 = nn.Conv2d(in_channels=8,
            ## Define the second conv layer
33                            out_channels=16,
34                            kernel_size=3,
35                            stride=1,
36                            padding=1)
37
38         self.pool = nn.MaxPool2d(kernel_size=2, stride=2)
            ## Define the max-pooling layer
39
40         self.fc1 = nn.Linear(16*7*7, 128)
            ## Define the hidden linear layer
41         self.fc2 = nn.Linear(128, 10)
            ## Define the out-put layer
```

Listing 5.2. CNN with PyTorch.

There are different types of supervised tasks that may involve time series. It could be a classification task, i.e. to classify a given time series, for instance, identifying a neurological disorder based on an EEG signal.

However, by far the most common type of task for time series is forecasting, i.e. prediction of the future of a time series. For instance, in the case of the sunspots dataset, the time series can be used to predict the number of sunspots in the next month or even the next six months.

Forecasting is one of the most popular machine learning applications and is used in a wide range of fields, from financial forecasting to natural language processing (NLP).

For most of this section we focus on forecasting. We start with the terminology and some notation. Then we explain the statistical methods to analyze time series. We then review the classical methods for analyzing time series and in the last part of this section will introduce a very powerful method based on the NNs.

Assume that we are given a time series

$$\{y^0, y^1, \dots, y^t\}.$$

For a forecasting problem the goal is to predict the future of this time series. The assumption is that

$$y^{t+1} = f(y^0, y^1, \dots, y^t). \tag{5.3}$$

In other words, we assume that the future of the series depends on its history. This is not always true, but when this assumption is valid it is possible to build powerful models to predict the future of the series.

The time steps in the history that are used for forecasting the future of the series are referred to as the 'lags'.

Question: Imagine that we have a time series for the position of a ball that is dropped from some height:

- Describe how you can find the function f for forecasting the future positions of the ball.
- How many lags do you need for forecasting the position?

Hint: You do not need to do the math, just a description of the process would be enough.

As you can see from the question above, usually we do not have the whole history (all the lags) for forecasting applications. Typically, it is enough to keep a window of recent history. Mathematically, this translates to

$$y^t = f(y^{t-1}, y^{t-2}, \dots, y^{t-n}). \tag{5.4}$$

Here n identifies how many lags (i.e. how much of the history) we are using or we need to estimate y^t. This often is specified based on our domain knowledge of the background dynamics. If the timescale of a process is about a second, we do not need to use a full day of history. On the other hand, keeping only one millisecond of the recent history would not be enough for a good forecast.

In the absence of any intuition or domain knowledge, n can be treated as a hyper-parameter and it can be tuned to find the model with the most accurate forecast.

However, there are also techniques that can help tune and optimize n.

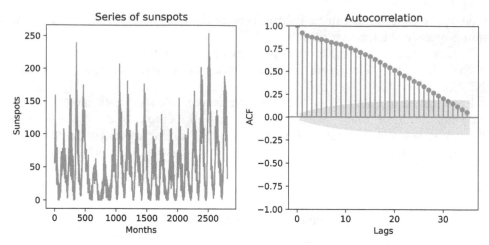

Figure 5.8. Auto-correlation between y^t and its lags for the series of sunspots.

ACF plot

The number of lags, n, is a key hyper-parameter. The ACF plot is a technique that can help specify n [15].

The ACF plot illustrates the autocorrelation between the y^t and its lags. This is often a bar plot where each bar shows the correlation between y^t and a lag $y^{t-\tau}$. It starts from $\tau = 0$ which is the correlation between y^t and itself and, therefore, it would be one. The right panel of figure 5.8 shows the ACF plot for the sunspots dataset. As you can see, the further we go back (increasing τ), the smaller the correlation becomes. We just consider the autocorrelation of lags with bars larger than the shaded region. Lags with bars within the shaded region are not statistically significant. The code is shown in listing 5.3.

5.2.1 Time series analysis

To better understand a time series it helps to decompose it into the different processes that contribute to the dynamics. Understanding different parts of the dynamics can provide a qualitative and even a quantitative description of a time series. Also, this helps with choosing the appropriate model for forecasting the time series.

Here we review two main components of a time series.

Trend

The trend describes the general trend and average behavior of the variable. For instance, a time series may have an increasing trend which means that it is on average increasing. As an example, figure 5.9 shows the global average temperature which has had an increasing trend over the past century [16, 17].

Note that there are fluctuations and for small windows, the dynamics may be decreasing. But the trend which describes the overall and global behavior of the dynamics is increasing. We refer to the trend as T.

```
42
     ## The input size is calculated with
43
     ## output_size = (input_size - kernel_size + 2*padding) / stride +
        1
44
     ## after pooling layer the output_size=output_size/2
45   def forward(self, x):
46       x = torch.relu(self.conv1(x))
     ## output_size=(28 - 3 + 2*1) / 1 + 1 = 28
47       x = self.pool(x)
     ## output_size=28/2 = 14
48       x = torch.relu(self.conv2(x))
     ## output_size=(14 - 3 + 2*1) / 1 + 1 = 14
49       x = self.pool(x)
     ## output_size=14/2 = 7
50       x = x.view(-1, 16*7*7)
     ## input_size=16*7*7
51       x = torch.relu(self.fc1(x))
52       x = LogSoftmax(dim=1)(self.fc2(x))
53       return x
54
55 criterion = nn.CrossEntropyLoss()
                    ## Define the loss
56 model = CNN_Net()
                    ## Make an object of the model
57 optimizer = optim.Adam(model.parameters(), lr=0.001)
                    ## Define the optimizer of the model.
58
59
60 num_epochs = 10
61 for epoch in range(num_epochs):
                    ## Train the model
62
63   outputs = model(X_train)
                      ## Compute the predictions.
64   optimizer.zero_grad()
                      ## Clear the gradient history
65   loss = criterion(outputs.squeeze(0), Y_train)
                      ## Compute the loss.
66   loss.backward()
                      ## Make the back-propagation.
67   optimizer.step()
                      ## Update the weights.
68
69   print(f'Epoch = {epoch} , Loss: {loss.item():.4f}')
                      ## Print the results.
```

Listing 5.3. Draw ACF plot.

For a stationary time series, the average of the time series remains relatively constant.

Also, for a non-stationary time series, if we remove the trend of a time series from its values, it will become stationary. Figure 5.10 shows a time series with a zero trend. Despite all the fluctuations, the average stays close to zero.

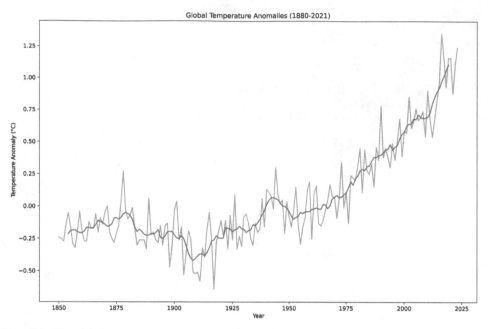

Figure 5.9. The global average temperature over the past century [16, 17]. Despite the fluctuations, the increasing trend is evident. The red curve shows the trend.

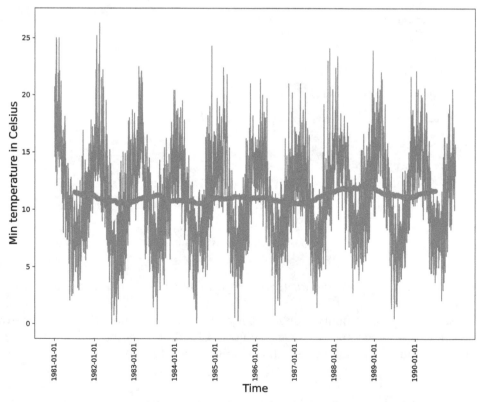

Figure 5.10. The time series of the minimum daily temperature in Melbourne in degrees Celsius [18].

Seasonality

Sometimes a time series exhibits a pattern that repeats over time. This kind of pattern is referred to as 'seasonality'. In figure 5.10 we can see that the minimum temperature in Melbourne oscillates with a frequency of 365 days. This indicates that this time series has an annual seasonality.

We refer to the seasonality as S.

Residual

It is possible to further decompose the dynamics and extract more components. However, for the purpose of this book we consider all the remaining processes of the dynamics as residual components and refer to them as the residual, R.

Understanding these components helps us understand the time series.

Sometimes the time series is additive [19]. This means that we can derive the value of the time series in each time step by adding the components of the series. Mathematically, it means

$$y^t = T^t + S^t + R^t. \tag{5.5}$$

This equation means that the value of the series in time t is derived by adding the value of trend, seasonality, and the residual at time t.

Sometimes it can be more complicated. For instance, in some cases it can be multiplicative [19]. When a time series is in the multiplicative mode, the value of a series at each time step is derived by multiplying the value of the trend and seasonality and the residual term:

$$y^t = T^t \times S^t \times R^t. \tag{5.6}$$

Series decomposition

For a time series in the additive mode, the values of the series would be the sum of the trend, seasonality, and residual. We can calculate the values of trend and seasonality and residual for any series. Decomposing the series to the trend, seasonality, and residual of the series is called decomposition. The decomposition gives us an overview of the behavior of trend and seasonality.

We can use the statsmodels library to decompose the series. The code in listing 5.4 gives an example.

Figure 5.11 shows the decomposition for the sunspot time series.

Test of stationarity

Some of the classical models are designed for stationary time series. There are several statistical tests for the stationarity of the time series. One of them is the Dickey–Fuller test. In this test y^t is expressed as

$$y^t = \rho y^{t-1} + R^t, \tag{5.7}$$

```
1 from statsmodels.graphics.tsaplots import plot_acf   ## Import the
      command
2 plot_acf(series)                                      ## Draw ACF plot
```

Listing 5.4. Series decomposition.

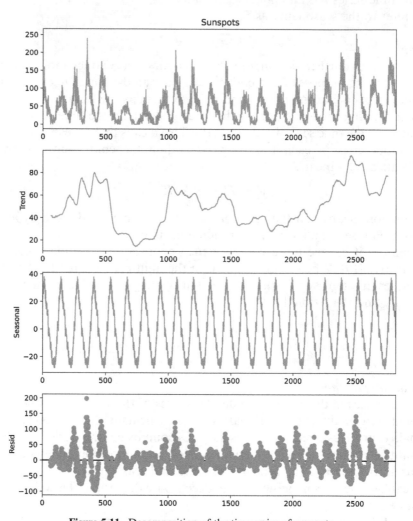

Figure 5.11. Decomposition of the time series of sunspots.

where R^t is the error term and ρ is the coefficient. If the coefficient $\rho = 1$ then the series is non-stationary. We use a variation of this test in Python, which is called the augmented Dickey–Fuller (ADF) test, known as the adfuller function in Python. In order to implement it in Python we use the statsmodels library as shown in listing 5.5.

```
1 from statsmodels.tsa.seasonal import seasonal_decompose ## Import the
     command.
2
3 result = seasonal_decompose(series,                        ## Make an
     object.
4                               model='additive',            ## Specify the
     decomposition mode.
5                               period=132)                  ##
6 result.plot()                                              ## Plot the
     decomposition result.
7 plt.show().
```

Listing 5.5. Implementation of the adfuller test.

If the *p*-value is less than 0.5, the null hypothesis would be rejected. It means that if the *p*-value <0.5 then the series is not non-stationary. In other words, the series is stationary.

5.2.2 Classical models in time series forecasting

There are different forecasting models. We may use deep learning models such as recurrent networks or we can use classical models that are not based on NNs. Here we review some of the more common techniques. For this section, we focus on classical (non-NN) techniques.

Autoregression
We can model a time series with a regression model using the lag values. We assume that the present value is derived from a linear combination of previous values:

$$y^i = w_1 y^{i-1} + w_2 y^{i-2} + \cdots + w_p y^{i-n} + w_0. \tag{5.8}$$

The y^i is a regressand and the $y^{i-1}, \ldots, y^{i-p}$ are regressors. This translates to training a forecasting model to optimize the w_i.

This approach turns the forecasting problem of a time series into a normal regression problem where in each step y^i is the label and the lags make the feature vector, i.e.

$$X^i = \{y^{i-1}, y^{i-2}, \ldots, y^{i-n}\}.$$

With this approach it is possible to extend the linear regression techniques that were introduced in chapter 3, for time series.

Before we use the autoregressive model to forecast a series, we should specify the n, the number of lags that we need to keep. We introduced the ACF plot earlier in this section that can be used for this.

We can also treat n as a hyper-parameter and use hyper-parameter tuning techniques such as grid search to optimize n.

The statsmodels library provides an efficient implementation of the autoregression model. The code in listing 5.6 shows how to use the autoregressive model in

```
1 from statsmodels.tsa.stattools import adfuller        ## Import the
    command
2 result = adfuller(series, autolag='AIC')              ## Run the ADFuller
    Test
3 print(f'ADF Statistic: {result[0]}')                  ## Print the results
    in detail
4 print(f'n_lags: {result[1]}')
5 print(f'p-value: {result[1]}')
6 for key, value in result[4].items():
7     print('Critial Values:')
8     print(f'    {key}, p= {value}')
```

Listing 5.6. Autoregressive model.

statsmodels for forecasting. We can use 80% of the series as train_set to train the model.

This is probably one of the simplest models that can be used for forecasting. There are also more sophisticated variations of the autoregressive model that are better at handling non-linearities. These include autoregressive-moving-average (ARMA) and autoregressive integrated moving average (ARIMA) which use the moving average of the series to better capture the trend [13, 15, 20]. There is also seasonal ARIMA (SARIMA) which to some extent can incorporate the seasonality of a time series [13, 20]. For the case of multivariate time series where different features are coupled and can all play some role in the dynamics and forecasting, there is the vector autoregressive model (VAR) which is a vector generalization of the autoregressive model [13, 20]. These are some of the more common techniques for forecasting, but this list does not cover all the methods that are used. Next, we will review a powerful classical technique known as the Facebook Prophet or Prophet technique.

Facebook Prophet

One of the most powerful classical models is Facebook Prophet [21]. It is designed for univariant time series.

The Facebook Prophet assumes that each time series at each time step is a summation of four terms at that time step. These four terms are the trend, the seasonality, the holidays, and the residuals or error terms:

$$y(t) = T(t) + S(t) + H(t) + E(t). \tag{5.9}$$

The holidays term, $H(t)$, helps with including the effects of recurring events such as holidays. Note that this is not limited to time series that deal with calendar holidays. Any irregular recurring effect can be included in the holiday term. In a way, the holiday term provides a tool to include domain knowledge in our model.

The trend of the series is modeled with a regression model. The Facebook Prophet model assumes a piecewise linear equation for the trend. The slope of the trend can change at some of the time steps. These time steps are referred to as the 'change-points'. Here is an example of a change point:

$$T(t) = \begin{cases} \alpha_0 + \alpha_1 t & t \leqslant c \\ \alpha_0 - \alpha_2 c + (\alpha_1 + \alpha_2)t & t > c \end{cases}. \tag{5.10}$$

In this equation $t = c$ is a change point. The model may have many change-points where the trend changes.

The model can detect and learn these change-points automatically. Alternatively, we can specify these points for the model.

Another possibility for the trend is to saturate. The value that the trend saturates to is called the 'capacity' if it is the upper bound or the 'floor' if it is a lower bound. For these cases, the trend would be modeled using the following logistic equation:

$$T(t) = \frac{C}{1 + e^{-k(t-m)}}, \tag{5.11}$$

where k and m are the parameters of the model and C is the capacity. The model is similar for the floor.

To model the seasonality, the model uses the Fourier analysis.

$$S(t) = \sum_{n=1}^{N} \left(a_n \cos\left(\frac{2\pi n t}{P}\right) + b_n \sin\left(\frac{2\pi n t}{P}\right) \right). \tag{5.12}$$

This includes N terms of the Fourier series. To model the series, the values of a_n and b_n should be identified. The periods of the seasonality could be 7 for weekly seasonality and 365.25 for yearly seasonality. The default seasonalities of Facebook Prophet are weakly and yearly seasonality. The daily seasonality would be included if the dataset has sub-daily data. We can turn off these seasonalities and define our own seasonality. Note that for a time series that has a different timescale (e.g. nanoscconds), these terms need to be adjusted accordingly.

Next is the holiday term. The holiday term could include any events that affect the series in a small time window. They may or may not repeat in the future. The holidays are introduced in the model as a list (pandas DataFrame) which shows when a holiday happens. Although it is called the holiday term, it includes any event with a sudden effect on the series. For example:

- a lockdown for the time series of the number of new Covid cases;
- a world cup for the series of the number of travelers.

Let us use this in an example. Assume that we have historical data such as a specific stock price. For the Prophet model, the input should be a pandas DataFrame where the first column indicates the time stamps and the second column includes the values of the time series.

The sample code in listing 5.7 shows how you can make a Prophet model and train it.

After training the model we can use it to make predictions for the future. In order to obtain a prediction, we need a pandas DataFrame of time stamps of the future.

```
1    from statsmodels.tsa.ar_model train_size=int(len(series)*.8)
                         ## 80% of series is for training
2  train_set=series.iloc[:train_size]              ## Specify the
       train_set
3  test_set=series.iloc[train_size:]               ## Specify the
       test_set
4  from statsmodels.tsa.ar_model import AutoReg     ## Import the
       command.
5  model=AutoReg(train_set,p).fit()                ## Make an
       object of the model
6                                                   ## and train
       it on the train set.
7  y_pred=model.predict(start=start,end=end)       ## Make
       prediction by specifying the
8                                                   ## start and
       end time.
```

Listing 5.7. Train the Facebook Prophet.

```
1  from prophet import Prophet                      ## Import the
       command.
2  model=Prophet()                                 ## Make an
       object of the model.
3  model.fit(df_train)                             ## Train the
       model on train dataframe
```

Listing 5.8. Make prediction with Facebook Prophet.

We can use the Facebook Prophet to make the time stamps. Then we can use the model to make predictions for the corresponding time stamps, see listing 5.8.

For more details see [22]. The predict method returns a pandas DataFrame which contains a lot of information. The YHAT contains the predicted y values. The YHAT_LOWER and YHAT_UPPER indicate the confidence intervals. Note that the future time stamps should be in the same format as the history. For example, if we do not have information about the hourly values of a series we cannot obtain predictions for hourly times in the future, or if we have data on business days of the week, we cannot obtain predictions for weekends.

5.2.3 Recurrent neural network

Next, we get to recurrent neural networks (RNNs). RNNs provide one of the most powerful tools for investigating time series [23, 24]. It is an NN architecture that is designed to use the temporal relation of a time series.

For this section, we use the dataset of sunspots, i.e. DTS-SS (1.2). In the case of the sunspots, imagine that we use a six month window for prediction. In other words, for predicting the sunspots in each month, we use the values for the six months leading to that month. In this case, we can treat the values from the previous six months as the input feature vector and the value for the target month as the label. So to generate the feature matrix, we can create six copies of the sunspot values and then shift them accordingly. For instance, the first column which should represent the number of sunspots one month ago, so we shift the data by one. Similarly, we do this for the second column that represents the data from two months ago and should be the same data shifted by two. Figure 5.12 shows this process schematically.

This way, we will create a dataset with seven columns, six of which represent the history of the sample, and the last one gives the number of sunspots in the target month.

If we want to use more of the history for this prediction, we can add more columns for that.

Remember that the historical window that we consider usually depends on the dynamic properties of the system that we are investigating. For one system, we may need to keep years of data for the prediction, and for another system, we may only need a few seconds of its history.

With a normal NN, every feature of an input sample is fed into the nodes in the first hidden layer with the corresponding weights. When the data are a time series, the input features is changing over time. To accommodate this, we can add a self-loop to the nodes in the NN. This means that all the elements of the time series are fed to the same node in sequence and the self-loop keeps track of the temporal relation.

Figure 5.13(A) shows a recurrent node schematically. We can add a new dimension to this picture over time. Figure 5.13(B) expands the node with the self-loop in time and shows how different elements of the time series interact with the node. Each element represents a time slice of the time series, $X^{(t)}$ going through the node.

For each step the internal memory of the unit is affected. This plays the role of the self-loop and is depicted by the arrows that connect the elements.

Once the tth element of the time series goes through the node, it affects the internal memory of the node. For the consecutive element, i.e. the $(t + 1)$th element, the node is affected by the previous element through the memory of the node. This enables the RNN node to learn the temporal patterns of the time series. We will discuss the mechanics and mathematics of the RNN in more detail.

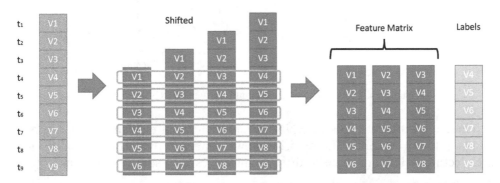

Figure 5.12. Schematic illustration of the process for extracting the feature matrix for a univariate time series. The left panel shows the time series. The middle panel shows four copies of the time series. Each copy is shifted compared to the original one. The rows identified by the gray boxes make the new data. Here we only kept three values in the history, but this can be extended to keep a larger window.

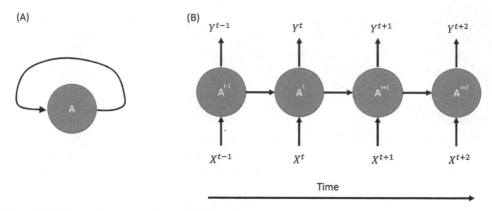

Figure 5.13. Schematic picture of a single RNN node. Panel (A) shows the node with its self-loop. Panel (B) expands the self-loop in time and shows how different elements of the time series are fed into the node and how the node keeps and carry forward an internal memory.

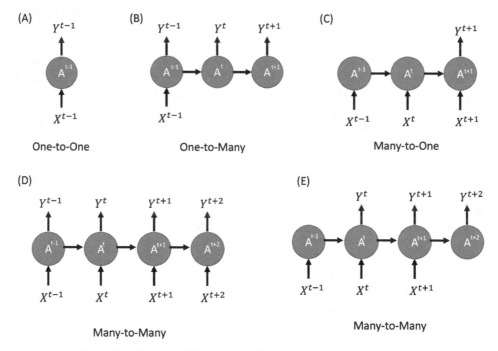

Figure 5.14. Schematic illustration of different types of RNN architectures.

There are different types of RNNs where each input element is not necessarily mapped to an output. Figure 5.14 shows some of the more common RNN architectures. Here are some of these architectures with some examples:

- Many-to-one: classification of patients from EEG signals.
- One-to-many: music generation.
- Many-to-many: translation of a text from one language to another.

There are also different types of structures for the internal architecture of RNN nodes. In the following sections we will review some of the most popular architectures. We start with the simple RNN structure.

Simple RNN

A simple RNN takes the input and evaluates two variables, the output, and the memory. Mathematically, they are given by

$$a^{\langle t \rangle} = g_a(W_a a^{\langle t-1 \rangle} + U_a X^{\langle t \rangle} + b_a),$$
$$y^{\langle t \rangle} = g_y(W_y a^{\langle t \rangle} + b_y),$$
(5.13)

where a represents the memory of the node and g_a and g_y are the activation functions for each variable.

In each time step the memory is re-evaluated based on the new element of the time series and the value of the memory from the previous step. W_a and U_a represent the learnable weights corresponding to the new input and the memory from the last step, respectively. As usual, we also consider a bias. Note that if the input has multiple features or if the hidden layer has multiple nodes, W_a and U_a would be tensors with matching dimensions.

The output is calculated using the memory. Note that the effect of the input is embedded in the memory, $a^{\langle t \rangle}$.

The common choices for the activation functions g_a and g_y are tanh and sigmoid, respectively.

We should add that this is not the only way that a simple RNN unit is designed and there are other variations [25, 26].

LSTM

One of the challenges with simple RNN is that the memory is replaced and re-evaluated in each step. This often means that the unit can only keep track of the short immediate history and the effect of an input vanishes after a few steps. For some applications, it is important to keep track of some of the inputs that may have a longer effect.

For instance, imagine that you are building a model to predict the price of fuel. A simple RNN would focus on the most recent trend of the price and would try to learn to predict the price from a few hours of history. Now imagine that there is news about changes in tariffs that are going to take place in six months. Normally, a simple RNN cannot remember this and when the tariffs are put in place, it would be surprised, i.e. its prediction would be off at least for a few hours. However, if it could keep track of inputs that have long-term effects, it would be able to do better.

This is the idea behind long short term memory (LSTM) RNNs [27]. Specifically, LSTM RNNs, in addition to the normal memory, have a memory that could keep track of longer changes (compared to the short term) [27].

There are different variations of the LSTM [25, 26]. The following equations describe the mathematics of one of the more popular LSTM designs:

$$c^{\langle t \rangle} = \tanh(W_m a^{\langle t-1 \rangle} + U_m X^{\langle t \rangle} + b_m),$$
$$\Gamma_s = \mathrm{sig}(W_s a^{\langle t-1 \rangle} + U_s X^{\langle t \rangle} + b_s),$$
$$\Gamma_f = \mathrm{sig}(W_s a^{\langle t-1 \rangle} + U_s X^{\langle t \rangle} + b_s),$$
$$c^{\langle t \rangle} = \Gamma_s c^{\langle t \rangle} + \Gamma_f c^{\langle t-1 \rangle}, \qquad\qquad (5.14)$$
$$\Gamma_r = \mathrm{sig}(W_r a^{\langle t-1 \rangle} + U_r X^{\langle t \rangle} + b_r),$$
$$a^{\langle t \rangle} = \Gamma_r c^{\langle t \rangle}.$$

Here c represents the long-term memory.

Each time the LSTM node receives an input, it calculates the value of the long-term memory in the new iteration, $c^{\langle t+1 \rangle}$. However, it does not necessarily use that. There are two processes involved in updating the long-term memory. The first one, identified by Γ_s, indicates if the $c^{\langle t+1 \rangle}$ should be stored or not. The second process, identified by Γ_f, indicates if the previous value of the long-term memory, $c^{\langle t \rangle}$ should be forgotten. These two, form the update rule for the long-term memory as indicated in the fourth equation in equation (5.14).

Once the long-term memory is set, it is used to evaluate the short term memory. For this, we need another process which is identified by the Γ_r. If $\Gamma_r = 1$, the information stored in the long-term memory is retrieved into the short term memory and used for the output. Otherwise, the long-term memory is left to be used in future iterations.

Note that all the Γ parameters are set using the input of the iteration $X^{\langle t \rangle}$ and the memory from the last iteration $a^{\langle t-1 \rangle}$. This means that depending on the new input and the memory from the previous iteration, any of the three processes above may be activated. For instance, for some input value, the node may decide that it needs to retrieve the long-term memory or for some other input, it may decide that it can forget the value of the long-term memory and replace it with a new value.

Figure 5.15 is a schematic illustration that shows the inner mechanics of an LSTM node [28].

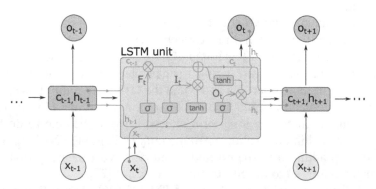

Figure 5.15. Schematic illustration of an LSTM node. (Image credit: Ixnay, from Wikipedia [28], CC BY-SA 4.0.)

GRU

For the LSTM, the update rule for the long-term memory involved two relatively independent processes, the storage given by Γ_s and the forgetting indicated by Γ_f.

It may seem more natural if these two were connected and there was only one variable that would decide when the short term memory should be updated with a new value and the previous values forgotten. This leads to a simplified version of LSTM where only one Γ is used to indicate when the long-term memory is updated. This is known as the 'gated recurrent unit' (GRU) [29]. Mathematically, for the GRU we have

$$\Gamma_f = 1 - \Gamma_s,$$
$$\Gamma_r = 1.$$

(5.15)

There is, however, an additional parameter Γ_l which indicates the impact of the memory for the evaluation of the long-term memory, i.e.

$$c^{\langle t \rangle} = \tanh(W_m \Gamma_l a^{\langle t-1 \rangle} + U_m X^{\langle t \rangle} + b_m).$$

(5.16)

Figure 5.16 shows schematically the internal design of a GRU node [28].

Note that there is a zoo of RNN architectures [25, 26] and the ones we described here are not the only ones. You probably can make your own variations and test how they perform for different problems. For a survey and benchmark of different RNN architectures see [25, 26].

5.2.4 Implementation of RNN

Here is a code snippet for the implementation of the RNN architectures that we discussed using TensorFlow and PyTorch.

The code in listing 5.9 shows how to implement an RNN model with Keras and TensorFlow.

The implementation in PyTorch is similar, see listing 5.10.

For LSTM, it is similar, i.e. listing 5.11.

Similarly for PyTorch, you use the code in listing 5.12.

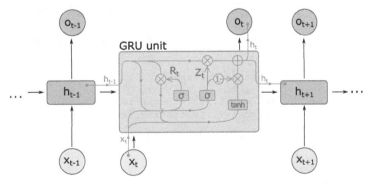

Figure 5.16. Schematic illustration of the GRU node. (Image credit: Ixnay, from Wikipedia [28], CC BY-SA 4.0.)

```
1 future_df=model.make_future_dataframe(            ## Make the
.     future dataframe
2     periods=n,                                    ## The length
      of future time to be
3     freq='D')                                     ## considered
      with frequency = 1 day
4 model.predict(future_df)                          ## Make the
      prediction on future dataframe
```

Listing 5.9. RNN with Keras.

```
1 Y = df.target.values
2 X = df.drop('target', axis=1).values
3
4 X = X.reshape(-1, n_ts, n_f )
              ## Convert into a 3D array.
5
6 from sklearn.model_selection import train_test_split
7 X_train, X_test, Y_train, Y_test = train_test_split(X, Y, random_state
      = 0)      ## Split data into train and test set
8
9 from tensorflow import keras
              ## Import library
10 from tensorflow.keras.layers import LSTM, SimpleRNN, Dense
              ## Import commands
11 from tensorflow.keras import layers
12 from tensorflow.keras import models
13
14 model = models.Sequential()
              ## Make a sequential object
15 model.add(SimpleRNN(64, input_shape =(n_ts, n_f) ,
              ## Add the rnn layer
16             activation='tanh',
17             return_sequences=True))
18
19
20 model.add(Dense(32,  activation='relu')  )
              ## Add a dense hidden layer
21 model.add(Dense(1,  activation='linear')  )
              ## Add the output layer
22
23 model.compile(loss = keras.losses.mean_squared_error,
              ## Define the loss
24             optimizer=keras.optimizers.Adam(learning_rate = .001) )
              ## Define the optimizer
25
26 history = model.fit(X_train, Y_train,
              ## Train the model
27                 epochs=10, batch_size=16,
28                 verbose=1, validation_data=(X_test, Y_test))
```

Listing 5.10. RNN with PyTorch.

```
 1 Y = df.target.values
 2 X = df.drop('target', axis=1).values
 3 X = X.reshape(X.shape[0],X.shape[1],1 )
                 ## Convert into a 3D array.
 4
 5 from sklearn.model_selection import train_test_split
 6 X_train, X_test, Y_train, Y_test = train_test_split(X, Y, random_state
     = 0)
 7
 8 import torch
 9 X_train=torch.from_numpy(np.array(X_train,dtype="float32"))
                 ## Convert into torch tensor
10 X_test=torch.from_numpy(np.array(X_test,dtype="float32"))
11 Y_train=torch.from_numpy(np.array(Y_train,dtype="float32"))
12 Y_test=torch.from_numpy(np.array(Y_test,dtype="float32"))
13
14 class RNN(torch.nn.Module):
15     def __init__(self, input_size, hidden_size, num_layers):
16         super(RNN, self).__init__()
17         self.hidden_size = hidden_size
18         self.num_layers = num_layers
19         self.rnn = torch.nn.RNN(input_size, hidden_size, num_layers,
    batch_first=True)
20         self.fc = torch.nn.Linear(hidden_size, 1)
21
22     def forward(self, x):
23         h0 = torch.zeros(self.num_layers, x.size(0),
                 # Initialize with a zero valued hidden state
24                     self.hidden_size).requires_grad_()
25         out, _ = self.rnn(x, h0.detach())
26         out = self.fc(out[:, -1, :])
27         return out
28
29 input_size = 1
30 hidden_size = 64
31 num_layers = 2
32
33 model = RNN(input_size=input_size,
                 ## Make an object of the model
34             hidden_size=hidden_size,
35             num_layers=num_layers)
36
37 criterion = torch.nn.MSELoss()
                 ## Define the loss
38 optimizer = torch.optim.Adam(model.parameters(), lr=0.001)
                 ## Define the optimizer
39
40 for epoch in range(200):
                 ## Train the model
41     outputs = model(X_train)
42     optimizer.zero_grad()
43     loss = criterion(outputs, Y_train)
44     loss.backward()
45     optimizer.step()
46
47     print(f'Epoch = {epoch} , Loss: {loss.item():.4f}')
```

Listing 5.11. LSTM with Keras.

```
1    from tensorflow import keras
                        ## Import the library
2 from tensorflow.keras.layers import LSTM, Dense
                ## Import commands
3 from tensorflow.keras import models
4
5 model = models.Sequential()
                ## Make a sequential object
6 model.add(LSTM(64, input_shape =(n_ts, n_f) ,
                ## Add the LSTM layer
7             activation='tanh',
8             return_sequences=True)
9         )
10
11 model.add(LSTM(32, activation='tanh') )
12
13 model.add(Dense(32, activation='relu') )
                ## Add a dense hidden layer
14
15 model.add(Dense(1, activation='linear') )
                ## Add the output layer
16
17
18 model.compile(loss = keras.losses.mean_squared_error,
                ## Define the loss
19         optimizer=keras.optimizers.Adam(learning_rate = .001) )
                ## Define the optimizer
20
21
22 history = model.fit(X_train, Y_train,
                ## Train the model
23             epochs=10, batch_size=16,
24             verbose=1, validation_data=(X_test, Y_test))
```

Listing 5.12. LSTM with PyTorch.

5.3 Graph neural network

So far we have seen two types of data structures where the features are related. The first one was images where the features are spatially structured. The second one was time series where the features were temporally connected. We saw that for these types of data it is better to exploit their structure to build more powerful models.

However, what if the data have some structure, but it is not as easy as the temporal or spatial structure? Many datasets have some sort of topological structure that can contain valuable information and help with building better machine learning models.

We need to find a way to capture the structure of the data. Graphs provide a powerful tool that can provide natural representations for complex structures in the data [30, 31].

Let us consider an example. Imagine that you want to build a model to predict the performance of students at a university. In addition to their individual features, the relations between students can play an important role in this prediction. Graphs are arguably the most natural representation that can capture the relations between students.

Graphs are capable of capturing complex relations and can be fairly generic. Also, graphs have been extensively studied in mathematics and are one of the more intuitive mathematical representations [30, 31]. This makes them a powerful representation for most structured datasets.

In this section, we will review graph representations for datasets and some of the machine learning tools that have been developed to work with graphs. Specifically, we will focus on graph neural networks (GNNs).

We start with reviewing the basics of graph theory. Then we will review some of the more common supervised problems for datasets with graph structure. We then introduce GNNs and specifically focus on graph convolutional neural networks (GCNs).

5.3.1 Brief review of graphs

Graphs are one of the most popular and intuitive mathematical representations. They are especially effective for capturing the relation between multiple objects. This representation can be applied to a wide range of applications, from a collection of masses that are attached with springs to abstract and complex networks such as a collection of people in a community.

Here we will briefly introduce the basics of graphs and our notation. At an abstract level, in discrete mathematics a graph is defined as a set of objects where some of those objects are paired based on some relation. The objects are represented by 'vertices' (also known as nodes). We refer to the set of vertices as V. This is a collection of vertices $\{V1, V2,..., Vn\}$. Also, the relationship between nodes that are paired is referred to as 'edges' (also known as links). We refer to the set of edges as E. An edge between $V1$ and $V2$ is represented by

$$(V_1, V_2). \tag{5.17}$$

A graph G is represented by the pair

$$G = (V, E).$$

Figure 5.17 shows a schematic example of a graph. The left panel indicates a vertex in blue. The right panel indicates an edge between $V1$ and $V2$ with a blue line.

Let us do some examples.

(a) (b)

Figure 5.17. (a) The vertex and (b) the edge.

Question: Find a graph representation for the following examples:

- A system of masses connected by springs.
- A circuit with resistors, capacitors, and inductors.
- The collection of neurons in some part of the brain.
- Cities in a country.
- Scientists working in the field of condensed matter physics.
- Users on a social network.

It is possible to find more than one graph representation for some of these examples. Also, the types of nodes and edges can be different. For instance, a graph may be simple or weighted, directed or undirected, and it may have parallel edges or even self-loops.

For example, if for the cities, we set $V = \{$ cities $\}$, then the edges between them could be the roads that connect them. There could be cities that have multiple roads connecting them (parallel edges).

Figure 5.18 shows examples of networks with parallel edges (a) or a self-loop (b).

Question: Can you think of an example where the graph would have a self-loop?

Question: Make schematics graphs such as the one in figure 5.17 and include:

- a self-loop;
- parallel edges;
- directed edges.

Also indicate the V and E set in each case.

Adjacency matrix

Two vertices are called adjacent if they are connected by an edge. A graph could be represented by expressing which nodes are neighbors. The adjacency matrix can be used to represent a finite graph based on the adjacency relationship of the nodes. This is a square matrix where each column and row represents a vertex. We show the adjacency matrix with A. For two nodes V_i and V_j that are adjacent, $A_{i,j} = 1$.

Figure 5.19 shows the graph from figure 5.17 and its adjacency matrix.

If the graph is not directed, the adjacency matrix would be symmetric. However, for a directed graph, it may be $A_{i,j} = 1$ while $A_{j,i} = 0$.

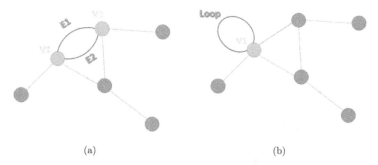

(a)   (b)

Figure 5.18. (a) The loop in graph and (b) parallel edges.

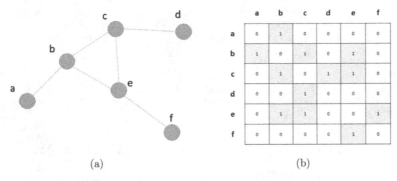

Figure 5.19. (a) The graph with labels for nodes and (b) the adjacency matrix.

For weighted graphs or graphs with parallel edges, the values in this matrix could be different from one or zero. For example, if there are two parallel undirected edges between vertices b and c, then

$$a_{b,c} = a_{c,b} = 2. \tag{5.18}$$

For simple graphs, the diagonal elements of the adjacency matrix are zero. However, if the graph has a loop, the corresponding diagonal elements would be non-zero. For example, if we have a loop for node f then

$$A_{f,f} = 1. \tag{5.19}$$

The adjacency matrix provides a compact and powerful representation of the graph. In particular, the spectrum of the adjacency matrix provides a lot of information about the properties of the graph [32]. However, we will not go into more detail. For more information, you are encouraged to see [32, 33].

Degree matrix
The degree matrix is another tool that provides information regarding the number of neighbors of each node in the graph. The degree matrix is a diagonal matrix and its diagonal elements show the number of connections for each node. For example, if the node b has three edges, then

$$d_{b,b} = 3. \tag{5.20}$$

Exercise: Find the degree matrix of the graph in figure 5.17.
The graph in the figure 5.17 is

$$
\begin{array}{c}
\quad\; a\,b\,c\,d\,e\,f \\
a\; 1\,0\,0\,0\,0\,0 \\
b\; 0\,3\,0\,0\,0\,0 \\
c\; 0\,0\,3\,0\,0\,0 \\
d\; 0\,0\,0\,1\,0\,0 \\
e\; 0\,0\,0\,0\,3\,0 \\
f\; 0\,0\,0\,0\,0\,1.
\end{array} \tag{5.21}
$$

```
 1 Y = df.target.values
 2 X = df.drop('target', axis=1).values
 3 X = X.reshape(X.shape[0],1,X.shape[1] )
                ## Convert into a 3D array.
 4 print(X.shape)
 5
 6 from sklearn.model_selection import train_test_split
 7 X_train, X_test, Y_train, Y_test = train_test_split(X, Y, random_state
       = 0)
 8
 9 import torch
10 X_train=torch.from_numpy(np.array(X_train,dtype="float32"))
                ## Convert into torch tensor
11 X_test=torch.from_numpy(np.array(X_test,dtype="float32"))
12 Y_train=torch.from_numpy(np.array(Y_train,dtype="float32"))
13 Y_test=torch.from_numpy(np.array(Y_test,dtype="float32"))
14
15 class NET(torch.nn.Module):
16     def __init__(self, input_size, hidden_size, num_layers,out_dim):
17         super(NET, self).__init__()
18
19         self.input_size=input_size
20         self.hidden_size = hidden_size
21         self.num_layers = num_layers
22         self.out_dim=out_dim
23
24         self.lstm = torch.nn.LSTM(input_size=self.input_size,
25                             hidden_size=self.hidden_size,
26                             num_layers=self.num_layers,
27                             batch_first=True)
28
29         self.lin = torch.nn.Linear(self.hidden_size, self.out_dim)
30
31     def forward(self, x):
32
33
34         h0 = torch.zeros(self.num_layers, x.size(0),
                ## Defining the initial hidden state
35                         self.hidden_size).requires_grad_()
                ## and cell state vectors.
36
37         c0 = torch.zeros(self.num_layers, x.size(0),
38                         self.hidden_size).requires_grad_()
39
```

Listing 5.13. Creating a graph.

There are other matrix representations of a graph like the 'incident matrix', but we will not cover them in this brief review. For more information see [30, 31].

Graphs in Python

In Python, we can use the NetworkX library to build, investigate and visualize graphs. The code in listing 5.13 shows how to construct a simple graph with NetworkX.

To visualize the graph, we can use the code in listing 15.14.

Question: Draw the graph in figure 5.19 with Networkx.

```
40
41        out ,(hn, cn) =self.lstm(x, (h0.detach(), c0.detach()))
42        out=self.lin(out[:,-1,:])
43        return out
44
45 input_size = 6
46 hidden_size = 64
47 num_layers = 2
48
49 model = NET(input_size=input_size,
                    ## Make an object of the model
50            hidden_size=hidden_size,
51            num_layers=num_layers,
52            out_dim=1)
53
54 criterion = torch.nn.MSELoss()
                    ## Define the loss
55 optimizer = torch.optim.Adam(model.parameters(), lr=0.001)
                    ## Define the optimizer
56
57 for epoch in range(50):
                    ## Train the model
58     outputs = model(X_train)
59     optimizer.zero_grad()
60     loss = criterion(outputs.squeeze(1), Y_train)
61     loss.backward()
62     optimizer.step()
63
64     print(f'Epoch = {epoch} , Loss: {loss.item():.4f}')
```

Listing 5.14. Draw the graph.

```
1 import networkx as nx
2 G = nx.Graph()                          ## Cunstruct an object of
3                                         ## networkx Graph
4 # Adding nodes
5 G.add_node(1)                           ## Add node, 1 to the graph
6 G.add_node(2)
7
8 #Adding an edge
9 G.add_edge(1, 2)                        ## Add Edge, from one node
      to the other
```

Listing 5.15. Graph from the pandas DataFrame.

We can also make a graph from an adjacency matrix or even from the pandas DataFrame. For the pandas Dataframe, there should be two columns representing the source and target vertices. Then the code in listing 5.15 would automatically generate directed edges between the source and the target nodes.

Note that the values of these two columns should be either an integer or a string. We can also assign some attributes for edges by using the option edge_attr which can be a list of columns. It is a fast method to make large-scale graphs.

5.3.2 Different types of problems

There are different types of machine learning problems that can involve graphs. Here we briefly review some of the most common ones. Later, we will explain how we can use GNNs to solve these problems.

Node classification

Consider a typical classification problem where we are given a set of samples and their corresponding labels, i.e. $\{X, Y\}$. Normally, when we dealt with this problem before, our assumption was that the samples in the dataset are independent of each other. However, what if they are connected and what if that connection would contribute to the label of the samples?

This is really common in complex network problems [34]. Often there is a graph where the nodes have some attributes and we are interested in predicting some properties of the nodes. For instance, consider students in a university and assume that there is an epidemic and we would like to predict who is likely to have the disease and who does not.

Normally we would take the attributes of the nodes (students) as the feature matrix X and the target property (sick or not) as the label. We then would train a supervised learning model with X and Y.

Exercise: What is the issue with this approach?

As you can guess, we are missing some key information in this approach, i.e. how the nodes are related to each other.

You can see why GNNs are important. For large classes of supervised problems, samples in the dataset are not independent and we cannot always ignore their connections. GNNs provide powerful tools to take relevant interactions between the nodes into account. Remember that a graph can be really flexible in the sort of relations that the represent. As a result, GNNs can often deal with even the most complex or abstract relations between the nodes.

Question: Before we reach the implementation of node classifications with GNN, for the classification problem above, try to find a way to take the graphs (i.e. the relations between the nodes) into account.

Link prediction

The link or edge prediction problem refers to predicting the presence and properties of edges on the basis of the local structure, topology, and labels of the graph [34–36].

Imagine that for a complex network problem, you have access to part of the graph but not all of it and we are interested in a specific edge and its properties.

One popular application of this is connecting people to friends on social media applications [37]. If you ever used LinkedIn, you have seen that it suggests people that you may know. In other words, the application is predicting that there should be an edge between you and those suggested individuals.

In addition to social networks, link prediction has wide applications in recommendation systems and drug side effect predictions as well [38].

Network classification

Another type of problem that we may face is when the samples in the dataset are graphs or can be represented as graphs and we would like to predict a global property of the graph.

For instance, imagine that we have a set of molecules and we are interested in their melting point or similar properties.

This is a popular type of problem in drug discovery [39, 40]. For instance, we may be interested in finding new antibiotics. It is interesting to train a model that can classify molecules that can be antibiotics [41].

We can treat the molecule as a collection of its atoms and their properties. However, we know that how those atoms are connected can significantly change the properties of the molecule.

In the case of molecules, graph representations for molecules have been used extensively in chemistry [42]. For the classification of the molecules we need to take the graph into account.

Question: Propose a way to take the graph into account.

5.3.3 GCN and embeddings

There are different neural network-based approaches to processing graphs. Here we focus on the graph convolutional network (GCN), which is one of the most popular techniques in GNN.

GCNs are inspired by CNNs. In each GCN layer the attributes of a node and its neighbors are used to find a new representation for that node.

One of the key issues that we need to address is how to represent the graph for the model. This representation should include the graph information as well the attributes of the samples.

The GCN takes a simple and relatively intuitive approach to finding these representations which is similar to what we did for CNNs. In fact, it builds an embedding for each node that depends on the node and its neighbors. The dependencies are determined by weights that are learned through the training process (similar to the convolution filters).

GCN for node classification

We will start with the node classification problem. Each node has its own feature vector. But it is not enough since the feature vector does not contain the graph and the relation between the node and its neighbors.

A simple approach is to aggregate the feature vectors of the node and its neighbors to build the embedding. Figure 5.19(a) shows this process schematically for some of the nodes. Mathematically, that is

$$h_b = (X_a + X_b + X_c + X_e)/3, \tag{5.22}$$

where we are focusing on node b. h_b represents the embedding for node b and X_i refers to the feature vectors of the nodes that are connected to b on the graph. With this, we are aggregating all the neighbors with uniform weights,

You may be wondering why we are limiting ourselves to the first neighbors. This is similar to CNN where in each layer we only consider the local neighborhood which is identified by the size of the filter. In order to go beyond the immediate neighbors, we can repeat the process. In other words, we can aggregate the embedding of the nodes h_i to find a new embedding. This is equivalent to two layers of CNN and expands the interactions beyond the immediate neighbors to the next nearest neighbors.

We use a superscript to refer to the number of layers of embedding. Initially, we have

$$h_i^0 = X_i.$$

Then we get to the first layer of embedding which is

$$h_b^{(1)} = \sigma(W^{(1)}(X_a + X_b + X_c + X_e)).$$

Note that we added an activation function σ. And next, we repeat this and obtain

$$h_b^{(2)} = \sigma(W^{(2)}(h_a^{(1)} + h_b^{(1)} + h_c^{(1)} + h_e^{(1)})).$$

Question: Find the relation for layer l, i.e. $h_b^{(l)}$.

Question: Show that $h_b^{(2)}$ take the second neighbors into account.

Figure 5.20(a) gives a schematic picture of the first two layers of the embedding. Similarly, figure 5.20(b) gives a schematic picture of the computation graph of the process. This approach is known as the GCN. Note that there are different types of GCN and here we covered one of the simpler versions.

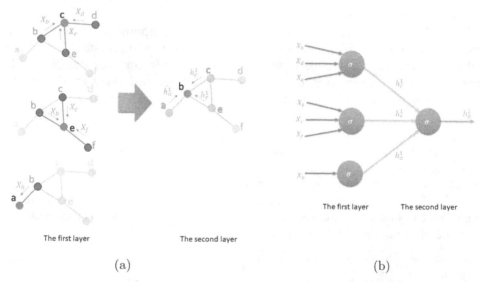

(a)   (b)

Figure 5.20. (a) The schematic view of the computation of node embeddings on the graph. (b) The computational graph of the GCN for one node. In the GCN, we first aggregate the feature vectors of all neighbors. Then, we aggregate the resulting vectors of the previous level.

Question: Find a vectorized and efficient implementation for the GCN as described above.

Tensor representation of GCN

One of the challenges of the process above is identifying the neighbors of each node. This can become especially challenging for large graphs.

Here we use the adjacency matrix of the graph to make an efficient version of the process that we described for building the embeddings.

The adjacency matrix can identify the neighbors for each node efficiently. To have a summation of the feature vectors of all neighbors we can use the product of the adjacency matrix, A, and the matrix of features of all nodes

$$(A + I)X, \tag{5.23}$$

where I is the identity matrix.

For example for the graph in figure 5.20, we would have

$$\begin{pmatrix} & a & b & c & d & e & f \\ a & 1 & 1 & 0 & 0 & 0 & 0 \\ b & 1 & 1 & 1 & 0 & 1 & 0 \\ c & 0 & 1 & 1 & 0 & 1 & 1 \\ d & 0 & 0 & 1 & 1 & 0 & 0 \\ e & 0 & 1 & 1 & 0 & 1 & 1 \\ f & 0 & 0 & 0 & 0 & 1 & 1 \end{pmatrix} \begin{pmatrix} \vec{X^a} \\ \vec{X^b} \\ \vec{X^c} \\ \vec{X^d} \\ \vec{X^e} \\ \vec{X^f} \end{pmatrix}. \tag{5.24}$$

Each row of the resultant matrix gives the uniform aggregation for the corresponding node. We define this matrix as $\hat{A}$ which is

$$\hat{A} = A + I. \tag{5.25}$$

To normalize the aggregation, we can use the degree matrix D. Specifically, we define

$$\hat{D} = D + I,$$

which gives the normalization factor for each node. The normalized aggregation can be calculated with

$$\text{aggr}(A,X)_i = \hat{D}^{-1}\hat{A}X \tag{5.26}$$

$$= \Sigma_j \frac{1}{\hat{D}_{i,i}} A_{i,j} \vec{X_j}, \tag{5.27}$$

where we use $\text{aggr}(A,X)_i$ to indicate the aggregation of node i. Also, note that $\hat{D}^{-1}$ is the inverse of the matrix.

To obtain the embedding, we multiply it with a weight matrix and apply the activation function which gives

$$h_i^1 = \sigma\left(\hat{D}^{-1}AXW\right). \tag{5.28}$$

We can repeat this process and use the final output vector as the embedding of the node. We refer to the embedding vector of node i as Z_i. Let us have a look at all calculations to reach Z:

$$h_i^0 = X_i$$
$$h_i^1 = \sigma\left(\hat{D}^{-1}Ah_i^0W_0\right)$$
$$h_i^2 = \sigma\left(\hat{D}^{-1}Ah_i^1W_1\right)$$
$$\vdots$$
$$Z_i = h_i^k = \sigma\left(\hat{D}^{-1}Ah_i^{k-1}W_{k-1}\right).$$

The Z matrix can be seen as the extracted features from the graph. It can be fed to an ordinary NN for a classification task.

The code in listing 5.16 shows how we can integrate a GCN layer in our model in PyTorch. It is similar to what we did for CNN layers.

You can see the GCN layers in the forward path need additional input, the edge_index. The edge index is commonly used for specifying a graph. It is a representation of the adjacency matrix where we keep the rows and columns of the non-zero elements. More specifically, the edge_index contains two lists, the list of the source nodes and the list of target nodes for all the edges in the graph. For a graph with e edges, this is a $2 \times e$ matrix.

One other step that is slightly different for GCNs is the specification of the training, test, and validation samples. For the training or validation, we run the model on all nodes but mask the output to only keep a subset of them that are used for training or for the test, see listing 5.17 for the code.

As you can see, when we generate the output, we use the train_mask to filter it out and keep only the relevant subset for training.

Similarly, for testing, we use a subset specified by the test_mask.

GCN for link prediction

We need to take a similar approach to link prediction. We need to find an embedding for each edge. There are different approaches to encoding the edges on the graph as well. Here we use a simple approach based on the embedding we found for nodes.

Exercise: How can we use the node embedding in the previous section to build an embedding for the edges in the graph?

```
1 import matplotlib.pyplot as plt
2 nx.draw_networkx(G, with_labels=True)           ## Draw the graph
    with matplotlib
```

Listing 5.16. NN with GCN layers.

```
1 G=nx.from_pandas_edgelist(df,                          ## Make a graph
    using a pandas dataframe
2                         source='source',               ## Edge would be
    directed from source column
3                         target='target',               ## to the target
    column
4                         edge_attr=Columns_list)         ## Assign
    attributes to the edges
```

Listing 5.17. Masking for GCN models.

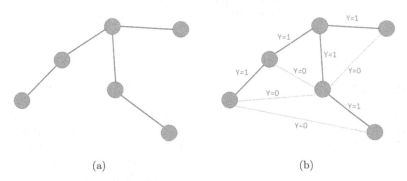

(a)   (b)

Figure 5.21. (a) Original graph and (b) graph with negative samples.

Similar to node embedding, there are different approaches to edge embedding. A simple approach would be to concatenate the embeddings of the source and target nodes. This leads to an embedding that is twice as long as the node embeddings.

The link prediction can be translated into a classification problem. The two classes are present (active) and absent (inactive) edges. Note that there could potentially be a link between any two nodes. If the edge is present in the graph, it would be labeled as 1 and if it is absent, it would be labeled as 0. Figure 5.21 shows this schematically.

There are two steps in training a GCN for link prediction. First, the edge embeddings need to be extracted from the graph. This is sometimes referred to as the 'encoder'. For this step, the absent edges (label 0) should not be included. The absent edges are not part of the graph and including them in the embedding extraction process would lead to fixed embeddings regardless of the graph structure.

Once the encoder is trained, it can be used to associate embeddings to both present and absent edges.

After the embeddings are extracted, we reach the second step where the embeddings are used to classify the edge as absent or present. This sometimes is referred to as the 'decoder'. At this step, all the edges, absent or present, should be included and the goal is to train a model that using the embeddings of each edge, would correctly predict if it should be part of the network or not.

There are more details that need to be considered for training a link prediction model such as splitting the data into training, testing, and validation sets. Check the code on GitHub for more details [43].

GCN for graph classification

Exercise: Based on what we have done for node classification and link prediction, propose a method for graph classification.

Similar to node classification and link prediction, we first need to find an embedding for the whole graph and then use the embeddings and the labels to train a model for the classification task.

Exercise: How can we find an embedding for a graph?

There are different approaches to graph embedding. One of the simplest ones is to aggregate the node embeddings. This can be done with a simple average. More specifically, in this approach, the embedding for the graph is built by averaging the vectors of node embedding.

Question: Build a model for graph classification in PyTorch.

5.4 Summary

There are many variations of the techniques that we discussed in this chapter and there are books dedicated to CNNs, RNNs, or GNNs. It was not our intention to cover all the details of these techniques. The goal is to provide a high-level understanding of these types of NN architectures and how and when you should use them. The reader is strongly encouraged to take these as the starting point and read on the specific architectures that may be relevant to the problems that they are solving.

Next, we will switch to unsupervised techniques and learn how to use the data when it is not labeled.

References

[1] Gu J *et al* 2018 Recent advances in convolutional neural networks *Pattern Recognit.* **77** 354–77

[2] Millstein F 2020 *Convolutional Neural Networks in Python: Beginner's Guide to Convolutional Neural Networks in Python* https://doi.org/abs/10.5555/3235272

[3] Aghdam H H and Heravi E J 2017 *Guide to Convolutional Neural Networks* vol 10 (New York: Springer) p 51

[4] Wikipedia 2023 Convolution *Wikipedia* https://en.wikipedia.org/wiki/Convolution (Accessed 10 April 2023)

[5] Smith S W *et al* 1997 *The Scientist and Engineer's Guide to Digital Signal Processing*

[6] Liu Y H 2018 Feature extraction and image recognition with convolutional neural networks *J. Phys.: Conf. Ser.* **1087** 062032

[7] Alaslani M G 2018 Convolutional neural network based feature extraction for iris recognition *Int. J. Comput. Sci. Inf. Technol.* **10** 65–78

[8] Dadhich A 2018 *Practical Computer Vision: Extract Insightful Information from Images Using TensorFlow, Keras, and OpenCV* (Birmingham: Packt)

[9] Ramo K 2019 *Hands-On Java Deep Learning for Computer Vision: Implement Machine Learning and Neural Network Methodologies to Perform Computer Vision-Related Tasks* (Birmingham: Packt)

[10] Alzubaidi L, Zhang J, Humaidi A J, Al-Dujaili A, Duan Y, Al-Shamma O, Santamaría J, Fadhel M A, Al-Amidie M and Farhan L 2021 Review of deep learning: concepts, CNN architectures, challenges, applications, future directions *J. Big Data* **8** 1–74

[11] Khan A, Sohail A, Zahoora U and Qureshi A S 2020 A survey of the recent architectures of deep convolutional neural networks *Artif. Intell. Rev.* **53** 5455–516

[12] Adaloglou N 2023 Best deep CNN architectures and their principles: from AlexNet to EfficientNet *The AI Summer* https://theaisummer.com/cnn-architectures/ (Accessed 10 April 2023)

[13] Hamilton J D 2020 *Time Series Analysis* (Princeton, NJ: Princeton University Press)

[14] Earthquake Hazards Program 2023 Earthquake magnitude, energy release, and shaking intensity *USGS* https://www.usgs.gov/programs/earthquake-hazards/earthquake-magnitude-energy-release-and-shaking-intensity (Accessed 10 April 2023)

[15] Nelson B K 1998 Time series analysis using autoregressive integrated moving average (ARIMA) models *Acad. Emerg. Med.* **5** 739–44

[16] National Centers for Environmental Information 2023 Global time series *Climate at a Glance* https://www.ncei.noaa.gov/access/monitoring/climate-at-a-glance/global/time-series (Acessed 19 April 2023)

[17] Rohde R 2021 Global temperature report for 2020 *Berkley Earth* https://berkeleyearth.org/global-temperature-report-for-2020/ (Accessed 2023)

[18] Brabban P 2018 Daily minimum temperatures in Melbourne *kaggle* https://www.kaggle.com/paulbrabban/daily-minimum-temperatures-in-melbourne (Accessed 2023)

[19] Australian Bureau of Statistics 2023 Time series analysis: the basics *Australian Bureau of Statistics* https://www.abs.gov.au/websitedbs/D3310114.nsf/home/Time+Series+Analysis:+The+Basics (Accessed 18 April 2023)

[20] Box G E P and Jenkins G M 1976 *Time Series Analysis: Forecasting and Control* (San Francisco, CA: Holden-Day) https://doi.org/10.1002/9781118619193

[21] Taylor S J and Letham B 2018 Forecasting at scale *Am. Stat.* **72** 37–45

[22] Time series/date functionality *pandas 2.0.0 documentation* https://pandas.pydata.org/pandas-docs/stable/user_guide/timeseries.html#timeseries-offset-aliases (Accessed 2023)

[23] Lipton Z C, Berkowitz J and Elkan C 2015 A critical review of recurrent neural networks for sequence learning arXiv preprint (arXiv:1506.00019)

[24] Salehinejad H, Sankar S, Barfett J, Colak E and Valaee S 2017 Recent advances in recurrent neural networks arXiv preprint (arXiv:1801.01078)

[25] Karpathy A and Fei-Fei L 2015 Deep visual-semantic alignments for generating image descriptions *Proc. IEEE Conf. on Computer Vision and Pattern Recognition* pp 3128–37

[26] Amidi A and Amidi S 2019 Recurrent neural networks cheatsheet *Standford* https://stanford.edu/~shervine/teaching/cs-230/cheatsheet-recurrent-neural-networks (Accessed 2023)

[27] Hochreiter S and Schmidhuber J 1997 Long short-term memory *Neural Comput.* **9** 1735–80

[28] Wikipedia 2022 Recurrent neural network *Wikipedia* https://en.wikipedia.org/wiki/Recurrent_neural_network (Accessed 10 April 2023)

[29] Cho K, Van Merriënboer B, Gulcehre C, Bahdanau D, Bougares F, Schwenk H and Bengio Y 2014 Learning phrase representations using RNN encoder–decoder for statistical machine translation arXiv preprint (arXiv:1406.1078)

[30] Bondy J A and Siva Ramachandra Murty U *et al* 1976 *Graph Theory with Applications* vol 290 (London: Macmillan)

[31] West D B *et al* 2001 *Introduction to Graph Theory* vol 2 (Upper Saddle River, NJ: Prentice-Hall)

[32] Spielman D A 2007 Spectral graph theory and its applications *48th Annual IEEE Symp. on Foundations of Computer Science (FOCS'07)* (Piscataway, NJ: IEEE) pp 29–38

[33] Biggs N, Biggs N L and Norman B 1993 *Algebraic Graph Theory* Number 67 (Cambridge: Cambridge University Press)

[34] Zhou J, Cui G, Hu S, Zhang Z, Yang C, Liu Z, Wang L, Li C and Sun M 2020 Graph neural networks: a review of methods and applications *AI Open* **1** 57–81

[35] Stamile C, Marzullo A and Deusebio E 2021 *Graph Machine Learning: Take Graph Data to the Next Level by Applying Machine Learning Techniques and Algorithms* (Birmingham: Packt)

[36] Wu L, Cui P, Pei J, Zhao L and Song L 2022 *Graph Neural Networks* (Berlin: Springer) https://doi.org/10.1007/978-981-16-6054-2_3

[37] Agrawal R and de Alfaro L 2019 Learning edge properties in graphs from path aggregations *The World Wide Web Conference* (Washington, DC: AAAI) pp 2684–90

[38] Catasta M 2022 The graph connection *Nat. Mach. Intell.* **4** 187–8

[39] Sun M, Zhao S, Gilvary C, Elemento O, Zhou J and Wang F 2020 Graph convolutional networks for computational drug development and discovery *Brief. Bioinform.* **21** 919–35

[40] Gaudelet T *et al* 2021 Utilizing graph machine learning within drug discovery and development *Brief. Bioinform.* **22** bbab159

[41] Stokes J M *et al* 2020 A deep learning approach to antibiotic discovery *Cell* **180** 688–702

[42] Trinajstic N 2018 *Chemical Graph Theory* (Milton Park: Routledge)

[43] Raeisi S 2022 Machinelearning_physics *GitHub* https://github.com/sraeisi/MachineLearning_Physics (Accessed 2023)

Part II

Unsupervised learning

IOP Publishing

Machine Learning for Physicists
A hands-on approach
Sadegh Raeisi and Sedighe Raeisi

Chapter 6

Unsupervised learning

Unsupervised techniques are another category of machine learning techniques. Unsupervised learning refers to a wide category of methods that are designed to work with and extract patterns from unlabeled datasets. This makes it one of the most important types of machine learning because most datasets are not labeled. Here we review some of the unsupervised techniques.

Up to this point we have focused on problems where we have access to labeled data. However, in reality data are not usually labeled. What that means is that we have a dataset with the feature matrix, X, but we do not know the labels of the samples.

Note that normally, when the data are collected they is not labeled automatically. The label is usually added in a separate process after the data are collected. For instance, for the Galaxy Zoo dataset, the images (the feature matrix) were collected through observations. However, the images do not automatically come with a label. For that, we need to get people to go through the images and label them manually [1]. As you can imagine, this is not easy. It takes a lot of time and it is an expensive process.

Usually labeling the data is expensive and in some cases it might be even impossible to label the data. There are different circumstances where the data cannot be labeled. A common case is when the data are too big. For example, some observatories or laboratories may collect millions or even billions of samples every day. It is not practically possible to label all of these data.

Exercise: Can you think of more examples of datasets that are hard to label?

This means that often our datasets are not labeled. What can we do with unlabeled data?

There is still a lot of information in a dataset that is not labeled. In this part of the book, we will review some techniques that are designed for unlabeled data. These kinds of tasks are referred to as 'unsupervised learning' [2, 3].

doi:10.1088/978-0-7503-4957-4ch6

Most of these techniques aim at finding patterns in the data without knowing the labels of the data. Depending on the specific task, we may be looking for different kinds of patterns.

There are different categories of unsupervised techniques. There are even different ways to categorize unsupervised techniques. For instance, one can divide these techniques into:

- *Unsupervised*: tasks that do not rely on labels [2, 3].
- *Semi-supervised*: tasks that use small labeled subsets of the data with a large amount of unlabeled data [4, 5].
- *Self-supervised*: tasks that automatically generate data from the input unlabeled data [6].

Sometimes these categorizations are not mutually exclusive.

In this part, we will mostly focus on unsupervised techniques. More specifically, we will cover:

- Clustering.
- Anomaly detection.
- Dimensionality reduction.

6.1 Clustering

Let us first obtain a sense of an unsupervised learning problem before moving on to the clustering problem.

Exercise: Look at the data in figure 6.1. Each sample has two features, $X1$, and $X2$.

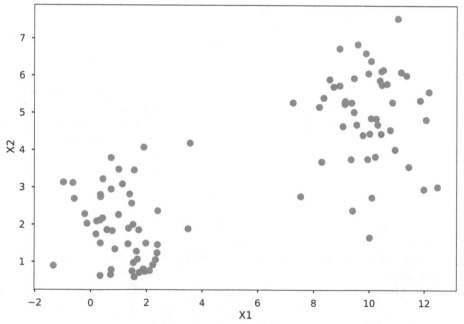

Figure 6.1. Some sample unlabeled data. Note that in contrast to the dataset that we saw in the previous chapters, the samples do not have distinctive colors. This is because they are not labeled. We only have the coordinates of each sample in the feature space.

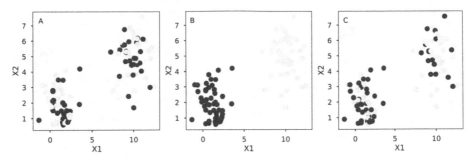

Figure 6.2. Which one seems more compatible for the proper labels of the samples in figure 6.1?

- How would you describe these data? What pattern(s) do you observe?
- The data are not labeled and that is why all the samples have the same color. If you were told that these data correspond to a binary classification (there are two classes), what would you guess the color of the samples to be? To make it easier, which of the options in figure 6.2 better fits your expectations?

You probably have picked option (B). This option probably provides a better classification in the sense that it clusters that sample into two linearly separable classes. However, this does not mean that the associated labels are real or correspond to anything meaningful. Note that we have not even specified what the problem is or what the features correspond to. Yet, (B) seems like to better fit. Why is that? Unconsciously, our brain is detecting a pattern, but what is this pattern? This is a 'clustering' [7–11]. Clustering is one of the most important types of unsupervised tasks and often one of the relatively easy patterns that can be detected in a dataset without labels.

In this section we plan to dive deeper into this concept and learn more about different types of clustering and what qualifies as a good clustering. Before we move forward, try to answer the following question.

Question: You probably have some intuition about clustering. Try to find a mathematical description/definition for clustering.

6.1.1 Mathematical definition

A clustering algorithm separates and puts samples in the dataset into different groups. We can define clustering as a function that assigns a group (or equivalently a group index) to each sample.

Definition: clustering
A function $\mathcal{F}_c$ that assigns a group to each sample (or its feature vector). In other words, it is a mapping from the feature vector of a sample to a group in the possible groups sets $\{g_1, g_2, \ldots, \}$.

Exercise: Which one of the following (figure 6.3) is a clustering? Different colors correspond to different clusters.

Exercise: Is there a unique clustering for the samples in figure 6.3?

Question: How many clusters do you see in the problem above?

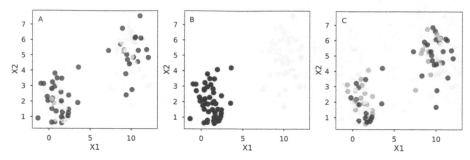

Figure 6.3. Which one(s) could be a clustering?

All three options provide a valid clustering. These do not necessarily provide meaningful or relevant clusterings. However, they still group all the samples into different clusters and, as such, meet the definition above.

Exercise: What makes a good clustering?

This is a difficult question to answer. It often depends on the specific problem and the domain information. We will investigate this question in more detail later.

Question: Make a clustering algorithm and test it on the data above. *Hint*: You can describe your algorithm by a pseudo-code or implement it in Python.

6.1.2 Different types of clustering

There are different ways to cluster given data [7–11]. Here we review some of the major attributes of a clustering and categorize these algorithms.

Number of clusters K
Some of the clustering algorithms need the number of clusters and the user should specify it. In contrast, some algorithms do not rely on the number of clusters as an input and can automatically find the number of clusters that matches the data.

For some problems, there may exist a natural number of clusters. For instance, imagine that you are collecting experimental data of measurements of bipartite quantum states. One natural clustering is based on entanglement, i.e. whether the state is entangled or not.

Question: Try to cluster the entanglement detection dataset, i.e. DTS-ED (table 1.2). *Hint*: ignore the labels and use only the feature vectors.

On the other hand, in some cases it is not possible to determine the number of clusters *a priori*. For instance, imagine that you want to cluster different hurricanes. Can you guess the number of clusters or determine your number of expected clusters?

In such cases, sometimes we may still set a number of clusters and use clustering algorithms that rely on the number of clusters. In the case of hurricanes, we may categorize them as mild, moderate, and severe.

The alternative is to use algorithms that do not need the 'number of clusters' as the input and let the clustering algorithm find the appropriate number of clusters.

Also, note that a dataset may be clustered based on different objectives. This means that the same dataset may be clustered with different values for the number of clusters.

Soft versus hard clustering

For some clustering problems, each sample is expected to fall into a specific cluster. For example, for the entanglement classification dataset above, each quantum state is either entangled or not. There are, however, other examples, for which it is not as easy to assign a category to each sample. For the example of hurricanes, a sample may fall between moderate and severe. In such cases, it is more fitting to assign a probability to each sample belonging to different categories.

This breaks clustering techniques into hard and soft [12]. Hard clustering algorithms are decisive and assign a unique cluster to a sample. In contrast, soft clustering algorithms do not necessarily assign a specific group to a sample and instead associate a probability to each sample for each cluster [12].

There are other ways to categorize clustering algorithms but these are two of the main categorizations. Moving forward, we will review some of the well-known clustering algorithms.

Hierarchical clustering

Hierarchical clustering refers to a family of clustering techniques that follows a hierarchical structure [13, 14]. This is one of the most basic approaches to clustering.

Here we focus on 'single linkage clustering' (SLC) which is one the more popular hierarchical clustering techniques [13–15]. These techniques are not used as widely as some of the other clustering algorithms, but they provide a simple and intuitive introduction to clustering algorithms.

Hierarchical clustering can be described as a greedy algorithm for clustering. It starts with assuming each sample is its own cluster. In each step it merges clusters that are closest to each other and reduces the number of clusters. It continues this process until it reaches the desired number of clusters [13–15]. Note that we need to specify the number of clusters, K.

Exercise: Apply the SLC algorithm to the data in figure 6.4 until you get to three clusters, $K = 3$.

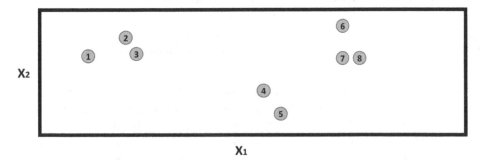

Figure 6.4. Apply the Hierarchical clustering algorithm to these data.

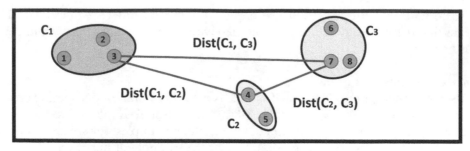

Figure 6.5. Distance between clusters. The red lines indicate the distance between clusters.

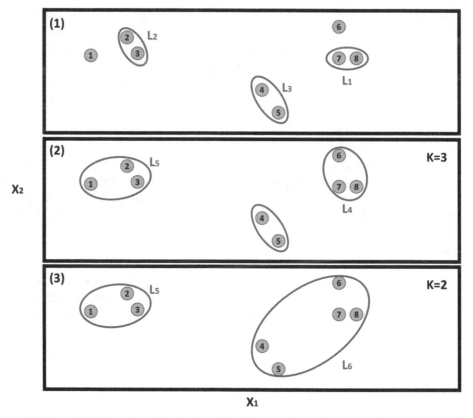

Figure 6.6. Hierarchical clustering with $K = 3$ and $K = 2$ for the data in figure 6.4. It shows how in each step clusters are merged together to make larger clusters. The second panel shows the result for $K = 3$ and the third panel shows the result for $K = 2$.

The distance between two clusters is defined as the distance between the closest samples of the two clusters. Figure 6.5 shows the result of hierarchical clustering for the data in figure 6.4. It also shows the distance between the clusters.

Exercise: For the example in figure 6.4, apply the algorithm above for $K = 3$ and for $K = 2$.

Figure 6.6 shows the solution. We use L_i to show the links and their order. As you can see, the first link connects samples 7 and 8 which are the closest to each other.

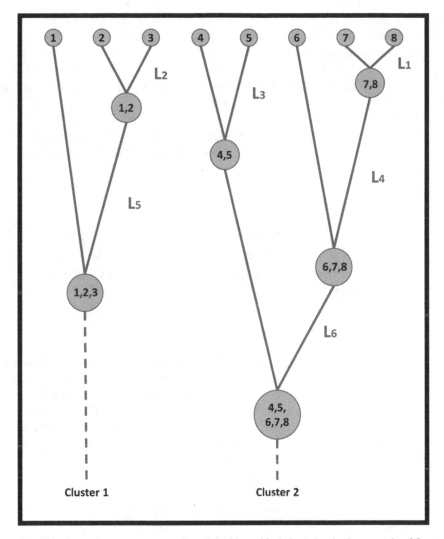

Figure 6.7. This shows the tree representation of the hierarchical clustering in the example of figure 6.4.

Similarly, L_2 and L_3 connect samples 2 and 3 and samples 4 and 5, respectively. At this point, we have five clusters, two of which consist of only single samples, and the other three have two samples each. The second panel (figure 6.6(2)) shows the process after making the next two links which lead to three clusters. So if $k = 3$, this is where we stop the algorithm. However, for $k = 2$, we need to go one step further and connect two of the clusters that are closest to each other. This is depicted in figure 6.6(3).

Hierarchical clustering creates a natural hierarchy or tree. Figure 6.7 shows this tree for the example in figure 6.4. This tree shows how clusters merge to make large clusters.

Question: Show that in hierarchical clustering, for k clusters, we need to make $n_s - k$ links. (*Hint*: this can be seen from the tree in figure 6.7.)

The hierarchical clustering algorithm above can be described by the pseudo-code in algorithm 3.

Exercise: Use the pseudo-code in algorithm 3 and implement the hierarchical clustering algorithms in Python.

Exercise: *Complexity*

Calculate the complexity of the hierarchical clustering. More precisely, estimate the number of mathematical operations needed to complete the algorithm.

Algorithm 3: Hierarchical clustering.

> **Data:** $1 < K \leq n_s$
> 1 **for** $n_{itr} = 1..n_s - k$ **do**
> 2 | Calculate the distance between all the clusters;
> 3 | Merge the two closest clusters into a new cluster;
> **end**

Let us start with the complexity of a single step. For each step we need to calculate the distance between all the clusters. For this we need the distance between all the points. For n_s samples, there are $O(n^2)$ distances to be calculated. This gives an estimate (upper bound) for the complexity of each step. The number of steps depends on the number of clusters and is $n_s - k$ (see the exercise above). This indicates that the complexity depends on the number of clusters. However, assuming that $n_s \gg k$, the complexity of the algorithm can be approximated as $O(n_s^3)$.

Exercise: *Deterministic or stochastic*

Is the hierarchical clustering algorithm a deterministic or stochastic algorithm? In other words, if we run the algorithm multiple times, does the algorithm always converge to the same set of clusters, or could the result change from one instance to the other?

As you can guess, this is a deterministic algorithm. The algorithm does not involve any random processes. Starting from a set of samples, the result only depends on the distances between the samples and would always lead to the same set of clusters. The reader is encouraged to run the algorithm a few times and check this for yourself.

As we mentioned at the beginning of this section, hierarchical clustering is not as popular as some of the algorithms that we will cover in this section. One of the reasons for this is the complexity of the algorithm. Another reason is that hierarchical clustering is more focused on individual distances and does not pay much attention to the geometry/topology of the clusters. As an example, look at the data in figure 6.8.

Exercise: Imagine that we want to cluster the samples in figure 6.8(A) in to $k = 2$ clusters:

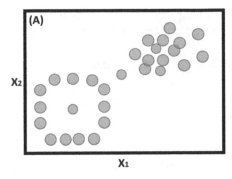 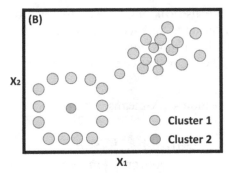

Figure 6.8. This figure shows one of the main weaknesses of the Hierarchical clustering algorithm. Panel (B) shows the result of the Hierarchical clustering which is not an intuitive clustering. The Hierarchical clustering algorithm only focuses on the distance between the points and cannot capture global patterns such as the geometry of the data points.

- Identify what makes sense to you for the two clusters.
- Identify what the hierarchical clustering leads to.

Hierarchical clustering, in this case, leads to a strange geometry for the clusters. This is because it only relies on the distances and not on the overall geometry of the clusters. This could lead to strange clusters with holes in the middle.

Another weakness of the hierarchical clustering is its sensitivity to noise and outliers. In the example of figure 6.4, if the middle point was removed the algorithm could converge to a more intuitive clustering.

There are different variations of the hierarchical clustering algorithm. We reviewed the SLC here [13, 14].

In the next section we will study a popular clustering algorithm that not only does not have the issues we discussed, but also is more efficient.

K-means clustering

K-means is one of the most popular and widely used clustering algorithms [16–18]. K-means assigns a center to each cluster, which intuitively, represents the center of mass of the cluster. The logic is that each sample belongs to the cluster with the closest center.

The idea seems intuitive and simple. However, the challenge is to find the centers. Note that for a given cluster, the center can be calculated easily. However, without knowing the clusters it is not obvious how to find the centers of the unknown clusters.

K-means takes an iterative approach to this [18]. Initially, it takes the number of input clusters, K, and randomly assigns the centers of the K clusters. Then it starts iterating.

Each iteration has two steps. First, all the samples are assigned the clusters with the closest center. Next, the cluster centers are updated [18].

We use $\{m_1, m_2,\ldots, m_K\}$ to refer to the cluster centers. In each iteration, the clustering is updated and so are the centers of the clusters. To start, the centers are initialized randomly.

The algorithm can be described by the following pseudo-code.

Algorithm 4: K-means.

> **Data:** $1 < K \leq n_s$
> 1 The centers, $\{m_1, m_2, \cdots, m_K\}$ are randomly assigned;
> 2 **repeat**
> 3   **for** s *in samples* **do**
> 4   Assign the cluster for s, i.e. $c^s = \arg\min_i \|X^s - m_i\|$;
>   **end**
> 5   **for** $i = 1$ *to* K **do**
> 6   Recalculate cluster centers, i.e. $m_i = \text{mean}\{X^s | c^s = i\}$;
>   **end**
> **until**;

Normally, we continue this until the algorithm converges. However, sometimes the stopping condition is set based on a preset number of iterations.

Exercise: Implement the K-means algorithm.

Let us go through one example to make this more clear. Figure 6.9 shows the first few iterations of K-means for $K = 2$ for a sample dataset.

Exercise: What happens if we re-do the K-means for the data in figure 6.9 but with three clusters?

Figure 6.10 shows how the K-means would iterate with three clusters.

Question: Prove that the K-means algorithm always converges.

Exercise: Does K-means always converge to the same clustering? Run your code for a dataset similar to the one here with $K = 10$ and check if your code always converges to the same results.

You probably noticed that it does not always converge to the same result. Why do you think that is?

The only stochastic step in the algorithm is the initial random assignment of the cluster centers. This can lead to different clusterings. An obvious variation is swapping the labels of the clusters. For instance, for $K = 2$, switching the random initial cluster centers would lead to switching the cluster labels. But it can be more than this. Consider the example in figure 6.11.

Exercise: How would you resolve the issue of variations of clustering due to random initializations?

As you probably have guessed, we can run the algorithm a few times and pick the best clustering. You may be wondering how to compare different clusterings and

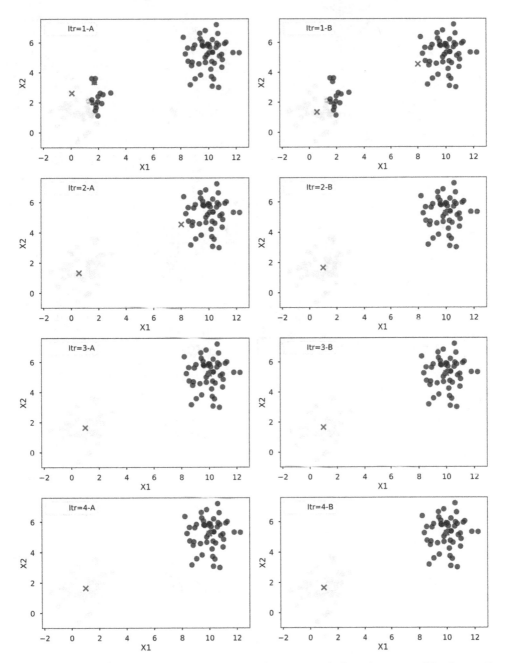

Figure 6.9. Iterations of K-means for a sample dataset. The red crosses indicate the centers of the clusters. For this case, $K = 2$, so there are two crosses. The clustering for the samples is identified by their colors. The plots in the first column indicated by A, show the first step of each K-means iteration where all the samples are clustered based on their proximity to cluster centers. The plots in the second column show the second step of each iteration where the cluster centers are recalculated. For the first one (Itr=1-A), the centers are randomly assigned and the samples are clustered (colored) based on the random centers. You can see that it is not a good clustering. But in the next step of the iteration, the centers are updated and start to approach the center of mass of the points of their cluster. After a few iterations, it converges and the centers stop moving.

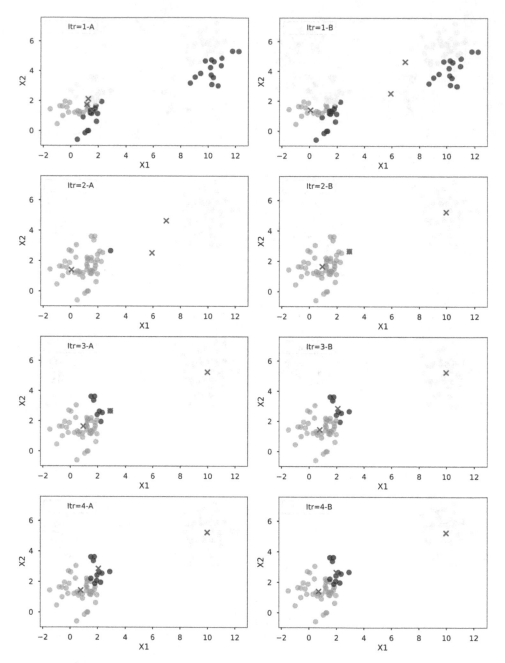

Figure 6.10. Iterations of *K*-means for a sample dataset with $K = 3$. This shows the *K*-means process for the same data as in figure 6.9 but with three clusters.

how to identify the best one. We will come back to this later. But for the case of *K*-means, it is possible to show that the objective is to minimize the overall distance between samples and their corresponding cluster centers. This means that the best clustering is the one that minimizes this objective.

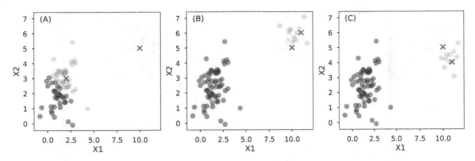

Figure 6.11. Different clustering of the same data. Different initializations for the centers could lead to different clusterings.

For K-means, it is important to specify the number of clusters as an input. K-means cannot automatically figure out the number of clusters. For any given data, you can apply K-means with different values of K. Each of them could provide a reasonable clustering for the number of clusters specified, but they are not necessarily a good clustering.

Exercise: What is the right number of clusters? How can we identify K?

One way to find the number of clusters is to use some domain knowledge from the application that the clustering is used for. We also may be able to use our intuition for determining the number of clusters. For instance, for the example in figure 6.9, visually, you probably would guess $K = 2$. The problem is that our visual intuition is usually limited to 2D or 3D data. In some cases, we can use dimensionality reduction techniques to reduce the data to 2D or 3D data and look for patterns visually.

An alternative approach is to try different values for K and choose the value that gives the best clustering. In other words, we can treat K as a hyper-parameter and fine-tune the model for it.

Exercise: Try K-means for the example in figure 6.8. Does K-means resolve the issue that the SLC had? (*Hint:* you do not need to write the code, just use a pen and follow the K-means procedure.)

Question: *Complexity*

Estimate the complexity of the K-means algorithm.

Soft clustering

Consider the distribution in figure 6.12. The red circle could potentially come from either of the two clusters. A hard clustering algorithm like K-means would assign the red sample to one of the two clusters. But in some cases it would be more informative to know that the red sample is as likely to belong to either of the clusters. In other words, it is more informative to assign a probability to the samples.

Soft clustering algorithms associate probability vectors to each sample where each probability corresponds to the sample belonging to the respective cluster [12]. In other words, for a clustering with k clusters, for a given sample x^i, we obtain

$$\{P(c(x^i) = 1), P(c(x^i) = 2),..., P(c(x^i) = k)\}.$$

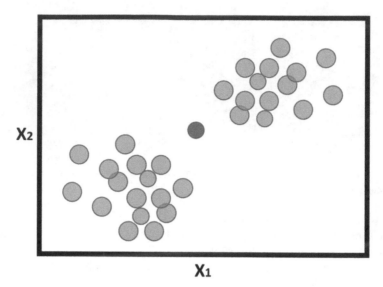

Figure 6.12. Schematic illustration of a situation where soft clustering could provide a better description of the data. There are two visibly distinct clusters. The sample indicated in red is as likely to belong to any of the two clusters.

These probabilities should add up to one for each sample. In the example above, for the red point, this probability would be close to 0.5 for each cluster.

Now the question is how to calculate these probabilities. Here we review a simple algorithm that is the probabilistic version of the K-means algorithm. It is known as 'expectation maximization' (EM) and was first introduced by Arthur Dempster, Nan Laird, and Donald Rubin in [19].

We assume that the samples of each cluster are distributed with a normal distribution. In other words, we are assuming that for each cluster, its samples make a Gaussian distribution around the center of the cluster.

Exercise: Consider the samples in figure 6.13(A). Which of the Gaussian clusterings describes the data better?

You probably picked the green one. But why does that make a good clustering? We will come back to this later when we talk about likelihood and likelihood maximization. But for now, it is enough to notice that the points fall closers to the center of the green curve. Remember that for Gaussian distribution, the probability of a sample being at distance d from the center of the Gaussian distribution scales as $e^{-\frac{d^2}{2\sigma}}$. Here we take $\sigma = 1$.

Exercise: Build an algorithm that finds the best clustering, i.e. a set of Gaussian distributions that are most likely to describe the distribution of the samples. (*Hint*: first, note that the Gaussian distribution is specified with two parameters, their center m_i and their standard deviation which we are assuming to be one. Second, try to use the iterative idea in the K-means algorithm to find the centers of the Gaussian distributions.)

The intuition of the EM algorithm is similar to the K-means algorithm. We start with a random set of cluster centers. Then we start iterating over updating the clustering and the cluster centers.

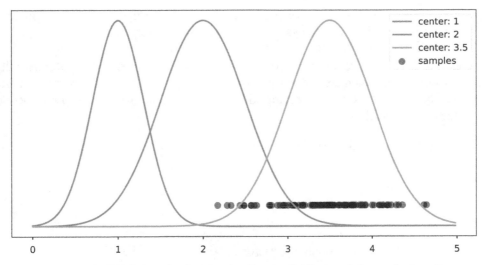

Figure 6.13. Which Gaussian function describes the distribution of the samples better?

The first difference with K-means is that, in each iteration, instead of assigning a unique cluster to each sample, we assign the probability of the sample belonging to each of the clusters. For this, we use the equation for the Gaussian distribution to find the probability for each sample. This associates K probabilities, i.e. the probability vector, to each sample.

We normalize the probability vectors, i.e. divide by the sum of the K probabilities. This vector specifies the probability with which the sample belongs to each cluster. However, since the centers are picked randomly, initially this is not going to give a good clustering. To improve this, we follow the K-means idea, i.e. update the cluster centers.

Note that for K-means, each sample belongs to a specific cluster, and for updating a cluster center, only the samples in that cluster are taken into account. For EM, each sample can be associated with all the clusters with some probability.

Exercise: How would you update the cluster centers?

For updating the cluster centers we take into account all the samples but with their corresponding probabilities. More specifically, for updating the center for cluster i, we calculate the weighted average of all the samples, where the weights are given by the probabilities of each sample belonging to cluster i. Mathematically that is

$$m_i' = \sum_j w_{i,j} x^j$$

$$w_{i,j} = \frac{P(x^j \in c_i)}{\sum_j P(x^j \in c_i)}, \qquad (6.1)$$

where m_i' represents the center of the ith cluster after the update. The weights are given by the probability of each sample belonging to cluster i. Note that we need to normalize the weights, hence the division by $\sum_j P(x^j \in c_i)$.

Next, we use the new centers to re-evaluate the probabilities for each sample and for the different clusters and then use the new probability vectors to calculate the cluster centers.

The algorithm involves repeating this iteration. The following pseudo-code describes the algorithm.

Algorithm 5: Expectation maximization (EM).

    Data: $1 < K \leq n_s$
1 $\{m_1, m_2, \cdots, m_K\}$ are randomly assigned;
2 **repeat**
3   **for** s *in samples* **do**
4   Evaluate the probability vector for the sample s, i.e.
          $p^s = [e^{-\frac{(X^s - m_i)^2}{2\sigma}}, i = 1, \cdots K]$;
    end
5   **for** $i = 1$ *to* K **do**
6   Recalculate cluster centers, i.e. $m_i' = \sum_j w_{i,j} x^j$ with $w_{i,j}$ as specified in
          Eq. 6.1;
    end
  until;

Figure 6.14 shows the animated process of EM in an example.

Exercise: Implement the EM algorithm.

It is possible to show that the EM algorithm tries to maximize the likelihood. More precisely, it is possible to show that the likelihood would either increase or stay the same in each iteration of the algorithm.

The EM algorithm converges for most problems. However, it is possible for the algorithm to get stuck. In fact, the algorithm converges to a point where the derivatives of the likelihood with respect to the Gaussian centers are zero. This means that it is possible for the algorithm to converge to a local minimum, maximum, or saddle point. In other words, the EM algorithm converges, but there is no guarantee that it would converge to the best possible clustering. For a detailed convergence analysis of the EM algorithm see [21].

In practice, the EM algorithm usually converges to a maximum, however, it may not necessarily be the global maximum. In other words, similar to the K-means, depending on the initial random centers, EM could end up with different clusterings.

For more details about the EM algorithm see [22–25]

DBSCAN clustering
Up to this point, all the clustering algorithms that we reviewed need the user to specify the number of clusters. Here we go over 'density-based spatial clustering of

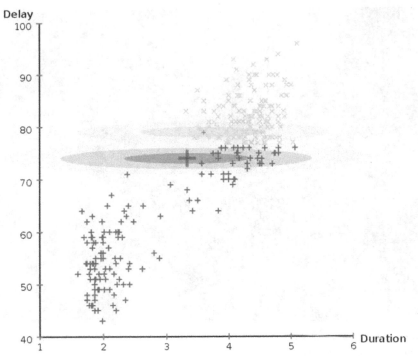

Figure 6.14. Animated process of EM. (Image credit: Chire, from Wikipedia [20]. CC BY-SA 3.0.)

applications with noise (DBSCAN)' which automatically clusters the dataset into the number of clusters that best fits the data [26–28].

DBSCAN goes over the samples and identifies where there is a high density of samples and clusters them together.

As suggested by the name, the algorithm assumes that the samples are distributed spatially and we can attribute density to the distribution of the points. In practice, the algorithm works for a wide range of problems and datasets, even when the features are not spatial features.

Exercise: Design an algorithm that uses the density of samples in the dataset to cluster them.

You probably noticed that we need to define a local measure of density first. The global density would be a fixed number (given by the total number of samples divided by the total volume) and is not going to be helpful for clustering.

We need to define a local density. The intuition is that the clusters are regions or clouds where the density is locally high.

Figure 6.15 shows a satellite image of North America at night. Can you identify where the cities are located? Think about what inspires your intuition.

There are different ways to define a local density. For the DBSCAN algorithm, we are going to use a smart idea that does not directly calculate the local density but rather measures the number of neighbors that each sample has.

For each sample, we look into its vicinity to see if the number of samples in its neighborhood is above some threshold. This defines a high-density region.

Figure 6.15. Satellite image of North America at night. Cities can be identified by the local density of light. (Image credit: https://unsplash.com/@nasa on https://unsplash.com/.)

Samples ⚬ Core Samples ● $N_c = 4$	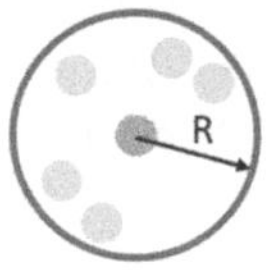	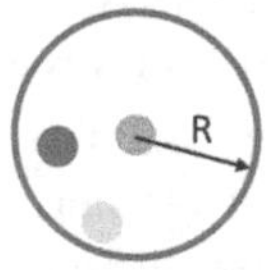	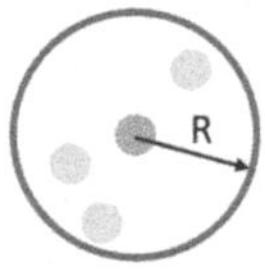
# Neighbors	N = 5	N = 2	N = 3
Does it have a core neighbor?	NA	Yes	No
Type	Core Point	Border Point	Noise Point

Figure 6.16. Different types of samples from the point of view of the DBSCAN algorithm.

For this, the DBSCAN algorithm needs two input parameters, the neighborhood radius, R, and the density threshold N_c. Using these two parameters, we can put the samples into three categories:

- *Core points*: Samples that have more than N_c neighbors in their R distance. These are the samples that identify a local high-density region. See figure 6.16(b) for a schematic example.

- *Border points*: Samples that are not core points (i.e. have less than N_c samples in their R neighborhood), but have at least one core point in their R neighborhood. See figure 6.16(c) for a schematic example.
- *Outliers or noise points*: Samples that are not core points (i.e. have less than N_c samples in their R neighborhood), and do not have any core points in their R neighborhood. See figure 6.16(d) for a schematic example.

Exercise: Using the categories of points defined above, design a clustering algorithm.

The algorithm starts by going over all the points and identifying which category they belong to. Next, we pick a random core point and assign it to the first cluster, i.e. c_1. Then we go over all of its neighbors and assign them to the same cluster. Some of these points are core points. We do the same thing for those core points that are neighbors with the initial points. We keep doing this until we cover all the points that either directly or indirectly are connected to the original core point.

Next, we check if there are more core points left. If there is, we pick one of them at random, cluster it as c_2 and repeat the process. This makes our second cluster.

We continue this until all the core points and their corresponding border points are clustered.

The outlier or noise points are not assigned a cluster and are treated as outliers. This is one of the advantages of DBSCAN. It does not force samples to be in a cluster and if a sample is far from all the clusters, it will be labeled as an outlier.

Another advantage of the DBSCAN algorithm is that it can capture clusters of strange shapes. Note that algorithms like the K-means base their clustering on the distance from the center of the cluster. While this could work well for clusters that are distributed spherically, it may not be as effective when the clusters have non-spherical shapes.

While DBSCAN does not take the number of clusters as an input, it still needs two input parameters. This may still be advantageous compared to getting the number of clusters as the input. This is because for a lot of practical applications, the neighborhood radius, R, and density threshold N_c can be specified based on domain knowledge of the problem. For instance, for a lot of physical problems, interactions decay with the distance and a scale for the neighborhood radius can be specified based on the range of the interactions. Similarly, often physical problems have some scale of critical mass or density that can be used as a threshold for DBSCAN.

This also suggests that DBSCAN is more powerful when there is a spatial distribution of the samples in some sense. Physical scales for mass or distance are more common for spatially distributed samples.

Question: Implement the DBSCAN algorithm. It may help to start with building the pseudo-code first.

6.1.3 Evaluation of a clustering algorithm

This is one of the main challenges with clustering, i.e. evaluating the result of a clustering algorithm. In the case of supervised algorithms we have the ground truth and there are a variety of metrics (e.g. the accuracy of the classification) that can be used for the evaluation of the performance of the models.

Exercise: Can we calculate a measure of accuracy for clustering? Take any of the examples in this chapter and try to measure the accuracy for them.

You probably have realized what the problem is. For the calculation of the accuracy of most of the metrics that we reviewed so far, we need to have ground truth values. But for an unsupervised problem, the samples do not have labels.

A metric such as accuracy is not even well-defined in this context. Let us think about a specific example. Assume that we have a dataset containing the records of the students at a university. Two different clustering algorithms may result in partitioning the data in two distinct yet accurate ways. For instance, one clustering may lead to a partitioning based on the performance of students. Another algorithm may result in a partitioning based on involvement in extracurricular activities. Both clusterings could be reasonable and accurate, but with respect to different objectives. In fact, the lack of ground truth makes clustering extremely subjective and application-specific.

With all of these, how would we characterize a good clustering? How can we evaluate the performance of a clustering algorithm or compare two different clustering algorithms?

Here we review two major approaches for the evaluation of the clustering.

Extrinsic measures for clustering

The first approach is to define an objective and evaluate the clustering with respect to that [29]. For the example of clustering students based on their records, we can specify the downstream task to be the categorization of the students based on their performance. You probably are wondering how this would go around the issue of the lack of ground truth. It does not, but it makes it easier to evaluate the performance of the clustering algorithm. It is often possible to manually label some random subsamples with respect to a defined objective and use that labeled subsample to calculate a measure of accuracy for the clustering algorithm.

In some cases, it is also possible to define a downstream task, where it is easier to label the samples. For instance, imagine that you are given a weather condition dataset. *A priori*, it is not clear what the clustering would lead to and what the clusters would correspond to. However, assume that we are interested in finding a clustering that is informative about the traffic. It is relatively easy to obtain the traffic data and label the samples. This can help us try different clusterings and see which one better correlates with the traffic. This helps tune the clustering toward a downstream task such as the traffic condition.

This further emphasizes that clustering is not objective. You can look at the same data for two different applications or downstream tasks and get two different notions of what good clustering means.

Some of the more popular extrinsic measures for clustering are the adjusted Rand index [30], mutual information-based scores [31], homogeneity [32], and V-measure [32]. The reader is encouraged to look up these metrics [29].

Intrinsic measures for clustering

Another approach for the evaluation of clustering is based on how we expect clusters to look.

To better understand this, let us do an exercise.

Exercise: In figure 6.17, which one is a better clustering and why?

Exercise: How would you characterize the quality of a clustering? Use your intuition from the previous exercise to define the objective you used for evaluating the clusterings.

The intuitive expectation is that, for good clustering, the samples in each cluster should be close to each other, and that clusters should be well-separated. Let us see how we can express these expectations mathematically.

The expectations above indicate that there are two important aspects of the evaluation of a clustering. First is the 'intercluster distance' which is the average distance of samples in the same cluster. Second is the 'intracluster distance' which is the average distance between the samples from different clusters.

There are different ways to characterize the intercluster distance and the intra-cluster distance. Here for simplicity, we use

$$d_{\text{in}} = \frac{1}{K} \sum_c \frac{1}{n_c} \sum_{i,j \in c} \sqrt{\sum_l \| x_l^{(i)} - x_l^{(j)} \|^2},$$

$$d_{\text{out}} = \frac{1}{K} \sum_c \frac{1}{n_c} \sum_{\substack{i \in c, \\ j \in c' \neq c}} \sqrt{\sum_l \| x_l^{(i)} - x_l^{(j)} \|^2},$$

(6.2)

where K is the number of clusters and n_c is the number of samples in cluster c. The inner sum goes over all the samples in cluster c. For d_{in} it measures the distance between points within that cluster and for d_{out} it measures the distance between each point in cluster c to points in other clusters. This gives an average intercluster distance and the intracluster distance for cluster c. The outer sum averages these distances over all clusters.

Finally, we need to merge these two distances into one quantity. There are different ways to do this. A common approach is to use the following:

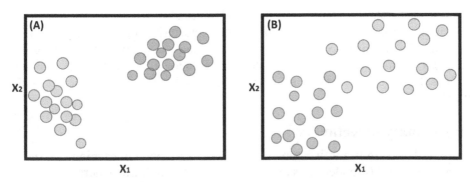

Figure 6.17. Which one is a better clustering?

$$s = \frac{d_{\text{out}} - d_{\text{in}}}{d_{\text{out}} + d_{\text{in}}}. \qquad (6.3)$$

This quantity is known as the 'silhouette metric' [33, 34]. The denominator is to normalize the quantity. Ideally, $d_{\text{out}} \gg d_{\text{in}}$ which leads to $s = 1$. But in principle, for a bad clustering, the silhouette metric can even become negative. Mathematically, $s \in [-1, 1]$.

The silhouette metric is one of the more well-known metrics for clustering. It is also possible to use different combinations of d_{out} and d_{in}. In fact, for the case of K-means, it is possible to show that the algorithm is minimizing d_{in}. There are also other metrics such as the Calinski–Harabasz index [35] and Davies–Bouldin index [36] that we will not get into.

Also note that sometimes, it is not possible to find any ideal clustering for the data. The samples may be scattered all over the feature space. Also, when the size of the data is too small or/and the data are too high dimensional, the distribution of the data in the feature space becomes sparse. Mathematically, in such situations d_{in} becomes too big and comparable to d_{out}. This means that you cannot expect to always be able to find a good clustering for your data.

6.1.4 Comparison of different clustering techniques

Figure 6.18 compares the algorithms that we have discussed here. You can see when and under what conditions each algorithm is performing well.

6.1.5 Implementation of clustering algorithms

The implementation of clustering in scikit-learn is similar to the implementation for supervised models. More specifically, it starts with constructing an object of the type of the clustering class. Then we use the 'fit' method to train the object which builds the clusters. Listing 6.1 shows a code snippet for implementing K-means and DBSCAN.

Note that the fit method only takes one input, i.e. the feature matrix. Remember that we do not have the labels for a clustering problem. After fitting the object, it generates the set of labels for the samples in the input. This can be accessed using 'labels_'.

For some clustering algorithms, it is possible to get predictions for new samples. Prediction is not necessarily meaningful for a clustering task. However, for some clustering algorithms it might be possible to extend predictions for new and unseen samples. For instance, in the case of the K-means, for a new sample it is possible to evaluate the distance from all the cluster centers and assign the sample to the cluster with the closest center.

6.2 Anomaly detection

Anomaly detection is another type of unsupervised machine learning. As the name suggests, the goal is to identify samples that do not match the general pattern of the samples [38, 39].

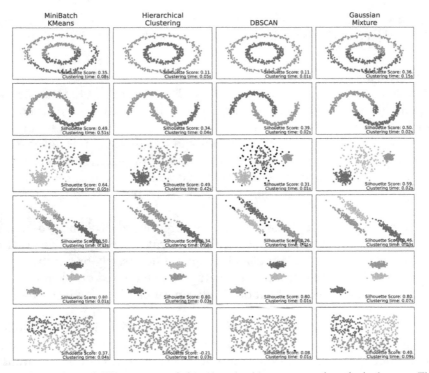

Figure 6.18. Comparison of different types of clustering algorithms on several synthetic datasets. The rows correspond to different datasets. Here we are generating the datasets based on different distributions. Columns represent clustering from different clustering techniques. The value of the silhouette metric and the clustering time are also included for each clustering. These are generated based on a code from the scikit-learn tutorials. (Image credit: scikit-learn library [37].)

```
1 from sklearn.cluster import KMeans
2 kmeans =  KMeans(n_clusters=3)
3 kmeans.fit(X)
4 Y_clstr = kmeans.predict(X)
5
6 %-----------------------------
7
8 from sklearn.mixture import GaussianMixture
9
10 gm = GaussianMixture( n_components=3 )
11 gm.fit(X)
```

Listing 6.1. Clustering.

Here we give a brief introduction to anomaly detection. It helps to start the discussions with some examples of some of the applications of anomaly detection. This provides some context for the problem statement. Then we will introduce one of the basic algorithms for anomaly detection.

Exercise: Can you think of any examples for the applications of anomaly detection?

Anomaly detection has a wide range of applications in fraud detection [40], fault detection [41], and cyber-security [42] among other things [38, 39]. Let us review an example.

Fraud detection

Imagine that you are a credit card company. The majority of the transactions are normal in the sense that they are done by your customers. However, there is usually a small portion of fraudulent transactions. It is important to identify and stop these fraudulent transactions. But how can you do that? It is not easy to label these transactions. You can try to label a subset of your data. But even if we assume that 0.1% of the transactions are fraudulent, we need to manually process over 10^6 transactions to obtain only 10^3 fraudulent samples. And this still is a small sample.

Additionally, these fraudulent transactions are always evolving. So even if you make a labeled dataset, it would only be able to catch the transactions that match the type of fraud it has seen before and would not necessarily be effective for a new kind of fraud. As you can see, this is a natural unsupervised problem.

What can we do in such a situation? How can we identify fraudulent transactions without a labeled dataset?

Normally, we become suspicious of a transaction when it does not follow the normal patterns or routines of a customer. For instance, if you live in the city of Istanbul, your transactions are normally in that city and if there is a transaction from your account in Berlin, it falls out of the normal pattern.

Exercise: Can you think of other ways that transactions can fall out of the pattern?

Question: Review the entanglement detection problem. Find a representation of the problem based on anomaly detection.

Question: Imagine that you want to build a model to detect if a patient has a sleep disorder from their EEG signal. Describe how anomaly detection can be used for this purpose.

6.2.1 Algorithms for anomaly detection

Exercise: In figure 6.19, identify the samples that you think are anomalous.

Think about your approach to this problem. You probably recognized that there is a central cluster and there are points that fall into the cluster. Every point that does not fall into the cluster is identified as an anomaly.

Exercise: Turn your intuition above into an algorithm. Note that the solution is not unique and there are many different ways to do this.

One simple example is to fit a Gaussian distribution to the data. This can be done using techniques such as likelihood maximization. Then we can assign a probability to each point (sample). If a probability is too low, it indicates that it is unlikely for that sample to come from the main distribution and is probably anomalous.

We can define a threshold such that if the corresponding probability falls below that threshold, the sample would be identified as an anomaly.

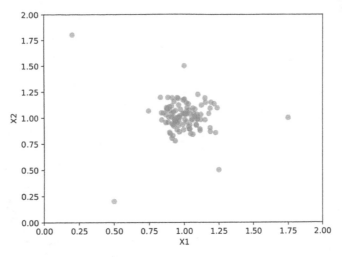

Figure 6.19. Example for anomaly detection: identify the samples that are anomalous.

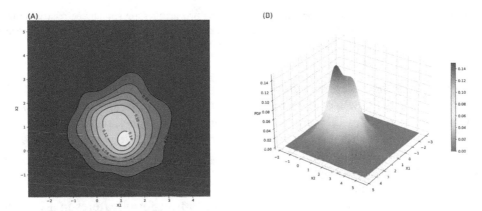

Figure 6.20. Samples from the figure 6.19 in a schematic contour plot. The counters indicate the likelihood of the points in the region of the feature space belonging to the Gaussian distribution that the samples are drawn from.

Figure 6.20 shows the samples in figure 6.19 in a contour plot. As expected, the samples that fall too far from the center of the Gaussian distribution would be associated with a small probability and are identified as anomalies.

Some clustering algorithms allow for anomaly detection as well. For instance, if you recall, the DBSCAN algorithm can detect outliers automatically. Some of the other algorithms may be modified to allow for the detection of outlier samples.

6.3 Dimensionality reduction

We already talked about dimensionality reduction when we were covering preprocessing techniques in chapter 3, but it is helpful to revisit this in the context of unsupervised machine learning.

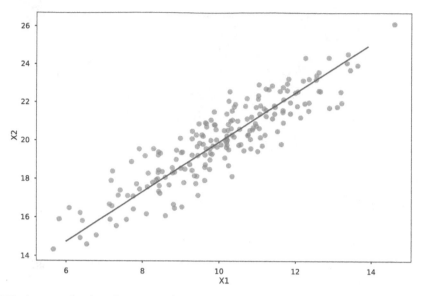

Figure 6.21. An example where features can be reduced. The two features are strongly correlated. In other words, by knowing one feature, it is possible to estimate the other feature with accuracy. In this case, keeping both features does not help any more than having one of them. So we can remove one of the two.

If you recall there were two classes of dimensionality reduction techniques. One approach uses the labels of the samples and reduces the dimension based on how informative or relevant they are toward the prediction of the labels.

The other approach relies only on the feature matrix and does not use labels. For instance, if there is a constant feature, i.e. a feature with no variance or small variance, it makes sense to ignore that feature as it is the same for all the samples and is not going to be helpful.

We also learned that sometimes it is possible to transform features in a way that the transformed features can be reduced. For instance, if two features are fully correlated, we do not need both of them. Figure 6.21 shows an example of such a situation.

As you can see, in such cases we do not need labels for dimensionality reduction.

We reviewed some of these techniques in chapter 3, including linear methods such as PCA and non-linear methods such as manifold learning.

There are other (arguably more sophisticated) unsupervised techniques that can be used for data reduction and feature engineering. Here we will review 'autoencoders' [43–45] and explain how they can be used for finding reduced representations of the input data.

Let us revisit the problem of dimensionality reduction, but let us try to use NNs to approach this problem.

Exercise: Try to design an NN for dimensionality reduction. Remember that our data are not labeled.

6.3.1 Auto-encoders

The main challenge that you probably faced for the exercise above is that we are dealing with unlabeled data. However, if you think carefully, you realize that for a dimensionality reduction task, we do have labels.

Exercise: What can we use as labels for a dimensionality reduction problem?

What is the goal of a dimensionality task? We are starting with our representation of the samples and want to map them to a reduced representation. This can always be done. What makes this task non-trivial is that we should be able to retrieve the original data from the reduced representation, at least to a good approximation. In other words, we should be able to both map the data into the reduced representation and reconstruct our samples from their reduced versions. Now can you guess how we can turn this into a supervised task?

We can use the data (i.e. X), both for the input and for the labels. This is because we want to be able to retrieve the inputs at the output (at least approximately).

Now that we have both the input and output, we just need one more idea to build an NN for dimensionality reduction.

Exercise: How would you design the architecture of the NN to find a reduced representation of input data? Note that we have a network that starts with the feature matrix and ends with the feature matrix.

The key is to make the NN compress the inputs in one of the hidden layers to fewer nodes and then recreate the inputs at the output. Figure 6.22 shows this idea schematically. We create a bottleneck in the middle of the network and then reproduce the input in the output layer. The objective is for the outputs to be as close to the input as possible.

This is called an 'autoencoder network' [43–45]. The first part of the network maps the inputs to the reduced representation and is referred to as the 'encoder'. The second part of the network retrieves the data from the compressed and reduced representation and is called the 'decoder' [43–45].

When the model is trained, the nodes in the bottleneck are pushed to learn or extract a representation of the input data that would be enough to reproduce the input again with the decoder.

For reducing the dimension of the data, the encoder part of the network is applied to the input data. Also, given the reduced representation of a sample, the decoder part of the network can be applied to it to reproduce the sample in the original space. Although for a typical dimensionality reduction task, we probably do not want to decode the reduced representation and instead may use the representation for other applications such as data visualization or training models using the reduced representation.

You can see that the complexity (the number of trainable layers/parameters) can grow fast in autoencoders. One way to control the complexity is to share the trainable parameters between the encoder and the decoder. This is known as an autoencoder with tied weights. Specifically, for an autoencoder with tied weights, the weights used for the decoder are the transposition of the weights for the encoder. This makes the network symmetric and reduces the number of parameters.

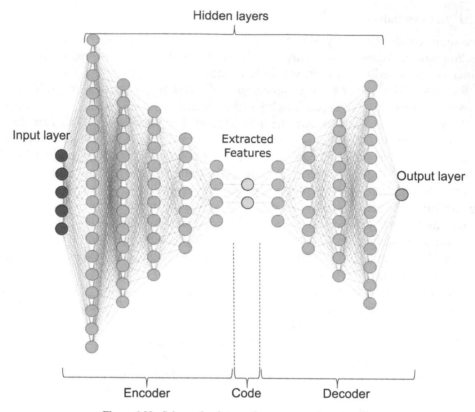

Figure 6.22. Schematic picture of an autoencoder network.

Question: Take the dataset of the hand-written images:

- Find a reduced representation of them using an autoencoder network.
- Retry the task above with an autoencoder with tied weights. How does this affect the training?
- Re-do the task above but design an autoencoder with a CNN architecture. Then try to see if you can use a pre-trained model to facilitate the training.

Exercise: *Linear autoencoder*

What happens if we remove the activation functions in an autoencoder network? Remember that for an NN without activation functions, the middle layers may be removed. In the case of an autoencoder, this means that there will be only one hidden layer which is the bottleneck. In fact, we can even get rid of this layer and map the input to itself. However, with the autoencoder architecture, the network is forced to find a linear encoder and decoder. In other words, the autoencoder is trained to find a reduced representation that is a linear transformation of the inputs.

You may be wondering how this is related to PCA. In fact, this is really close to PCA, although it would not be exactly the same. The linear transformation that is applied for PCA can be described as a linear autoencoder network. The matrix that represents the transformation of the PCA can be used for the values of the weights of the encoder. Similarly, the decoder can be specified based on the PCA transformation.

In this sense, autoencoders can be seen as a non-linear generalization of the PCA algorithm [43]. The advantage is that we can systematically add non-linearity (and complexity) by increasing the depth of the network and finding complex maps for reducing the feature space.

Question: *PCA versus autoencoders*

For the previous question, try to find a reduced representation using PCA. How effective is this? What do you learn from this?

You may be wondering how autoencoders compare to manifold learning algorithms. There are two points we should consider here. First, autoencoders provide a scalable way to increase the complexity of reduced features. Second, autoencoders are normally faster to train compared to most manifold learning transformations. You are encouraged to test the t-distributed stochastic neighbor embedding (TSNE) technique and compare the speed to an autoencoder for some of the examples in this book.

The applications of autoencoder networks are not limited to dimensionality reduction. There are different variations of autoencoders [45, 46]. We will not cover all of these applications, but we will review denoising autoencoder networks briefly [46–48].

In contrast to the architecture in figure 6.22, with a denoising autoencoder the middle layer can have more nodes than the input features.

For a reconstruction task this will become trivial as the middle layer has enough nodes to memorize the input nodes.

Exercise: If the number of nodes in the middle layer is more than the input features, propose a network (with explicit values for the weights) to reconstruct the input samples in the out of the network.

First, note that the network does not need any non-linearity. All it needs is to preserve the exact values of the input features on a subset of the nodes for the middle layer and then pass them to the output.

To do this, we can set the weights as

$$W_{i,j} = \begin{cases} 1, & \text{if } i = j, \\ 0 & \text{otherwise.} \end{cases}$$

Exercise: If the middle layer has more nodes than the input, what is useful for?

We can use this architecture to learn a representation of the input that is robust to noise and use it for denoising the samples.

For instance, imagine that we add some Gaussian noise to the input features or randomly set some of the features to zero. Clearly, if the network only memorizes the input features, it is not going to be able to reconstruct the samples.

However, the information on the missing or noisy features may be retrieved (at least partially) from the other features of the sample. If we add the noise while we are training the network, the middle layer is forced to learn a representation that is more robust to the noise. This means that if the network is given a noisy sample, it would be able to provide a less noisy reconstruction. In fact, it learns to rely more on the collection of the features and less on the individual features that may be affected by the noise.

Also, note that the extracted representation is only robust for the noise that is considered for training. If the noise model changes, it may not be as effective.

Historically, autoencoders were proposed in [43], although there were similar ideas in [49, 50]. However, except for the linear case, there was not much progress in their practical applications until [51]. This is because the performance of training autoencoders was relatively poor. This changed when, in 2006, Hinton and Salakhutdinov proposed the idea of pretraining the autoencoders [51]. They used a construct known as the restricted Boltzmann machine (RBM) for initializing the weights of an autoencoder. RBMs are another class of unsupervised techniques that can be used both for dimensionality reduction and generative models [52–55]. We will cover RBMs when we encounter the generative algorithms.

6.4 Summary

In this chapter, unsupervised machine learning was reviewed. These are techniques that deal with unlabeled data. Considering that the vast majority of the available data are not labeled, these techniques are very important for making good use of our available data.

We reviewed clustering techniques, anomaly detection, and dimensionality reduction in this chapter.

In the next chapter, we will study generative machine learning. We categorize generative models under unsupervised techniques as they work with unlabeled data, but they are sometimes categorized differently.

References

[1] Willett K W *et al* 2013 Galaxy Zoo 2: detailed morphological classifications for 304 122 galaxies from the Sloan Digital Sky Survey *Mon. Not. R. Astron. Soc.* **435** 2835–60

[2] Patel A A 2019 *Hands-On Unsupervised Learning Using Python: How to Build Applied Machine Learning Solutions from Unlabeled Data* (Farnham: O'Reilly Media)

[3] Hiran K K, Jain R K, Lakhwani K and Doshi R 2021 *Machine Learning: Master Supervised and Unsupervised Learning Algorithms with Real Examples* (Noida: BPB Publications)

[4] Zhu X J 2005 Semi-supervised learning literature survey *Department of Computer Science, University of Wisconsin-Madison, Madison, WI* https://pages.cs.wisc.edu/~jerryzhu/pub/ssl_survey.pdf

[5] Padmanabha Reddy Y C A, Viswanath P and Eswara Reddy B 2018 Semi-supervised learning: a brief review *Int. J. Eng. Technol.* **7** 81

[6] Jaiswal A, Babu A R, Zadeh M Z, Banerjee D and Makedon F 2020 A survey on contrastive self-supervised learning *Technologies* **9** 2

[7] Mirkin B 1996 *Mathematical Classification and Clustering* (Berlin: Springer) **11**

[8] Rokach L and Maimon O 2005 *Clustering Methods* (Boston, MA: Springer) pp 321–52

[9] Rai P and Singh S 2010 A survey of clustering techniques *Int. J. Comput. Appl.* **7** 1–5

[10] Popat S K and Emmanuel M 2014 Review and comparative study of clustering techniques *Int. J. Comput. Sci. Inf. Technol.* **5** 805–12

[11] Saxena A, Prasad M, Gupta A, Bharill N, Patel O P, Tiwari A, Er M J, Ding W and Lin C-T 2017 A review of clustering techniques and developments *Neurocomputing* **267** 664–81

[12] Peizhuang W 1983 Pattern recognition with fuzzy objective function algorithms (James C Bezdek) *SIAM Rev.* **25** 442

[13] Murtagh F 1983 A survey of recent advances in hierarchical clustering algorithms *Comput. J.* **26** 354–9

[14] Murtagh F and Contreras P 2012 Algorithms for hierarchical clustering: an overview *Wiley Interdiscip. Rev. Data Min. Knowl. Discov.* **2** 86–97

[15] Sibson R 1973 SLINK: an optimally efficient algorithm for the single-link cluster method *Comput. J.* **16** 30–4

[16] Forgy E W 1965 Cluster analysis of multivariate data: efficiency versus interpretability of classifications *Biometrics* **21** 768–9

[17] Hartigan J A and Wong M A *et al* 1979 A k-means clustering algorithm *Appl. Stat.* **28** 100–8

[18] Steinley D 2006 K-means clustering: a half-century synthesis *Br. J. Math. Stat. Psychol.* **59** 1–34

[19] Dempster A P, Laird N M and Rubin D B 1977 Maximum likelihood from incomplete data via the EM algorithm *J. R. Stat. Soc.* B **39** 1–22

[20] Wikipedia 2022 Expectation-maximization algorithm *Wikipedia* https://en.wikipedia.org/wiki/Expectation%E2%80%93maximizationalgorithm

[21] Jeff Wu C F 1983 On the convergence properties of the em algorithm *Ann. Stat.* 95–103

[22] Sundberg R 1972 Maximum likelihood theory and applications for distributions generated when observing a function of an exponential family variable *PhD Thesis* University of Stockholm

[23] Meng X-L and Van Dyk D 1997 The EM algorithm—an old folk-song sung to a fast new tune *J. R. Stat. Soc.* B **59** 511–67

[24] Ng S K, Krishnan T and McLachlan G J 2012 The EM algorithm *Handbook of Computational Statistics: Concepts and Methods* (Berlin: Springer) pp 139–72

[25] Gupta M R and Chen Y *et al* 2011 Theory and use of the EM algorithm *Found. Trends Signal Process.* **4** 223–96

[26] Ester M, Kriegel H-P, Sander J and Xu X 1996 A density-based algorithm for discovering clusters in large spatial databases with noise *Proc. 2nd Int. Conf. on Knowledge Discovery and Data Mining, KDD'96* (Washington, DC: AAAI) pp 226–31

[27] Khan K, Rehman S U, Aziz K, Fong S and Sarasvady S 2014 DBSCAN: past, present and future *5th Int. Conf. on the Applications of Digital Information and Web Technologies (ICADIWT'2014)* (Piscataway, NJ: IEEE) pp 232–8

[28] Schubert E, Sander J, Ester M, Kriegel H P and Xu X 2017 DBSCAN revisited, revisited: why and how you should (still) use DBSCAN *ACM Trans. Database Syst.* **42** 1–21

[29] Amigó E, Gonzalo J, Artiles J and Verdejo F 2009 A comparison of extrinsic clustering evaluation metrics based on formal constraints *Inf. Retr.* **12** 461–86

[30] Rand W M 1971 Objective criteria for the evaluation of clustering methods *J. Am. Stat. Assoc.* **66** 846–50

[31] Xu W, Liu X and Gong Y 2003 Document clustering based on non-negative matrix factorization *Proc. 26th Annual Int. ACM SIGIR Conf. on Research and Development in Information Retrieval* pp 267–73

[32] Rosenberg A and Hirschberg J 2007 V-measure: a conditional entropy-based external cluster evaluation measure *Proc. 2007 Joint Conf. on Empirical Methods in Natural Language Processing and Computational Natural Language Learning (EMNLP-CoNLL)* pp 410–20

[33] Rousseeuw P J 1987 Silhouettes: a graphical aid to the interpretation and validation of cluster analysis *J. Comput. Appl. Math.* **20** 53–65

[34] Dudek A 2020 Silhouette index as clustering evaluation tool *Studies in Classification, Data Analysis, and Knowledge Organization* (Cham: Springer) pp 19–33

[35] Caliński T and Harabasz J 1974 A dendrite method for cluster analysis *Commun. Stat.* **3** 1–27

[36] Davies D L and Bouldin D W 1979 A cluster separation measure *IEEE Trans. Pattern Anal. Mach. Intell.* **PAMI-1** 224–7

[37] scikit-learn user guide *skicit-learn* https://scikit-learn.org/stable/user_guide.html (Accessed 2023)

[38] Patcha A and Park J-M 2007 An overview of anomaly detection techniques: existing solutions and latest technological trends *Comput. Netw.* **51** 3448–70

[39] Chandola V, Banerjee A and Kumar V 2009 Anomaly detection: a survey *ACM Comput. Surv.* **41** 15

[40] Kou Y, Lu C-T, Sirwongwattana S and Huang Y-P 2004 Survey of fraud detection techniques *IEEE Int. Conf. on Networking, Sensing and Control* vol 2 (Piscataway, NJ: IEEE) pp 749–54

[41] Purarjomandlangrudi A, Ghapanchi A H and Esmalifalak M 2014 A data mining approach for fault diagnosis: an application of anomaly detection algorithm *Measurement* **55** 343–52

[42] Ahmed M, Mahmood A N and Hu J 2016 A survey of network anomaly detection techniques *J. Netw. Comput. Appl.* **60** 19–31

[43] Kramer M A 1991 Nonlinear principal component analysis using autoassociative neural networks *AIChE J.* **37** 233–43

[44] Kramer M A 1992 Autoassociative neural networks *Comput. Chem. Eng.* **16** 313–28

[45] Chen S and Guo W 2023 Auto-encoders in deep learning–a review with new perspectives *Mathematics* **11** 1777

[46] Goodfellow I, Bengio Y and Courville A 2016 *Deep Learning* (Cambridge, MA: MIT Press)

[47] Vincent P, Larochelle H, Lajoie I, Bengio Y, Manzagol P-A and Bottou L 2010 Stacked denoising autoencoders: learning useful representations in a deep network with a local denoising criterion *J. Mach. Learn. Res.* **11** 3371–408

[48] Wang W, Huang Y, Wang Y and Wang L 2014 Generalized autoencoder: A neural network framework for dimensionality reductionr *Proc. IEEE Conf. on Computer Vision and Pattern Recognition Workshops* pp 490–7

[49] Rumelhart D E, Hinton G E and Williams R J 1985 Learning internal representations by error propagation *Technical Report* La Jolla Institute for Cognitive Science, California University at San Diego

[50] Ballard D H 1987 Modular learning in neural networks *AAAI-87 Proc.* **647** 279–84

[51] Hinton G E and Salakhutdinov R R 2006 Reducing the dimensionality of data with neural networks *Science* **313** 504–7

[52] Smolensky P 1986 Information processing in dynamical systems: foundations of harmony theory *Technical Report* Department of Computer Science, Colorado University at Boulder

[53] Hinton G E 2012 A practical guide to training restricted Boltzmann machines *Neural Networks: Tricks of the Trade* (Berlin: Springer) 2nd edn pp 599–619

[54] Fischer A and Igel C 2012 An introduction to restricted Boltzmann machines *Proc. Progress in Pattern Recognition, Image Analysis, Computer Vision, and Alications: 17th Iberoamerican Congress (Buenos Aires, Argentina, 3–6 September)* (Berlin: Springer) pp 14–36

[55] Zhang N, Ding S, Zhang J and Xue Y 2018 An overview on restricted Boltzmann machines *Neurocomputing* **275** 1186–99

Chapter 7

Generative models

Generative models are an extremely powerful class of machine-learning models that has driven a lot of progress in this field over the past few years. Generative models are capable of 'being creative' and generating new paintings, pieces of music, and more. Here we review the generative models.

Imagine that you are given a dataset and you want to generate samples that match the pattern and structure of the samples in the dataset. A generative model is trained based on the samples in the dataset such that it can generate samples that mimic the samples in the training data.

An example of this is building models that would generate music or art. In physics, generative models have been used for a wide range of applications, including high-energy physics [1, 2] and quantum information science [3].

There are two approaches to building generative models [4]. One approach is to estimate the probability distribution function (PDF) of the samples in the dataset. If the probability distribution of the samples is known, new samples can be drawn from it and they would match the patterns of the samples in the dataset. We will review some basic examples including the maximum likelihood approach.

The second approach is to build models that can generate samples compatible with the samples in the dataset without actually learning the probability distribution. We will review a technique with this approach too.

Generative models fall between supervised and unsupervised techniques. They can be categorized as unsupervised because usually they do not require labeled data and work with unlabeled samples. However, similar to supervised techniques, they can be described as a function estimation problem. The difference is that the target function is the probability distribution of the samples.

Let us start with a simple example.

Example: Gaussian data

Exercise: Build a generative model for the data in figure 7.1.

For a dataset with a Gaussian distribution such as the one in figure 7.1, the easiest approach is to estimate the probability distribution.

As we have discussed before, the Gaussian distribution is specified by two parameters, the center, and the standard deviation. The average of the features of samples gives the center of the Gaussian distribution and the standard deviation can be calculated from the data.

Figure 7.2 shows this PDF for the data in figure 7.1.

Once we have the probability distribution of a dataset, we can use it to generate new samples.

Question: How do you generate samples from a probability distribution?

Question: Repeat the exercise above for the data in figure 7.3.

Next, we will explore the logic behind the example in this section in a more systematic way and explain how it may be extended to other situations. We will also review one of the main assumptions behind this approach.

7.1 Maximum likelihood estimation

As you saw in the previous section, if we have the PDF of the samples we can use it to make a generative model.

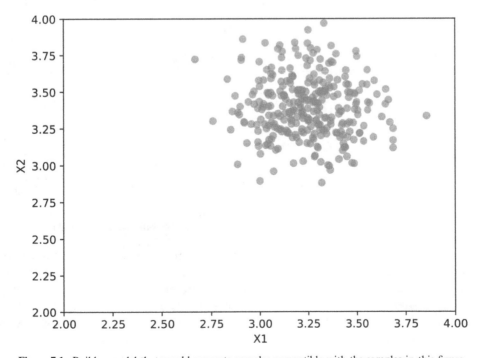

Figure 7.1. Build a model that would generate samples compatible with the samples in this figure.

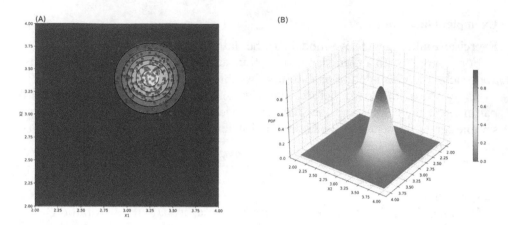

Figure 7.2. The PDF for the samples in figure 7.1. The left panel shows the contours corresponding to the probability and the right panel shows the PDF itself.

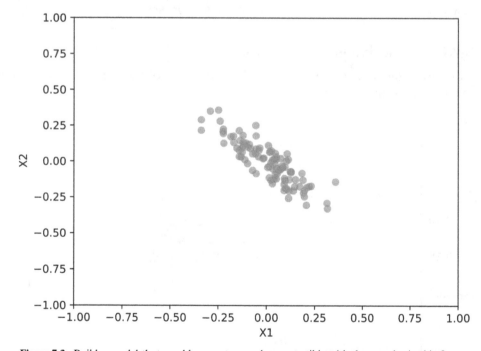

Figure 7.3. Build a model that would generate samples compatible with the samples in this figure.

However, what if the data are not as simple as those in figure 7.1? What if the underlying phenomenon that generated the data is not Gaussian? In this section we extend the intuition of the previous section to more general distributions.

Imagine that we are given a sequence of samples and that all the samples are specified with one feature. In other words, we have a 1D dataset. These samples are generated from a PDF that is unknown to us. The problem that we are trying to solve here is to estimate the PDF that the data are drawn from.

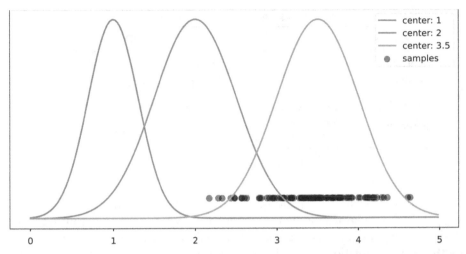

Figure 7.4. Finding the best estimation to the probability distribution: which PDF better describes the 1D data here?

The first approach is to use 'maximum likelihood estimation' [5, 6]. You may be familiar with the content of this section from courses such as statistics. We cover the basics of this technique briefly.

Exercise: Figure 7.4 shows some 1D samples. Each sample has one feature that is indicated by $X1$.

Which of the PDFs gives a better estimation of the probability distribution? Can you explain your intuition?

To answer this question we will take an approach similar to the one for a supervised problem. Specifically, we start with a hypothesis about the PDF. This hypothesis, similar to the ones we used for supervised tasks, has some parameters. Also similar to a supervised learning task, we define a loss function and try to minimize it to find the best estimate for the PDF.

Let us take these steps one by one. We start with the hypothesis. We indicate this with

$$P_\theta(x). \tag{7.1}$$

P indicates the PDF, θ indicates the trainable parameters of the PDF, and x is the feature vector of a given sample. The PDF returns the probability of given samples with features given by x.

Table 7.1 shows some examples for the choice of hypothesis as well as the related parameters.

The choice of the hypothesis is often motivated by our domain knowledge about the problem.

Next, we need to tune θ to find the best estimate for the PDF. Let us assume that the original PDF that generated the data is compatible with our hypothesized PDF. We refer to the original PDF as P_θ with θ the target parameter values. We also refer to our estimate as $P_{\hat\theta}$ with $\hat\theta$ as the estimated values for the parameters.

Table 7.1. Some of the popular probability distribution functions.

Hypothesis	x	θ	PDF
Gaussian	Continuous	μ, σ	$P_{(\mu,\sigma)}(x) = \frac{1}{z}e^{-(\frac{x-\mu}{\sigma})^2/2}$
Poisson	Discrete	$\lambda > 0$	$P_\lambda(x) = \frac{\lambda^x e^{-\lambda}}{x!}$
Gamma	Continuous, $x > 0$	$\alpha, \beta > 0$	$P_{(\alpha,\beta)}(x) = \frac{x^{\alpha-1}e^{\beta x}\beta^\alpha}{\Gamma(\alpha)}$
Bernoulli	Discrete	$p > 0$	$P_\theta(x) = \frac{1}{z}e^{-(\frac{x-\mu}{\sigma})^2/2}$

We need to define a loss function that describes how far our estimate is from the target parameters. Unfortunately we do not have access to the probabilities. This is a probabilistic process and unlike the supervised case, the outcomes are not fixed. Note that for the function estimation case, for every input x, the output y is unique and for a supervised task we try to find a function that reproduces similar outputs. However, for the probabilistic case, for an input x, we obtain a probability $P(x)$. This means that for different times that we try this process, we may obtain different outcomes, and $P(x)$ gives the probability of x. This is what makes this problem more challenging.

Exercise: What would be a good objective or loss function for this problem?

Let us go back to the data in figure 7.4 again. What can we use for the objective function?

A simple solution is to use the probability of the data points given in each of the PDFs. The PDF with the higher probabilities is more likely to be the underlying PDF. More specifically, we can use the likelihood of the whole sequence of points, $\{x_1, x_2,..., x_{n_s}\}$ as the objective function, and the goal would be to find the $\hat{\theta}$ that maximizes this probability. This probability is referred to as the 'likelihood' and mathematically, it is given by

$$\mathcal{L}(P) = P(x_1, x_2,..., x_{n_s}). \tag{7.2}$$

It is sometimes written as $\mathcal{L}(\theta)$ as well. This is in fact $P(x_1, x_2, \ldots, x_{n_s}|\theta)$, i.e. the probability of obtaining the sequence conditioned on θ being the parameters of the PDF.

To better understand this let us look at an example. Assume that the likelihood is zero for a specific PDF. This means that it is impossible to obtain that sequence of samples from the given PDF. Similarly, a high likelihood for a PDF indicates that the corresponding PDF can be a good fit for the distribution of the samples. Generally, the higher the likelihood, the more likely it is for the samples to come from the corresponding PDF.

You are probably wondering how we can calculate the likelihood, $\mathcal{L}(\mathcal{P})$. In general, this is a complex problem and is not always tractable. But we can make an assumption that would significantly simplify the problem. We are going to assume that the samples $\{x_1, x_2, \ldots\}$ are random and independent. This simplifies the likelihood to

$$\mathcal{L}(P) = P(x_1, x_2, \ldots, x_{n_s}) = P(x_1) \times P(x_2) \times \cdots P(x_{n_s}). \qquad (7.3)$$

We now can use our hypothesis for the PDF to calculate the $P(x_i)$. We will do some examples to make this clear.

Question: Assume that we are given the following ten samples each of which has one feature (1D data):

$$\{6.79, 5.44, 5.1, 3.14, 4.72, 4.65, 4.92, 4.37, 4.96, 4.52\}.$$

Also, assume a Gaussian hypothesis with $\sigma = 1$. Calculate the likelihood for

- $\mu = 0$,
- $\mu = 5$,
- $\mu = 7$.

Which value gives a better fit for the data?

Question: We flip a coin ten times and we obtain $\{h, h, h, t, h, t, t, t, h, h\}$, where h and t are heads and tails, respectively. The probability distribution for this would be a binomial distribution. Calculate the likelihood for:

- $p = 0.2$,
- $p = 0.5$,
- $p = 0.7$,

with p the probability of obtaining head in one flip.

Question: For the question above, plot the likelihood for different values of $p \in [0, 1]$. What does this tell you?

It is common to use the log of the likelihood function. We use l to indicate the log-likelihood. This is specifically useful for estimating the maximum likelihood. Since log is a monotone and increasing function, finding the maximum of the likelihood and its log are the same. This, however, turns the products into a sum, i.e.

$$l(P) = \log(P(x_1, x_2, \ldots, x_{n_s})) = \sum_i^{n_s} \log(P(x_i)). \qquad (7.4)$$

Now let us go back to the problem of estimating the maximum likelihood. Let us do another exercise.

Exercise: Consider the coin flip question above. Find p such that it maximizes the likelihood.

Let us start with the log-likelihood for this problem and let us indicate the number of times that we obtained heads with m. For the binomial probability distribution, we have

$$P_p(n, m) = \binom{n}{m} p^m (1 - p)^{n-m}.$$

This gives

$$l = \log\left(\binom{n}{m}p^m(1-p)^{n-m}\right) = c + m\log(p) + (n-m)\log(1-p),$$

where $c = \log\left(\binom{n}{m}\right)$ is a constant and does not depend on p.

To maximize the likelihood we need to find the value p for which the derivative of the likelihood or similarly the log-likelihood vanishes. Doing the derivative, we obtain

$$\frac{dl}{dp} = \frac{m}{p} - \frac{n-m}{1-p} = 0.$$

Solving for p, as expected, we obtain

$$p = \frac{m}{n}.$$

Exercise: Similar to one of the earlier questions, assume that we are given the following ten samples

$$\{6.79, 5.44, 5.1, 3.14, 4.72, 4.65, 4.92, 4.37, 4.96, 4.52\}.$$

Assume a Gaussian hypothesis with $\sigma = 1$ and find $\hat{\mu}$ that maximizes the likelihood.

We first calculate this symbolically and then replace the values for the samples. The log-likelihood is

$$l_\mu = \sum_i^{n_s} \log\left(\frac{1}{z}e^{-(x_i-\mu)^2/2}\right) = \sum_i^{n_s}\left[\log\left(\frac{1}{z}\right) + \log(e^{-(x_i-\mu)^2/2})\right]$$

$$= n_s \log\left(\frac{1}{z}\right) - \sum_i^{n_s}\frac{(x_i-\mu)^2}{2}.$$

Next, we need to calculate the derivative with respect to μ which leads to

$$\frac{dl}{dp} = \sum_i^{n_s}(x_i - \mu) = 0.$$

This gives

$$\hat{\mu} = \frac{\sum_i^{n_s}x_i}{n_s}.$$

This is compatible with using the average of the samples for the center of the Gaussian distribution.

Question: Repeat the procedure above for a Poisson distribution.
Does this match your expectations for the Poisson distribution?

One of the main assumptions that enabled us to use this approach is that the samples are random and independent. But what if this is not the case? For a large class of problems in physics, the sequence of samples or measurements could be correlated. For instance, consider the sequence of measurements on a quantum system. We know that each measurement changes the system and consequently would affect the result of the following measurements. Even for classical problems, measurements could have back-actions and change the system.

Generative problems could become complex in other aspects too. For instance, samples usually have more than just one feature. Consider a generative model that generates images of an object. Each sample, in this case, would be a matrix with possibly hundreds of input features.

For such problems, it is not easy to find a closed form for the probability function $P(x_1, x_2, \ldots, x_{n_s})$. How should we deal with these sorts of problems? Here we introduce two different approaches. The first one focuses on estimating the $P(x_1, x_2, \ldots, x_{n_s})$ and the second one gives a generative model without directly estimating the probability distribution.

7.2 Restricted Boltzmann machines

With restricted Boltzmann machines (RBMs) we take a different approach to estimating the probability distribution [7–9]. You may have already guessed it from the name.

If you recall from your statistical physics course, the Boltzmann distribution attributes probabilities to different states of a system based on the energy of the corresponding state [10]. In other words, it gives a mapping between the energy and the probability distribution. The lower energy states are more likely (higher probability) and high-energy states are less likely (low probability). Mathematically, the probability of a given state s with energy $\mathcal{E}_s$ is given by

$$P(s) = \frac{e^{-\mathcal{E}_s/K_b T}}{z},\tag{7.5}$$

where K_b is the Boltzmann constant, T is the temperature, and z is the normalization factor.

With RBMs, instead of training for the probabilities to match the likelihood of the samples of the data, we try to find or learn an energy landscape that could be mapped to the data using the Boltzmann distribution [7–9]. It may seem that we are over-complicating the problem, but as we will see this works well in practice.

For simplicity, we are going to assume that our data are binary, i.e. the features of each sample are either 0 or 1.

Let us first start with how we define a trainable energy landscape. We start with a small unit. Figure 7.5 shows a model with two nodes that are connected with an edge. These types of models are known as energy-based models [11]. The unit in figure 7.5 makes a small energy-based model with two nodes.

The energy for this unit can be written as

Figure 7.5. Schematic illustration of a small unit of an energy-based model.

$$\mathcal{E}(S_1, S_2) = b_1 S_1 + b_2 S_2 + w_{1,2} S_1 S_2, \tag{7.6}$$

where S_1 and S_2 are the values of the two nodes and b_1, b_2, $w_{1,2}$ are the parameters that define the energy landscape based on the values of the nodes. This can be seen as a simple Ising model where the nodes are the particles and the energy is determined by the couplings and on-site fields. For different states, this gives different energies and consequently different probabilities.

Exercise: Map this energy to a probability for one node.

For a given configuration, $\{S_1, S_2\}$ for the states of the two nodes, the probability can be calculated as

$$P(\{S_1, S_2\}) = \frac{e^{-\mathcal{E}/K_b T}}{z} = \frac{e^{-(b_1 S_1 + b_2 S_2 + w_{1,2} S_1 S_2)/K_b T}}{z}. \tag{7.7}$$

For this network, there are four different configurations, i.e. $\{(0, 0), (0, 1), (1, 0), (1, 1)\}$. Knowing b_1, b_2, $w_{1,2}$ we can calculate the energy of a given state and its corresponding probability.

Exercise: *Normalization factor*

Calculate the normalization factor.

We need to sum over all the configurations and make sure that they add up to one. That is

$$\sum_{s_1, s_2} P(\{s_1, s_2\}) = \sum_{s_1, s_2} \frac{e^{-\mathcal{E}(\{s_1, s_2\})/K_b T}}{z} = 1.$$

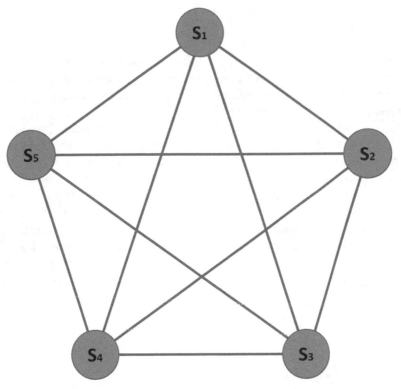

Figure 7.6. Schematic picture of an energy-based model. This is a combination of units like the one in figure 7.5.

This gives

$$z = \sum_{s_1, s_2} e^{-\mathcal{E}(\{s_1, s_2\})/K_b T}.$$

If you recall from statistical physics, this is the partition function. As we will see later, this could become complex for larger systems.

Question: For the network above, assume that $b_1 = -1$, $b_2 = 2$, $w_{1,2} = 1$.

- Calculate the energy of each configuration.
- Calculate the probability of each configuration.
- How can we change the parameters to make $(0, 1)$ the most likely configuration?

Now let us consider a more general setting. Consider a generalization of the model above, i.e. an energy-based model with m nodes. Figure 7.6 shows a schematic picture of such a network.

Exercise: Generalize the energy function in equation (7.6) for the model in figure 7.6.

Similar to the simple unit, we can assign a bias to each node and a coupling for each edge [11]. This gives

$$\mathcal{E}(S_1, S_2, \ldots S_n) = \sum_i b_i S_i + \sum_{i,j} W_{i,j} S_i S_j. \tag{7.8}$$

We can use this to calculate the probability distributions. One challenge is that as the system grows, the number of configurations grows exponentially with it. This makes calculations of the probabilities challenging and intractable.

Exercise: How can we simplify this?

RBMs in some aspects are a simplified energy-based model. Imagine that the samples in the dataset have n_f features. An RBM network is comprised of an input layer with n_f nodes and one hidden layer. The number of nodes in the hidden layer is one of the hyper-parameters of the model. For simplicity, in this section, we refer to the number of nodes in the input layer and hidden layer as n and m, respectively.

The samples are fed into the input layer [9]. The input layer is also referred to as the visible layer since this is the layer that is not hidden. RBM networks are not like the normal feed-forward networks that we have worked with. The data can propagate in both directions, i.e. from the visible layer to the hidden layer and vice versa. Figure 7.7 shows the structure of an RBM network schematically.

The values of the visible nodes are used to calculate the hidden layer, i.e.

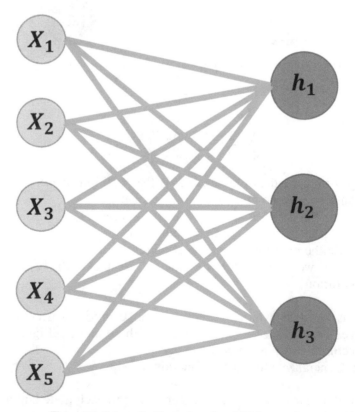

Figure 7.7. Schematic illustration of an RBM network.

$$h_j = \sigma\left(\sum_i (a_i + w_{i,j}v_i)\right),$$

where σ is the sigmoid function and the sum is over all the inputs nodes. We use the sigmoid activation function because the v_i are binary and the sigmoid function can give the probabilities.

Similarly, the values of the hidden layer can be used to evaluate the nodes in the visible layer

$$v_i = \sigma\left(\sum_j (b_j + w_{i,j}h_j)\right).$$

This is the reverse pass that can be used for the generation of new samples.

RBM networks have one key simplifying attribute compared to general energy-based models which makes RBMs much easier to train compared to general energy-based models. As you can see, the number of nodes in an RBM network is more than the number of input features. However, the network is partitioned into two parts, the visible layer, and the hidden layer. There is no edge between the nodes in the visible layer. Similarly, the nodes in the hidden layer are not connected to each other.

Question:
- How many edges are there in an RBM network with n input features and m nodes in the hidden layer?
- How many edges would there be if this was an energy-based model with $n + m$ nodes?

At this point, you may be wondering how this kind of model can be helpful for estimating the probability distribution. Imagine that we could find an energy function that associates lower energy to the configurations that we observe in the samples and higher energy to the rest of the configurations. In other words, we want to build an energy landscape that has lower values for configurations that happen more frequently in the dataset. This is how we build and train RBM models [9].

But why do we need the hidden layer? Why do we not just use a simple energy-based model with n nodes?

Exercise: How does the hidden layer help?

Note that without the interconnections in the visible layer, the model may be unable to capture the correlations and higher-order relations between different features. The hidden layer is designed to compensate for that. But where is this intuition coming from?

The idea is that sometimes random variables corresponding to the input nodes can be inferred from latent or hidden variables [12, 13]. The intuition behind RBMs is that we design a network that can accommodate and learn these hidden variables as the nodes in the hidden layer. With successful training, the nodes in the hidden layer would learn to capture the hidden variables.

Interestingly, these nodes can be used as a reduced representation of the input samples too. In other words, this approach can also be used as a dimensionality reduction technique.

Now that we have some high-level understanding of RBMs, let us dive into the technical aspects and learn how the mechanics of RBMs works.

We start with the energy function.

Exercise: Find the energy function of an RBM.

You can follow the equation (7.8). Note that there is no edge between the nodes in the visible layer and similarly no edge between the nodes in the hidden layer. It is easier to partition the nodes into two sets. Mathematically, this can be written as

$$\mathcal{E}(v, h) = -\sum_i a_i v_i - \sum_j b_j h_j - \sum_{i,j} W_{i,j} v_i h_j, \qquad (7.9)$$

where v_i and h_j represent the nodes from the visible and hidden layer, respectively. Note that we added a negative sign to all the terms This is a reparametrization of the old b_i and $w_{i,j}$ into the new a_i, b_j, $w_{i,j}$. It will become clear how this notation is more convenient. We can rewrite the energy in a vectorized form as

$$\mathcal{E}(v, h) = -a^T \cdot v - b^T \cdot h - v^T \cdot W \cdot h. \qquad (7.10)$$

Note that the input features and the values of the nodes in the hidden layer are treated as vectors.

Next, we need to calculate the probability distribution. We can use the equation (7.5) to find $P(v, h)$. This includes the state of both the visible nodes as well as the hidden ones.

Since we only interact directly with the visible layer, we are more interested in the marginal probability distributions. Specifically, we are interested in $P(v)$, the probability of getting a sample with the specific set of features v. We also need the conditional probabilities, i.e. $P(v|h)$ and $P(h|v)$, for inference and training the model.

This involves some straightforward but rather long calculations [9]. You are encouraged to do the following questions to become more familiar with these calculations and the structure of the probability distributions for an RBM model.

Question: Use the energy function and the Boltzmann probability to show that

$$P(v_i = 1|h) = \sigma\left(a_i + \sum_j w_{i,j} h_j\right).$$

Question: Use the energy function and the Boltzmann probability to show that

$$P(h_j = 1|v) = \sigma\left(b_j + \sum_i w_{i,j} v_i\right).$$

You can see that these are consistent with the forward and backward equations for the RBM network.

Question: Use the energy function and the Boltzmann probability to show that

$$P(v) = \frac{e^{-F(x)}}{z}, \tag{7.11}$$

where $F(x)$ is the free energy and is

$$F(x) = -a^T v - \sum_j \log(1 + e^{b_j + \sum_i (w_{i,j} v_i)}).$$

For the questions above, note that both the hidden variables and the visible variables are binary and only take 0 and 1 for the values.

7.2.1 Training an RBM: contrastive divergence algorithm (CDA)

Next, we are going to see how we can train an RBM model. But let us first see what it means to train the RBM network. We do not have any labels. The goal is to present the model with the samples in the dataset and tune the parameters a, b, w such that the probability of getting those samples are high and the probability of getting samples that are not part of the dataset is low.

To better understand the challenge, we can start with the equation (7.11) which gives $P(v)$. Assume that we have one sample. To maximize the probability, we need to maximize

$$-F(x) = a^T v + \sum_j \log(1 + e^{b_j + \sum_i (w_{i,j} v_i)}).$$

Maximizing the first term means that we need to pick a such that it is aligned with the feature vector of the sample. Similarly, we can tune b and w in the second part (also known as the 'softplus' function) to increase the probability. This, however, only works for that one sample. We cannot choose a to be aligned to all the samples at the same time. Thus we need to set up the parameters to maximize the likelihood of the whole dataset. If we only had the first term, this would not work. However, with the hidden nodes and the second term, we can tune the parameters such that if the samples and their corresponding hidden variables fit specific patterns, this PDF associate a high probability to them.

To this end, we want to massage the energy landscape and lower it where the samples from the dataset are located, and increase it everywhere else [9].

The objective of the optimization is the likelihood function, but it is a convention to use the negative log-likelihood (Nll), i.e.

$$\text{Nll}(P(x)) = -\frac{1}{n_s} \sum_l \log(P(x^{(l)})), \tag{7.12}$$

where n_s is the number of the samples and the sum is over the feature vectors for different samples. The Nll is a proper loss function that can be minimized for training the RBM.

One of the most effective techniques to minimize the negative log-likelihood for RBM is the 'contrastive divergence algorithm' (CDA) [9]. It is based on using the gradient descent algorithm. However, there are some challenges and to overcome them CDA makes some simplifications that we will review here.

Let us do the gradient descent one sample at a time. With some calculation, we obtain

$$-\frac{\partial \log(p(x^{(l)}))}{\partial \theta} = \mathbb{E}_{h}\left(\frac{\partial \mathcal{E}(x^{(l)}, h)}{\partial \theta} \,\middle|\, x^{(l)} \right) - \mathbb{E}_{x,h}\left(\frac{\partial \mathcal{E}(x, h)}{\partial \theta} \right), \tag{7.13}$$

where $\partial \mathcal{E}(\cdot)$ indicates the expectation value.

Question: Derive the equation (7.13).

The first term is positive and increases the likelihood of the samples that are observed. But we also need to reduce the likelihood of samples that do not fit the patterns of the samples in the dataset. This is what the second term does.

The first term in equation (7.13) is the expectation value for the specific sample. The second term however is more challenging as it needs to average overall values of x according to the model.

The CDA uses a trick to approximate the second term. It deploys Gibbs sampling with one sample. Specifically, we start with a sample and propagate it forward to calculate the hidden variables. Then we propagate it back to calculate the values of the visible nodes, given the hidden values. We repeat this k times. We use the final values of the visible layer for the calculation of the second term. In other words, it is calculated the same as the first term, except that instead of $x^{(l)}$, we use the values that we got after the k passes through the network. This may seem counter-intuitive, however, it works well in practice. One way to make sense of this is that, if the model is trained perfectly, it would be able to retrieve the $x^{(l)}$ after a pass, i.e. evaluation of the hidden variables from the input and then the input from the hidden variable. If this happens, the first and the second term of the equation (7.13) become equal and the derivative gets zero. In other words, if the model is trained to a point where it can retrieve the input from the hidden variables, it stops training. Similarly, the closer it gets to reproducing the input, the smaller the derivative gets and the smaller the changes to the network become.

We are not covering all the details of the CDA here and this is only meant to give you a high-level understanding of what the algorithm involves. For more details see [9].

Once the RBM model is trained, it can be used for different applications. First, it can be used for dimensionality reduction. For this, the hidden layer should have fewer nodes than the input. We can feed the samples into the visible layer of the RBM and let it transform them into the hidden layer. Then the hidden variables can serve as a reduced representation of the inputs.

A similar idea can also be used for the initialization of other model architectures. For instance, one of the early successful attempts to train autoencoders used RBMs to initialize the weights layer by layer [14]. For each layer of the autoencoder, they trained an RBM with the nodes from the previous layer as the input (visible layer) and the nodes of the new layer as the hidden layer. Then they used the weights as the initial weights of the autoencoder and started the training from there.

However, the application that is of interest in this section is that by training the RBM network, we can find the probability distribution of the data using the hidden variables in the hidden layer. More specifically, the training leads to the optimal values for a, b, and W. These parameters can be used to calculate the energy and then the probability distribution of the visible layer. This enables us to generate new samples that have a high likelihood according to the estimated PDF.

There are other ways to make generative models based on estimating the PDF of the samples. One such example is variational auto encoders (VAE) [15, 16]. However, investigating all generative techniques is beyond the scope of this book. The reader is encouraged to see [4] to learn more about this topic.

Next, we review a generative approach that does not rely on approximating the PDF.

7.3 Generative adversarial networks (GAN)

Next, we get to, arguably, one of the smartest architectures in deep learning. This is known as generative adversarial networks (GAN) and was first proposed recently by Ian Goodfellow and his colleagues in [17]. GANs are composed of two competing models. One model generates fake samples, also known as the 'generator'. The second model tries to figure out if a given sample is fake and generated by the generator model or if it is real and coming from the actual dataset. The second model is known as the 'discriminator'. The training is also comprised of training both models together [17–21].

To better understand GANs, let us go through an analogy. Imagine that there is an art forger and an art inspector. They compete against each other. Every time the forger forges a new piece of art, the inspector needs to put some effort and learn how to identify the fake art. For this, the forger needs to discover patterns in the real art and mimic them in their forgeries. At the same time, the inspector needs to learn the pattern in the real art too and identify which patterns are missing from the forgeries.

The forger and the inspector help improve each other. Eventually, this process converges into forgeries that could be extremely difficult to distinguish from real ones. Similarly, the inspector will become really good at identifying patterns in real artworks and detecting forgeries.

This is an adversarial approach. We let the two models compete against each other. As one model gets better, the loss for the other model increases which forces it to do better to keep up with its adversary. Similarly, if the second model gets better, it forces the first model to improve. As a result, they help each other improve.

Exercise: Try to design a model architecture for the idea above. Describe what the inputs and outputs are. This can be a schematic design and does not need to include actual layers and nodes.

Figure 7.8 shows a schematic architecture for a GAN. As you can see there are two models, the generator and the discriminator. The input to the discriminator is a sample that may be coming from the dataset (i.e. real) or may be generated by the

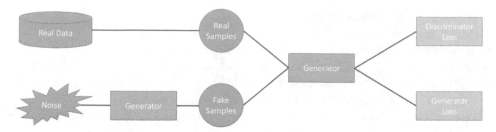

Figure 7.8. Schematic picture of a GAN model. The generator takes a random noise vector as an input and makes fake samples. These fake samples are mixed with real samples from the dataset and are passed to the discriminator. Note that the real samples are labeled as 0 and the fake ones are labeled as 1. The discriminator tries to distinguish the fake samples. There are two types of loss, one for the discriminator and one for the generator.

generator network (i.e. fake). The discriminator is a binary classifier and its output indicates if the input is real or fake (0 or 1).

The generator model generates samples that are expected to mimic the samples in the dataset. The generator model takes a random vector in the input. This random input is needed to generate different samples. If the input is fixed, the model will always generate one fixed forgery. This random vector can also be seen as a reduced representation of the generated images. This is because, after the training, there is a network that can map the vector to the generated image.

We will refer to networks for the generator and the discriminator as 'G-network' and the 'D-network', respectively. We also will use the subscripts G and D to refer to the generator and the discriminator. We refer to the random input to the generator by ξ.

Now that we have specified the model structure we need to train them.

Exercise: How would you train a GAN model as specified in figure 7.8?

The training process of a GAN involves two steps, training the generator and training the discriminator [18–21]. We need to train both models simultaneously. Intuitively, this is because if each of the two models is superior to the other one, the other model cannot be trained. For instance, imagine that the generator generated different forgeries, each of which is trying to mimic a different pattern or aspect of the inputs. If the discriminator is significantly better than the generator, it would identify all the samples as fake. But this does not give the generator any information on how to improve. However, if the discriminator is at the same level as the generator, it would miss some of the better forgeries and catch some of the worse ones. This indicates to the generator which forgeries are better and helps the generator learn and improve the successful forgeries and move away from repeating the detected forgeries.

Figures 7.9 and 7.10 show the two steps of the training.

In one step, we train the discriminator without changing the generator. In a way, we treat the generator as the environment or the circumstances that the discriminator is exposed to during its training step. Figure 7.9 shows this process schematically. The gray elements are either frozen or are not part of the pipeline at this step.

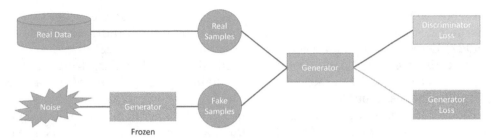

Figure 7.9. Schematic illustration of training the discriminator of the GAN model. The generator is frozen, i.e. it does not train. It only generates some samples that are used for training the discriminator.

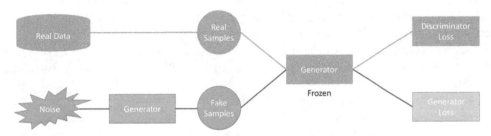

Figure 7.10. Schematic illustration of training the generator of the GAN model. At this step, the discriminator is frozen, i.e. it does not train. The generator generates new fake samples. Only the fake samples are passed to the discriminator. Also, we only calculate the loss for the generator and train the generator at this step.

After a phase of training the discriminator, it is time to train the generator using the updated discriminator. This time the discriminator is fixed and the weights of the generator network are updated. Figure 7.10 shows this process schematically. The gray elements are either frozen or are not part of the pipeline at this step.

The key ingredient here is defining the right loss functions. In other words, we need to identify the objective for which we are training each model.

Exercise: What loss function would you use for training?

The discriminator is a binary classifier. If you recall from the supervised techniques, cross-entropy is a popular choice for such problems, so we use cross-entropy for training the GAN model.

The discriminator is given a set of samples that are randomly chosen from the samples in the dataset and samples generated by the generator. The discriminator assigns a probability to each sample for being fake. The cross-entropy loss function quantifies how accurately the discriminator has identified the samples.

For the steps when the discriminator is trained, first the generator generates a set of samples from random noise vectors. Then the fake samples are mixed with real samples from the dataset. They are also labeled based on coming from the dataset (i.e. 0) or being generated by the generator (i.e. 1). The samples and their labels are then used to train the discriminator. The discriminator returns a vector of probabilities for the input samples. Then the cross-entropy loss is calculated based on the predicted probabilities and the actual labels. Next, the back-propagation is done but only for the discriminator network. This means that the weights of the discriminator network are updated according to the optimization technique (e.g. gradient descent) while the weights of the generative model are kept fixed.

Next, the generator has to go through a training step. For this, the objective is different. The goal is for the generative model to build samples that are all classified as real by the discriminator.

Again, the generator generates some samples from the random noise vectors. This generates the samples as we did before. But this time, we do not mix them with samples from the dataset. We also set all the labels to zero. This is because the objective of this step is to fool the discriminator, i.e. for the discriminator to label all of the samples as real. Next, we pass the samples and their labels to the discriminator and then use the cross-entropy to calculate the loss. We then back-propagate and calculate the derivatives of the trainable parameters of the generator. Finally, we update the weights of the generator while keeping the discriminator fixed.

GANs are different from the previous generative approaches that we studied in the sense that GANs do not provide a direct estimation of the probability distribution [4].

Also, note that GANs provide two models. For the purposes of this section we are more interested in the generator. However, the discriminator can also provide a strong classifier or anomaly detector. The discriminator can recognize the patterns of samples from the dataset and identify samples that do not match those patterns [22, 23].

Question: Design a schematic approach based on GANs for building a model for entanglement detection. Remember that entanglement detection is generally an NP-hard problem. There have been supervised approaches to this problem for specific dimensions such as two quantum bits. However, it is hard to extend these ideas to higher dimensions because it is not easy to label the data samples. While entanglement detection is hard, generating separable states is easy and we can build large datasets of separable states for any dimension.

Question: Design a schematic approach for generating synthetic data using GANs.

Question: Design a GAN architecture that can generate 2D images from images in a dataset. This can be used for the generation of samples like the ones in the Galaxy Zoo dataset.

Try to use what you have learned from CNNs and combine it with the GAN architecture. See [24] for more details.

7.4 Summary

This section reviewed generative machine learning and studied some of the more popular generative techniques. Some of these techniques estimate a PDF for the input data and build a generative model based on the PDF. We reviewed maximum likelihood estimation and restricted Boltzmann machines in this chapter.

In contrast, there are generative techniques that build models for generating new samples without estimating the PDF. Arguably, the most important techniques in this chapter are generative adversarial networks, which were reviewed in the last section.

There are other generative techniques, such as variational autoencoders, that were not covered here. Also, there are many variations of the techniques that were reviewed here that were beyond the scope of this book. Generative machine learning is one of the most active and agile fields of machine learning. Many of the major milestones were only achieved recently. Some of the most powerful techniques such as GANs are not even a decade old. It is important to actively engage with research in this field and keep up with the fast pace of new ideas and techniques.

References

[1] de Oliveira L, Paganini M and Nachman B 2017 Learning particle physics by example: location-aware generative adversarial networks for physics synthesis *Comput. Softw. Big Sci.* **4** 4

[2] Paganini M, de Oliveira L and Nachman B 2018 Accelerating science with generative adversarial networks: an application to 3D particle showers in multilayer calorimeters *Phys. Rev. Lett.* **120** 042003

[3] Chen Y, Pan Y, Zhang G and Chong S 2021 Detecting quantum entanglement with unsupervised learning *Quantum Sci. Technol.* **7** 015005

[4] Foster D 2019 *Generative Deep Learning: Teaching Machines to Paint, Write, Compose, and Play* (Sebastopol, CA: O'Reilly Media)

[5] Eliason S R 1993 *Maximum Likelihood Estimation: Logic and Practice* Number 96 (Thousand Oaks, CA: SAGE) https://doi.org/10.4135/9781412984928

[6] Rossi R J 2018 *Mathematical Statistics: An Introduction to Likelihood Based Inference* (New York: Wiley)

[7] Fischer A and Igel C 2012 An introduction to restricted Boltzmann machines *Progress in Pattern Recognition, Image Analysis, Computer Vision, and Applications: 17th Iberoamerican Congress (Buenos Aires, Argentina, 3–6 September)* (Berlin: Springer) pp 14 36

[8] Zhang N, Ding S, Zhang J and Xue Y 2018 An overview on restricted Boltzmann machines *Neurocomputing* **275** 1186–99

[9] Hinton G E 2012 A practical guide to training restricted ed G Montavon, G B Orr and K-R Müller *Neural Networks: Tricks of the Trade* 2nd edn (Berlin: Springer) pp 599–619

[10] Kardar M 2007 *Statistical Physics of Particles* (Cambridge: Cambridge University Press)

[11] Du Y and Mordatch I 2019 Implicit generation and generalization in energy-based models arXiv preprint (arXiv:1903.08689)

[12] Borsboom D 2008 Latent variable theory *Meas. Interdiscip. Res. Perspect.* **6** 25–53

[13] Everett B 2013 *An Introduction to Latent Variable Models* (Berlin: Springer)

[14] Hinton G E and Salakhutdinov R R 2006 Reducing the dimensionality of data with neural networks *Science* **313** 504–7

[15] Kingma D P and Welling M *et al* 2019 An introduction to variational autoencoders *Found. Trends Mach. Learn.* **12** 307–92

[16] Doersch C 2016 Tutorial on variational autoencoders arXiv preprint (arXiv:1606.05908)

[17] Goodfellow I, Pouget-Abadie J, Mirza M, Xu B, Warde-Farley D, Ozair S, Courville A and Bengio Y 2020 Generative adversarial networks *Commun. ACM* **63** 139–44

[18] Gonog L and Zhou Y 2019 A review: generative adversarial networks *2019 14th IEEE Conf. on Industrial Electronics and Applications (ICIEA)* (Piscataway, NJ: IEEE) pp 505–10

[19] Hany J and Walters G 2019 *Hands-On Generative Adversarial Networks with PyTorch 1.x: Implement Next-Generation Neural Networks to Build Powerful GAN Models Using Python* (Birmingham: Packt) https://download.packt.com/free-ebook/9781789530513

[20] Langr J and Bok V 2019 *GANs in Action: Deep Learning with Generative Adversarial Networks* (Shelter Island, NY: Manning)

[21] Cheng J, Yang Y, Tang X, Xiong N, Zhang Y and Lei F 2020 Generative adversarial networks: a literature review *KSII Trans. Internet Inf. Syst.* **14** 4625–47

[22] Di Mattia F, Galeone P, De Simoni M and Ghelfi E 2019 A survey on GANs for anomaly detection arXiv preprint (arXiv:1906.11632)

[23] Xia X, Pan X, Li N, He X, Ma L, Zhang X and Ding N 2022 GAN-based anomaly detection: a review *Neurocomputing* **493** 497–535

[24] Radford A, Metz L and Chintala S 2015 Unsupervised representation learning with deep convolutional generative adversarial networks arXiv preprint (arXiv:1511.06434)

Printed in the USA
CPSIA information can be obtained
at www.ICGtesting.com
JSHW061340241223
54197JS00004B/62